FINAL FANTASY ANTHOLOGY™
OFFICIAL STRATEGY GUIDE

By David Cassady

SQUARESOFT®

BRADYGAMES
TAKE YOUR GAME FURTHER

Table of Contents

OFFICIAL FINAL FANTASY ANTHOLOGY™
STRATEGY GUIDE

Brady Publishing
An Imprint of
Macmillan USA, Inc.
201 West 103rd Street
Indianapolis, Indiana 46290

Please be advised that the ESRB rating icons, "EC", "K-A", "T", "M", and "AO" are copyrighted works and certification marks owned by the Interactive Digital Software Association and the Entertainment Software Rating Board and may only be used with their permission and authority. Under no circumstances may the rating icons be self-applied to any product that has not been rated by the ESRB. For information regarding whether a product has been rated by the ESRB, please call the ESRB at (212) 759-0700 or 1-800-771-3772. Please note that ESRB ratings only apply to the content of the game itself and do NOT apply to the content of the books.

ISBN: 1-56686-925-0

Library of Congress Catalog No.: 99-073671

Printing Code: The rightmost double-digit number is the year of the book's printing; the rightmost single-digit number is the number of the book's printing. For example, 99-1 shows that the first printing of the book occurred in 1999.

03 02 01   5 4

Manufactured in the United States of America.

BradyGAMES Staff

Publisher
Lynn Zingraf

Editor-In-Chief
H. Leigh Davis

Licensing Manager
David Waybright

Marketing Manager
Janet Eshenour

Acquisitions Editor
Debra McBride

Creative Director
Scott Watanabe

Marketing Assistant
Tricia Reynolds

Credits

Development Editor
David Cassady

Project Editor
Tim Cox

Screenshot Editor
Michael Owen

Book Designer
Scott Watanabe

Production Designers
Bob Klunder
Jane Washburne

We would like to extend an extra special thanks to Rick Thompson and Fernando Bustamante for all their help and dedication to making a great guide. Also, we can't forget to thank Square's Customer Service Reps for all their assistance. In particular, a special thanks goes to Patrick Cervantes, Caroline Liu, Alaine Deleon, James Dilonardo, John Montes, Art Yang, Ryan Riley, Mark Acero, Mark Abarca, and Alan Deguzman. This book would not have been possible without all your support and help!

The Characters

It should be noted that the following are the base stats for each character.

Bartz

Bartz is a simple traveler, who aimlessly wanders into Tycoon territory. The sudden impact of a massive meteor initiated the beginning of a quest that would span worlds. In addition, this sole event would reveal to Bartz the towering legacy that lies beneath his simple exterior.

Comes With: Broadsword, Leather Armor, Memento

Vigor	Speed	Stamina	Mag.Pwr	Bat.Pwr
28	25	27	25	3

Reina

Princess Reina, the youngest daughter of the King of Tycoon, is a kind-hearted, yet adventurous, young woman. Her plan to follow in her father's footsteps nearly ends in disaster when she is caught by the blast from a falling meteor. A wanderer named Bartz saved Princess Reina, enabling her to journey to the Wind Shrine in search of her father.

Comes With: Knife, Leather Armor, Pendant

Vigor	Speed	Stamina	Mag.Pwr	Bat.Pwr
25	26	25	28	3

Galuf

Galuf, an original Warrior of Light, seeks to return to his home world after sensing a disturbance in the elemental crystals. Unfortunately, however, Galuf develops a case of amnesia due to the violent impact when his ship lands. This horrible incident robbed Galuf of all his memories, but not his name and sense of purpose.

Comes With: Leather Armor

Vigor	Speed	Stamina	Mag.Pwr	Bat.Pwr
27	24	28	24	3

Faris

The leader of a band of salty, but surprisingly loyal pirates, Faris has more than a few secrets to share with the rest of the group. Faris' strong nature and questions about the past help foster a close bond, thus creating more devotion to the quest at hand.

Comes With: Dirk, Leather Shield, Leather Armor

Vigor	Speed	Stamina	Mag.Pwr	Bat.Pwr
27	27	26	26	3

Jobs

Wind Crystal Jobs

Wind Shrine

New jobs gained from Crystals in Wind Shrine

Name	Vigor	Speed	Stamina	Mag.Pwr
Knight	+27	+1	+20	-14
Monk	+26	+1	+26	-23
Blue Mage	-8	+1	+3	+23
Thief	+1	+16	+2	-6
Black Mage	-9	0	-2	+21
White Mage	-7	+1	0	+25

Knight

Valiant warriors. Covers allies nearing KO status.

2nd Slot Default Ability: !Guard

Level#	ABP Needed	Ability Name	Description
Level 1	10	Cover	Protect injured allies
Level 2	30	!Guard	Defends from physical attacks
Level 3	50	2-handed	Can hold sword/katana/axe with 2 hands for 2x effect
Level 4	100	EqShield	Can equip shield
Level 5	150	EqArmor	Can equip armor
Level 6	350	EqSword	Can equip sword

Monk

Expert martial artist. Powerful critical attacks & counterattacks.

2nd Slot Default Ability: !Kick

Level#	ABP Needed	Ability Name	Description
Level 1	15	!Store	Charge energy for 1 turn and cause 2x damage on next attack
Level 2	30	Barefist	Gain same attack power as Monk
Level 3	45	!Chkra	Restore HP. Heals poison, blind, and other conditions
Level 4	60	Counter	Counter attacks when attacked
Level 5	100	HP +10%	Max HP 10% up
Level 6	150	HP +20%	Max HP 20% up
Level 7	300	HP +30%	Max HP 30% up

Blue Mage

Mages with enemies' skills. Learn special monster skills.

2nd Slot Default Ability: !Blue

Level#	ABP Needed	Ability Name	Description
Level 1	10	!Check	Checks enemy's HP/weakness
Level 2	20	Learning	Learn monster special attacks
Level 3	70	!Blue	Cast Blue Magic

Condemnd	Roulette	AquaRake
L5 Doom	L4 Qrtr	L2 Old
L3 Flare	ToadSong	LitlSong
Flash	TimeSlip	MoonFlut
DoomClaw	Aero	Aero 2
Aero 3	Burn Ray	GobPunch
BlakShok	GuardOff	Pep Up
MindBlst	RedFeast	MagHammr
Guardian	Exploder	????
Blowfish	Whitwind	Missile

Level#	ABP Needed	Ability Name	Description
Level 4	250	!View	See enemy's level/HP/weakness/condition

Thief

Expert bandits. Dash with cancel button.

2nd Slot Default Ability: !Steal

Level#	ABP Needed	Ability Name	Description
Level 1	10	Secret	Can find "hidden rooms"
Level 2	20	!Flee	Escape quickly from some enemies
Level 3	30	Dash	Use direcitonal key while holding the 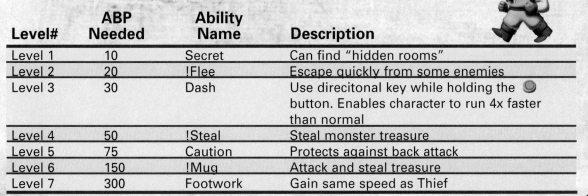 button. Enables character to run 4x faster than normal
Level 4	50	!Steal	Steal monster treasure
Level 5	75	Caution	Protects against back attack
Level 6	150	!Mug	Attack and steal treasure
Level 7	300	Footwork	Gain same speed as Thief

Black Mage

Battle mages. Use Black magic.

2nd Slot Default Ability: !Black

Level#	ABP Needed	Ability Name	Description
Level 1	10	!Black	Can use Level 1 Black magic Fire, Ice, Bolt
Level 2	20	!Black	Can use Level 2 Black magic Poison, Sleep, Toad
Level 3	30	!Black	Can use Level 3 Black magic Fire2, Ice2, Bolt2
Level 4	50	!Black	Can use Level 4 Black magic Drain, Break, Bio
Level 5	70	!Black	Can use Level 5 Black magic Fire3, Ice3, Bolt3
Level 6	100	!Black	Can use Level 6 Black magic Flare, Doom, Asper
Level 7	400	MP +30%	Max MP 30% up

White Mage

Protective mages. Use White magic.

2nd Slot Default Ability: !White

Level#	ABP Needed	Ability Name	Description
Level 1	10	!White	Can use Level 1 White magic Cure, Scan, Antdot
Level 2	20	!White	Can use Level 2 White magic Mute, Protes, Mini
Level 3	30	!White	Can use Level 3 White magic Cure2, Raise, Muddle
Level 4	50	!White	Can use Level 4 White magic Blink, Shell, Esna
Level 5	70	!White	Can use Level 5 White magic Cure3, Rflect, Bersrk
Level 6	100	!White	Can use Level 6 White magic Arise, Holy, Dispel
Level 7	300	MP + 10%	Max MP 10% up

Walz Tower

New jobs gained from Crystals in Walz Tower

Name	Vigor	Speed	Stamina	Mag.Pwr
Berserker	+21	-5	+25	-23
Sorcerer	+14	+14	+14	+1
TimeMage	-5	+2	-3	+24
Summoner	-10	-4	+1	+23
Red Mage	+8	+5	-6	+8

Berserker

Bestial Warriors. Always Berserk in battle.

2nd Slot Default Ability: None

Level#	ABP Needed	Ability Name	Description
Level 1	100	Berserk	Attack until enemy dies
Level 2	400	EqAxe	Can equip axe

Sorcerer

Sword-using mages. Cast Mbarrier while near KO.

2nd Slot Default Ability: !Sword

Level#	ABP Needed	Ability Name	Description
Level 1	10	Magiwall	Auto-Mbarrier when KO'ed
Level 2	20	!Sword	Can use Level 1 Sword magic Fire/Ice/Bolt
Level 3	30	!Sword	Can use Level 2 Sword magic Poison/Mute/Sleep
Level 4	50	!Sword	Can use Level 3 Sword magic Fire2/Ice2/Bolt2
Level 5	70	!Sword	Can use Level 4 Sword magic Drain/Break/Bio
Level 6	100	!Sword	Can use Level 5 Sword magic Fire3/Ice3/Bolt3
Level 7	400	!Sword	Can use Level 6 Sword magic Holy/Flare/Asper

Time Mage

Masters of space & time. Use Time & Space magic.

2nd Slot Default Ability: !Time

Level#	ABP Needed	Ability Name	Description
Level 1	10	!Time	Can use Level 1 Time magic Speed, Slow, Regen
Level 2	20	!Time	Can use Level 2 Time magic Mute, Haste, Float
Level 3	30	!Time	Can use Level 3 Time magic Demi, Stop, Telepo
Level 4	50	!Time	Can use Level 4 Time magic Comet, Slow2, Return
Level 5	70	!Time	Can use Level 5 Time magic Demi2, Haste2, Old
Level 6	100	!Time	Can use Level 6 Time magic Meteo, Quick, X-zone
Level 7	250	EqRod	Can equip Rod

Summoner

Mages with summoning magic. Summon magic beings.

2nd Slot Default Ability: !Summn

Level#	ABP Needed	Ability Name	Description
Level 1	15	!Summn	Can use Level 1 Summon magic Chocobo, Sylph, Remora
Level 2	30	!Summn	Can use Level 2 Summon magic Shiva, Ramuh, Ifrit
Level 3	45	!Summn	Can use Level 3 Summon magic Titan, Golem, Shoat
Level 4	60	!Summn	Can use Level 4 Summon magic Carbuncl, Hydra, Odin
Level 5	100	!Summn	Can use Level 5 Summon magic Phoenix, Leviathan, Bahamut
Level 6	500	!Call	Randomly summons a beast w/o using MP

Red Mage

Versatile Mages. Use Black & White magic.

2nd Slot Default Ability: !Red

Level#	ABP Needed	Ability Name	Description
Level 1	20	!Red	Can use Level 1 Red magic Cure/Scan/Antdot/Fire/Ice/Bolt
Level 2	40	!Red	Can use Level 2 Red magic Mute/Protes/Mini/Poison/Sleep/Toad
Level 3	100	!Red	Can use Level 3 Red magic Cure2/Raise/Muddle/Fire2/Ice2/Bolt2
Level 4	999	!Redx2	Back-to-back spells

Fire Ship

New jobs gained from Crystals on Fire Ship

Name	Vigor	Speed	Stamina	Mag.Pwr
Trainer	+21	-5	+25	-23
Geomancer	+4	+2	+4	+24
Ninja	+15	+14	+3	-10

Trainer

Monster Trainers. Control & capture monsters.

2nd Slot Default Ability: !Catch

Level#	ABP Needed	Ability Name	Description
Level 1	10	!Tame	Calm monster
Level 2	50	!Cntrl	Control monster
Level 3	100	EqWhip	Can equip whip
Level 4	300	!Catch	Catch certain monsters

Geomancer

Masters of the elements. No damage on damage floors.

2nd Slot Default Ability: !Earth

Level#	ABP Needed	Ability Name	Description
Level 1	25	!Earth	Attack enemy with nature's power
Level 2	50	Findhole	Can find trap doors
Level 3	100	Antitrap	No damage on damage floors

Ninja

Stealth fighters. Use two swords.

2nd Slot Default Ability: !Throw

Level#	ABP Needed	Ability Name	Description
Level 1	10	!Dustb	Escape quickly from some enemies
Level 2	30	!Twin	Creates an illusion causing the enemy to miss
Level 3	50	Firstatk	Raises % of first attack
Level 4	150	!Throw	Throw/attack with weapon. Use with Ninja/shuriken "throw"
Level 5	450	2-swords	Hold weapon in each hand. Bow/Harp excluded

Chocobo Forest

New jobs gained from Crystals in Chocobo Forest

Name	Vigor	Speed	Stamina	Mag.Pwr
Bard	-8	+8	-9	+11
Hunter	+16	+12	+1	-5

Bard

Singing fighters. Sing in battle.

2nd Slot Default Ability: !Sing

Level#	ABP Needed	Ability Name	Description
Level 1	25	!Hide	Evade attack when hidden
Level 2	50	EqHarp	Can equip harp
Level 3	100	!Sing	Sing Magic songs

PowerSong	SpeedSong
Str.Song	MP Song
LVL Song	Requiem
Love Song	TemptSong

Hunter

Nature loving Hunters. Call on friendly critters.

2nd Slot Default Ability: !Aim

Level#	ABP Needed	Ability Name	Description
Level 1	15	!Critt	Calls friends from the woods

Mindia Rabbit Lv. 1	Nightingale Lv. 11	Skunk Lv. 31
Squirrel Lv. 1	Tree Squirrel Lv. 16	Wild Boar Lv. 41
Bee Swarm Lv. 6	Falcon Lv. 21	Unicorn Lv. 51

Level#	ABP Needed	Ability Name	Description
Level 2	45	!Aim	Raise accuracy
Level 3	135	EqBow	Can equip bow
Level 4	405	!Sshot	4x attack

Earth Shrine

New jobs gained from Crystals in Earth Shrine

Name	Vigor	Speed	Stamina	Mag.Pwr
Samurai	+19	+2	+19	-12
Lancer	+18	+5	+15	-12
Dancer	+5	+5	-10	-5
Chemist	+2	+3	+6	-4

Samurai

Master swordsmen. Toss & sword catch.

2nd Slot Default Ability: !$toss

Level#	ABP Needed	Ability Name	Description
Level 1	10	!Sslap	Petrify enemy
Level 2	30	!$toss	Throw GP, damage enemy
Level 3	60	Swrdgrab	Catches attack
Level 4	180	EqKatana	Can equip katana
Level 5	540	!Fdraw	Randomly attacks enemy with katana

Lancer

Dragon knights. Jumping lance attacks.

2nd Slot Default Ability: !Jump

Level#	ABP Needed	Ability Name	Description
Level 1	50	!Jump	Jumping attack. 2x stronger with spear attack
Level 2	150	!Lance	Drain HP/MP
Level 3	400	EqLance	Can equip spear

Dancer

Dancing fighters. Dance to confuse enemies.

2nd Slot Default Ability: !Dance

Level#	ABP Needed	Ability Name	Description
Level 1	25	!Flirt	Thwart an attack by "attracting" your enemy
Level 2	50	!Dance	Dance the forbidden dance

Temptango	Sword Dance
WonderWaltz	Jitterbug

Level#	ABP Needed	Ability Name	Description
Level 3	325	EqRibbon	Can equip ribbon

Chemist

Medicine users. 2x effect of Potions/Ether.

2nd Slot Default Ability: !Drink

Level#	ABP Needed	Ability Name	Description
Level 1	15	Medicine	2x Potion/Ether
Level 2	30	!Mix	Mix items in battle to make special drinks
Level 3	45	!Drink	Drink certain items
Level 4	135	!Recvr	Recover from various conditions
Level 5	405	!Rvive	Restore KO'ed ally

Job Gained on World 3

Mimic

Battle mime. Mimic allies' attacks.

2nd Slot Default Ability: !Mimic

Note that Mimic is actually in the first slot, and all of the other 3 slots are open for customization. !Fight and !Item will appear in your list of Abilities when the Mimic class is selected.

Level#	ABP Needed	Ability Name	Description
Level 1	999	!Mimic	Mimic preceding command

FINAL FANTASY ANTHOLOGY™

FINAL FANTASY® V
Walkthrough

THE BEGINNING

After the opening scenes end, use the Chocobo to enter the forest, where you will discover that a meteorite has crashed into the earth. You meet up with Reina, who claims that she is looking for her father, who hasn't returned from the Wind Shrine. In addition, you discover that a third civilian has been injured.

The injured civilian, named Galuf, eventually comes to but he remembers little else about himself, other than his name and that he was also heading to the Wind Shrine. After Reina and Galuf head to the Wind Shrine, you should return to your Chocobo.

NOTE

Make sure you pick up the Phoenix Down (1) in the chest near the meteorite.

Earthquake!

Ride your Chocobo to the only available path on the map to the northwest. However, as you enter, an earthquake hits and the ground begins to separate.

After disposing of the goblins in the canyon, carry Reina and Galuf to safety in the hills.

As they regain consciousness, Bartz agrees to join them on their quest to reach the Wind Shrine. The only problem is that the earthquake and the meteor have blocked the only passages to the Shrine. You are then forced to enter a small cave that was created during the commotion. Save your game and head inside.

PIRATE COVE

Enemies
Stroper

Items
Leather Cap

Upon entering the cave, replenish your health at the underground spring located in the second cave to the right. As you head through the cave, you'll eventually sneak up on what looks like a pirate. The pirate then flicks a switch on one of the cave walls, which opens a secret doorway leading deeper into the caverns.

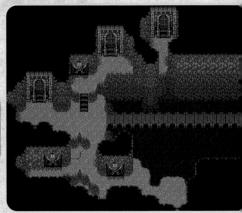

Follow him into the cave by flipping the switch on the wall, and head through the doorway to emerge in what resembles a secret underground harbor for pirate ships!

Your only hope for finding the Wind Shrine at this point is to sneak onto one of the boats. However, the place is crawling with pirates, so you must be careful! Head up and to the right to cross a long wooden pier.

Captured by Faris!

After boarding one of the ships, check the wheel at the front of the boat. Once you do, you'll get caught! The pirate leader, Faris, and the rest of the gangly crew will descend upon you.

Puzzled by Reina's amulet gleaming in the sunlight, Faris chooses to throw your group into a cell. However, Faris soon releases your party because Faris realizes that the amulet that Reina is wearing is similar to the one Faris is also wearing. Faris then agrees to help you reach the Wind Shrine!

You then meet Hydra, the great water dragon, who has helped Faris since childhood. Hydra pulls the boat through the water, making travel a cinch with or without the wind's assistance.

Enemies
None

Items
Ether (1)
Phoenix Down (2)
Tonic (3)
100 GP (4)
Tent (5)
150 GP (6)
Tonic (7)
Tent (8)
Leather Shoes (9)
Phoenix Down (10)
Leather Shoes (11)

TULE VILLAGE

Checklist

☐ Play Piano #1

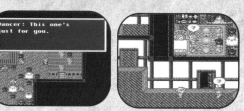

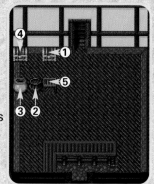

Sail your ship to the northwestern shore along the inner sea to find the small village of Tule. While there, stock up on items, weapons and armor, but don't forget to visit the House of Learning to bone up on some of the basics of the game. You can also pick up some items in the house as well.

You'll learn that a man named Zok lives in the big mansion at the far end of town. Reina knows him through her father, but upon visiting the mansion, you learn that he is not home. It's time to head to the Wind Shrine!

Enemies

Money Mage
Mauldwin
BlakGoblin
Whitesnake

Items

Tonic (x5)
Tent (1)
Leather Cap (2)
Broadsword (3)
Staff (4)

WIND SHRINE

The Wind Shrine is located on the north shore across the inner sea to the east. As you enter, you discover that several of the King's attendants have occupied the rooms on the first floor.

After speaking with them, you learn that the king hasn't returned from his trip. Something's definitely wrong. Take a moment to speak with the two guards at the south end of the room, and they'll give you five **Tonics** and let you use the **Recovery Water Jug** to replenish your health.

When you are ready, head up the staircase through the door at the back of the 1st floor to start your long climb to the Wind Crystal Room. On the 2nd floor, you should save your game and pick up the **Tent** from the chest.

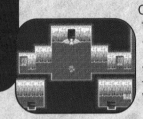

On the 3rd floor, you can fetch the **Leather Cap** and **Broadsword** from the two chests. When you reach the 4th floor, you'll meet an obstacle blocking your path: the Boss Wingrapter!

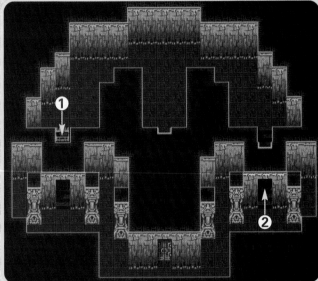

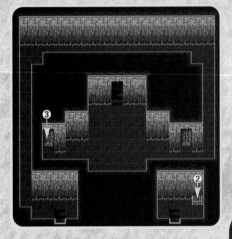

Boss: Wingrapter

LV: 1
HP: 250

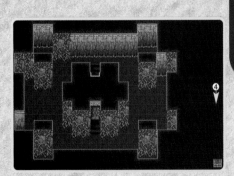

To reach Reina's father, you must fight this tough battle. Make sure that each party member is equipped with the most powerful weapon available: the Broadsword. Hack away at Wingrapter, and avoid attacking it when its wings are not extended. Doing so provokes a powerful counterattack called Iron Nail, which causes damage to the entire party.

The Wind Crystal

You are then given the first set of **Crystal Shards**, which contain the power of ancient warriors and grant you the ability to take on new jobs. You can now change your party members' abilities to the following:

Name	Vigor	Speed	Stamina	Mag.Pwr
Knight	+27	+1	+20	-14
Monk	+26	+1	+26	-23
Blue Mage	-8	+1	+3	+23
Thief	+1	+16	+2	-6
Black Mage	-9	0	-2	+21
White Mage	-7	+1	0	+25

To exit the Wind Shrine, step onto the transport to visit the outside world.

Enemies

None

Items

Ether (1)
Phoenix Down (2)
Tonic (3)
100 GP (4)
Tent (5)
150 GP (6)
Tonic (7)
Tent (8)
Leather Shoes (9)
Phoenix Down (10)
Leather Shoes (11)

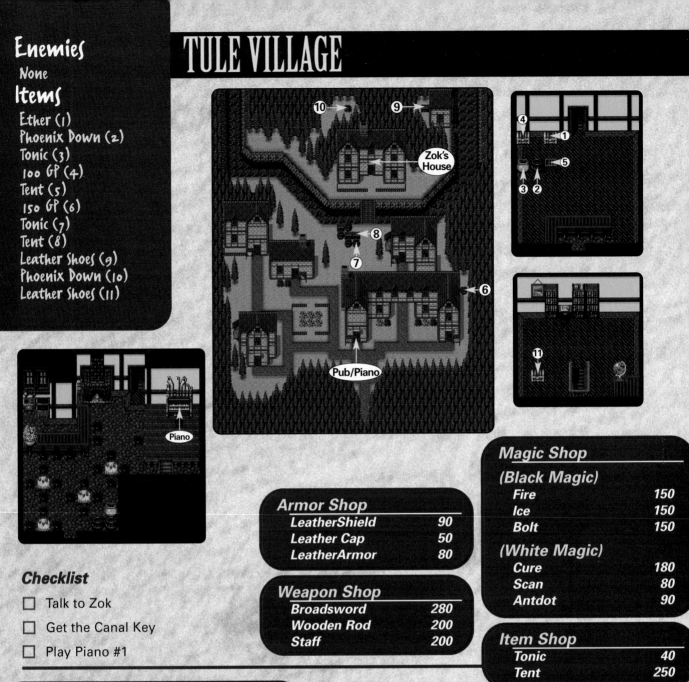

Zok's House

Pub/Piano

Piano

Checklist

☐ Talk to Zok

☐ Get the Canal Key

☐ Play Piano #1

Armor Shop

LeatherShield	90
Leather Cap	50
LeatherArmor	80

Weapon Shop

Broadsword	280
Wooden Rod	200
Staff	200

Magic Shop

(Black Magic)

Fire	150
Ice	150
Bolt	150

(White Magic)

Cure	180
Scan	80
Antdot	90

Item Shop

Tonic	40
Tent	250

Around Town

After clearing the Wind Shrine, visit Tule Village to the west from the Shrine so you can rest, stock up, and chat with the villagers.

Make sure you visit the House of Learning. This is where you'll learn the basics of playing FINAL FANTASY® V, plus you'll learn about the jobs and the battle system.

Getting the Canal Key

To reach the next Shrine, you must speak with Zok in the mansion at the back of town. He informs you that he lost the **Canal Key**, but offers you his home to rest in.

During the night, Bartz will speak with Zok, who admits that he has the Canal Key. However, he was afraid that he would jeopardize Reina to the monsters that have overrun the waterway. Zok hands you the Canal Key.

Enemies

Fins
Cybis
Thunderpit
Karl Boss (Boss)

Items

None

TORNA CANAL

Checklist

☐ Unlock the Canal   ☐ Fight Karl Boss (Boss)

Reina: Think they'd give us a ride...?

Take the pirate ship to the canal south of the Wind Shrine, and use the Canal Key to enter. As you proceed further into the Canal, a whirlpool nearly sucks your ship underwater.

It's time to fight Karl Boss, the Boss of Torna Canal!

Suggested Level: 5
Weakness: Bolt
Item Won: Tent

LV: 5
HP: 650

Karl Boss

The best way to defeat Karl Boss is to make your entire party Black Mages, and purchase the Bolt spell in Tule Village. Have each party member cast Bolt during each turn to defeat Karl Boss in no time.

Also, you may want to make one party member into a White Mage to heal during rounds, especially after Karl Boss casts the Tail Screw attack.

Tentacle / Tail Screw

Karl Boss   Bartz 195 Reina 129 Galuf 93 Faris 93
Karl Boss   Bartz 95 Reina 129 Galuf 93 Faris 93

Enemies

Skeleton
CrystalSlug
LumberBeast
Psychoheds

Items

Flail (1)
Tent (2)
990 GP (3)
Tonic (4)
Phoenix Down (5)
World Map (6)
Antidote (7)
Antidote (8)
Phoenix Down (9)

SHIP GRAVEYARD

Navigating the Graveyard

Checklist

☐ Get the World Map

☐ Raise the sunken ship

☐ Fight Siren

Beginner's house

Faris: Are ye gonna pass thru here? ...gonna get wet...

Received 990GP!

After the Boss fight with Karl Boss, you will find yourself in a Ship Graveyard. You must find your way across the water by using the skipping stone bridges while passing through different sunken ships.

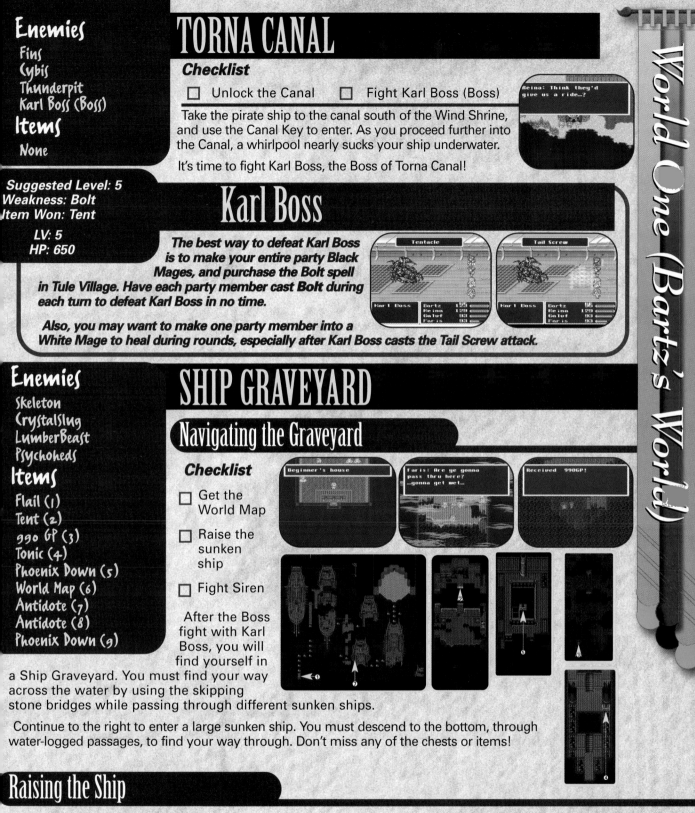

Continue to the right to enter a large sunken ship. You must descend to the bottom, through water-logged passages, to find your way through. Don't miss any of the chests or items!

Raising the Ship

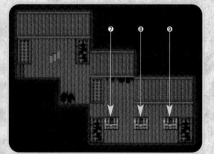

After resting, exit the ship and cross over to the next one. Inside the short hall, pick up the **World Map** from the chest. Continue across the rocks to the right to find the chest on the next ship. Upon opening it, the ship will suddenly rise to the surface.

Now just hop across the rocks leading north to finally reach dry land! Unfortunately, something's waiting for you on the shore.

Received "World Map!"

LV: 2
HP: 900

Suggested Level: 7
Weakness: Cure
Item Won: Bronze Armor or Bronze Shield

Siren

Siren has two distinctly different forms to fight. The first form can heal itself for up to 60 HP, while its second form is that of a zombie.

The best way to fight Siren is to have a party consisting of characters who can use powerful attacks and use **Cure** spells. You can either have White Mages with the **Barefist** ability, or any other class using the White ability.

Enemies

None

Items

Antidote (1)
Ice Rod (2)
1000 GP (3)

TOWN OF KERWIN

Magic Shop

(Black Magic)

Fire	150
Ice	150
Bolt	150
Sleep	300

(White Magic)

Cure	180
Antdot	90
Mute	280
Protes	280

Weapon Shop

Dirk	300
Long Sword	480
Wooden Rod	200
Staff	200

Checklist

- [ ] Learn about the Dragon at North Mountain
- [ ] Rest and stock up
- [ ] Get the Ice Rod
- [ ] Play Piano #2

Armor Shop

Bronze Shield	290
Bronze Helmet	250
Bronze Armor	400
Bronze Plate	350
Cotton Robe	300

Item Shop

Tonic	40
Antidote	30
Eye Drop	20
Maiden's Kiss	60
Cornucopia	50
Soft	150
Phoenix Down	1000
Tent	250

Where's Walz?

After you rest and stock up, speak with the townspeople to learn more about the situation in the town of Walz. You also learn that there have been sightings of a Dragon atop North Mountain near Kerwin.

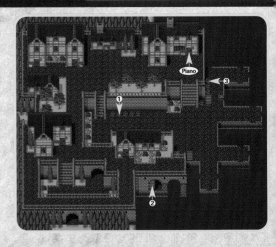

A woman mentions that her husband in the Pub recently saw the Dragon. Head to the Pub and look for her hubby on the second floor. After talking to him, Reina insists that the Dragon is her father's. Now it's on to North Mountain.

Getting the Ice Rod

From the entrance leading to the town of Kerwin, head to the right through the tunnel, then take a right toward the boxes in the small corridor. Make your way to the left and pass under the Item Shop to grab the **Ice Rod** from one of the boxes.

Enemies

Rockcutter
Ghilcat
Stones
Cockataur
Magissa (Boss)

Items

Soft (1)
Phoenix Down (2)

NORTH MOUNTAIN

Checklist

☐ Beat Magissa (Boss)

☐ Find the Dragon

Across the Divide

North Mountain is located northeast of Kerwin. Upon entering, pass through the first set of caves, making sure to pick up the **Soft** and **Phoenix Down**. You must weave in and out of the caves by passing along the outer mountainside through a few more caves until you reach a Save Point. Heal your party members and save your game, and then head outside to cross the bridge.

NOTE

Avoid touching the purple Dragon Grass when traveling outside the cave. Touching it will poison your party! If you get poisoned, you'll notice that the screen will look unusual as you walk around.

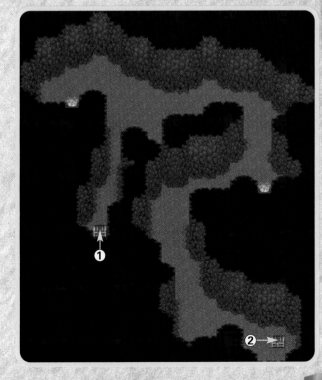

Magissa & Faltzer

Magissa	Faltzer
LV: 8	LV: 8
HP: 650	HP: 850

Suggested Level: 8
Weakness: None
Item Won: Power Drink, Whip

Magissa isn't exactly an easy fight, but it's fairly easy compared to the beast this Boss summons named Faltzer. To really speed through this fight, create four Monks out of your party, and use their powerful physical attacks and high critical hit rates to whittle down Magissa's HP before Faltzer is even summoned.

If you want, place a White Mage in your party so he/she can heal party members after getting hit with the Magissa's magic spells. Note that any type of magic works against Magissa and Faltzer.

The Dragon

You're now free to continue up the mountainside. At the top, you'll discover King Tycoon's Dragon lying injured among the Dragon Grass. After Reina heals the Dragon, you can then ride it down to the town of Walz.

Enemies
ElfToad
IceSoldier

Items
SilvrGlasses (1)

TOWN OF WALZ

Checklist
- ☐ Gather information about Water Crystal
- ☐ Stock up

Magic Shop

(Time Magic)

Slow	80
Regen	100
Mute	320
Haste	320

(Summon Magic)

Chocobo	300
Sylph	350
Remora	250

Item Shop

Tonic	50
Antidote	30
Eye Drop	20
Maiden's Kiss	60
Cornucopia	50
Soft	150
Phoenix Down	1000
Tent	250

Armor Shop

Iron Shield	390
Iron Helmet	350
Iron Armor	500
Kung-fu Suit	450
Cotton Robe	300

Weapon Shop

Battle Ax	650
Long Sword	480
Dirk	300

The Water Crystal

You discover from the townspeople that King Walz has been using a machine to draw more power out of the Water Crystal. You must talk with him and make him stop before the Crystal shatters!

Take a moment to acquaint yourself with Garula, who's in the lower, right-hand section of the town. Garula's role in the game will come into play later. Now head to Walz Castle next to the town.

Enemies

Paddlethru
ElfToad
Y Burn
RicardMage
IceSoldier

Items
(B.1 Floor)

Elf Cloak (1)
1000 GP (2)
"Learned Speed!" (3)
1000 GP (4)

Items
(Storehouse)

Tent (5)
490 GP (6)
Phoenix Down (7)

WALZ CASTLE

Checklist

☐ Speak with King Walz

The Walz Meteor!

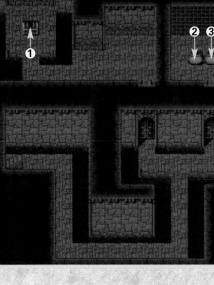

After entering the Castle, head to the throne room and speak with King Walz. Upon doing so, a loud crash signifies the arrival of the second meteor! At this point, a guard notifies you that Walz Tower has been overrun with monsters, and that Garula has stormed the tower to get to the Crystal!

King: Assemble the guard! To the tower at once!
Soldier: Yes sir!

Reina: I'm afraid we must ask you to please stop amplifying the Water Crystal!

NOTE

The Harpy in the basement of Walz Castle is one tough enemy! However, if you choose to fight it, you can learn the Moon Flute. It does have a weakness to water-based spells, so keep that in mind as you fight it.

Enemies
ElfToad
IceSoldier
Shiva (Boss)
Items
None

WALZ WATER TOWER

Checklist

☐ Beat Shiva (Boss) and receive Shiva summon.

Finding Shiva

To enter the Water Tower behind Walz Castle, head down one floor from the entrance by using the staircase to the right of the double doors. On the lower floor, exit the castle by passing through the doorway to the lower right.

Walz Water Tower

This places you outside the castle. Follow the waterway around to the back of the castle, and pass through the center of the waterfall. This takes you to the Water Tower.

Follow the path until you reach a room filled with raised platforms. Climb to the center platform to meet Shiva.

NOTE

Create a Blue Mage to learn the Elftoad's Toad Song skill. This enemy will only cast it if it is alone, so eliminate all the enemies until there is only one Elftoad.

LV: 11
HP: 1500

Suggested Level: 7
Weakness: Fire
Item Won: Shiva summon

Shiva

This fight is easy if you create four Red or Black Mages and use Fire2 spells on the entire party of enemies from the start of the battle. Keep plugging away with either a Ninja throwing Fireskill or Fire2, and Shiva and its cohorts will be history.

Enemies
PaddleThru
ElfToad
Y Burn
RicardMage
IceSoldier
Garula (Boss)

Items
Silk Robe (1)
Maiden's Kiss (2)
Ether (3)
SilvrArmBand (4)

WALZ TOWER

Checklist

☐ Find King Walz

☐ Save the Water Crystal

☐ Defeat Garula (Boss)

Find the King

Helpless and injured, the King is on the middle floor of the tower. He urges you to continue and stop Garula from destroying the Water Crystal.

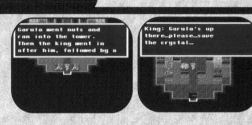

Find the Water Crystal!

From the King's location, proceed to the left and walk straight into the water. Follow the path to the ivy-covered wall, and climb the vines to grab the **Silk Robe**.

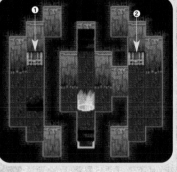

Jump down the opening to proceed back up through the middle hole to save your game. Explore a little to find all the chests, and then continue to climb up the floors to locate the Crystal Room, where Garula awaits!

LV: 3
HP: 1200

Suggested Level: 6
Weakness: None
Item Won: Potion

Garula

This Boss fight can be difficult if you don't know exactly what to do. If you learned the **Toad Song** *from the Elftoad in the Walz Water Tower, cast it on Garula to turn it into a frog. You can also cast* **Mute** *to silence Garula from recovering from the spell. When turned into a frog, Garula is easy to defeat.*

However, if you don't have the Toad Song spell, simply cast defensive spells on your party using a White Mage. It's also wise to create a few Knights to protect party members from Garula's most powerful attack, Charge.

Get the Crystal Shards!

After fighting Garula, pick up the **Crystal Shards** so you can gain new jobs for your party. After doing so, you're automatically transported outside the tower.

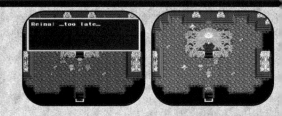

New jobs gained from Crystals in Walz Tower

Name	Vigor	Speed	Stamina	Mag.Pwr
Berserker	+21	-5	+25	-23
Sorcerer	+14	+14	+14	+1
Time Mage	-5	+2	-3	+24
Summoner	-10	-4	+1	+23
Red Mage	+8	+5	-6	+8

Next Stop, Karnak!

Return to Walz Castle and speak to the King, who is in his room upstairs. He informs you that Karnak is in need of your attention, because the **Fire Crystal** is being threatened.

Also, don't forget to speak to the Karnak Soldier in the castle.

Head to the Walz Meteor and enter. Step on the warp tile to get transported to the western continent, where you'll find the Town of Karnak and Karnak Castle.

Enemies

None

Items
(Inside Castle)

Potion (1),
Cottage (2)
Ether (3)
Phoenix Down (4)
Elixir (5)
Ether (6)
Elixir (7)
Phoenix Down (8)
Maiden's Kiss (9)
Healing Staff (10)
Shuriken (11)
Monster Bell (12)
Katana (13)

TYCOON CASTLE (OPTIONAL)

Checklist

☐ Get the Healing Staff

Getting the Healing Staff

After fighting Garula, stop by Tycoon Castle. You can stay overnight for free, plus you get to see a cool event. Afterwards, visit the Storage Room to the left of the castle in the courtyard, and find the switch at the back of the room.

Use the Thief's **Secret** ability to see the hidden path leading to the Chancellor. He'll give you the **Healing Staff**, plus you can pick up more items in the chests behind him.

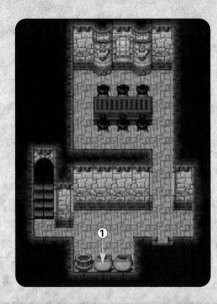

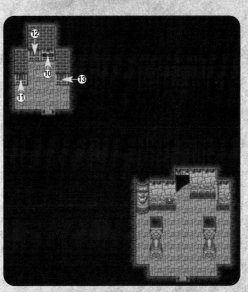

Enemies
None

Items
Fire Rod (1)

TOWN OF KARNAK

Checklist

☐ Find Professor Cid

☐ Get info on the Fire Crystal

☐ Play Piano #3

Armor Shop

MythrilShield	590
MythrilHelmet	550
Plumed Hat	350
MythrilArmor	700
Silver Plate	600
Silk Robe	500
MythrilGlove	600
SilvrArmBand	500

Weapon Shop

MythrilKnife	450
MythrilSword	880
MythrilHammer	1050
Fire Rod	750
Ice Rod	750
Lightning Rod	750
Flail	750

Item Shop

Tonic	40
Antidote	30
Eye Drop	20
Maiden's Kiss	60
Cornucopia	50
Soft	150
Phoenix Down	1000
Tent	250

Magic Shop

(White Magic; left counter)

Cure2	620
Raise	700
Muddle	650
Mute	280
Protes	280
Cure	180
Scan	80
Antdot	90

(Black Magic; center counter)

Fire2	800
Ice2	600
Bolt2	600
Poison	290
Sleep	300
Fire	150
Ice	150
Bolt	150

(Time Magic; right counter)

Demi	620
Stop	580
Haste	320
Mute	320
Slow	80
Regen	100

Reaching Karnak

Piano

From the meteor site, head north around the mountain range, and then go southwest through the forest to reach Karnak.

Karnak's Most Wanted

When you reach town, you learn that the Queen has imprisoned Professor Cid and that monsters have attacked the Fire Crystal. Head into one of the shops in town and purchase an item.

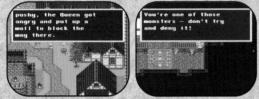

The moment you do, you get arrested for being a monster and are promptly thrown into a cell neighboring Cid's. While in the cell, constantly move around it and, eventually, Cid will bust through the wall.

Professor Cid

Cid introduces himself as the inventor who built the crystal amplifier for Karnak. He explains that he was imprisoned for trying to stop the amplifier from destroying the Fire Crystal. Soon after, you get released from prison by the Chancellor, who has come to free Cid.

He informs you that the Fire Crystal is indeed shattering, and he needs Cid's help to stop it. Cid suggests that the Fire Ship is the culprit, and asks you to meet him at the boat.

Karnak in Flames!

Upon leaving the prison and Karnak Castle, you discover that everything is in flames. Note that all the treasure chests around the castle are blocked, but remember their locations for later.

Exit Karnak and head to the shore to reach the Fire Ship.

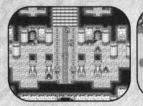

Enemies

Cool Dust
Defeater
Mottletrap
Poltergeist
Liquid Flame (Boss)

Items

MythrilGlove (1)
Elixir (2)
Cottage (3)
Elixir (4)
Phoenix Down (5)
Green Beret (6)
Thief'sGlove (7)
Moonring (8)
Elixir (9)

FIRE SHIP

Checklist

☐ Find the Queen

☐ Find the engine room

☐ Fight the Liquid Flame (Boss)

> **NOTE**
> Avoid casting Bolt on the Mottletrap enemies. Doing so causes them to spontaneously explode, inflicting damage to your party.

> **NOTE**
> When you run into the Cool Dust enemies, destroy them immediately or else they will cast Flash, which blinds your party.

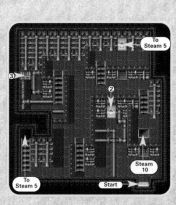

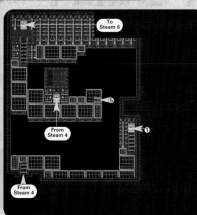

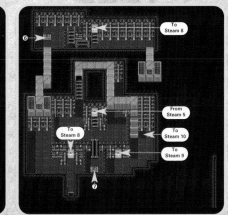

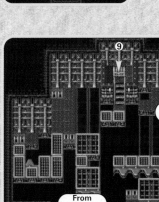

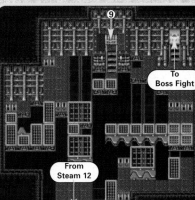

27

Find the Queen

Upon entering the Fire Ship, follow Cid until you reach the maze within the boat. You must find the Queen, who has run off to the deepest part of the ship.

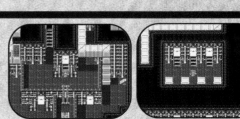

Chutes and Ladders

The inside of the Fire Ship maze is riddled with conveyor belts, ventilation chutes, and short trams that will both help and hinder you. Explore as many routes as possible so you can pick up all the items scattered throughout the maze. You'll discover many dead ends, but you'll eventually enter the heart of the Fire Ship maze. This is where you can save and heal your party.

Liquid Flame

Suggested Level: 12
Weakness: Ice
Item Won: Fire Rod or Fire Skill

*Create three party members as Black or Red Mages who can cast **Ice2** spells, while having one Mage play the role of medic by casting **Cure2** or using the **Healing Staff**. Also, it's important to equip as many of the remaining mages with **Ice Rods** to increase the power of Ice spells.*

When the Boss forms the shape of a hand, avoid casting magic spells. If you do cast any spells, make sure you heal your entire party before it counterattacks!

Enemies

None

Items

Monsters/Elixir (1)
2000 GP (2)
Monsters/Shuriken (3)
Monsters/Ribbon (4)
Monsters/Esna (5)
Monsters/Lgtningskill (6)
Monsters
Elixir (7 & 8)
2000 GP (9)
Monsters
Elixir (10-12)
Monsters/Elf Cloak (13)
Monsters/HuntingKnife (14)

ESCAPING KARNAK CASTLE!

Escaping the Castle

Checklist

☐ Escape Karnak Castle within 10 minutes!

☐ Defeat Iron Claw (boss)

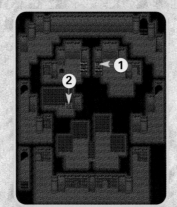

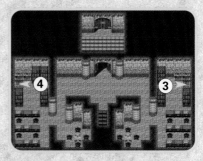

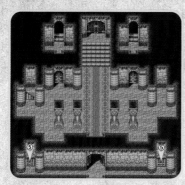

Save your game the moment you escape the Fire Ship, and then use a Tent to heal your party members. Now your job is to escape from Karnak Castle before it completely disintegrates. You have 10 minutes to do so, and there are lots of treasure chests to plunder on your way through.

Try to avoid wasting too much time fighting enemies, and only fight those enemies you encounter when opening some of the chests. After exiting the castle, prepare for another Boss fight.

NOTE
Use your Thief's Flee ability to quickly escape from unnecessary battles.

Iron Claw

LV: 39
HP: 900

Suggested Level: 12
Weakness: None
Items Won: None

Iron Claw has no real weakness, so you must hit it with your strongest attacks and magic spells. Make sure your Blue Mage learns the **Doom Claw** *attack from this Boss, and use Monks to cause as much damage as possible.*

When Iron Claw has sustained enough damage, it will change into the real thing. When this occurs, cure your party or use healing items to survive.

The Castle Destroyed!

After defeating Iron Claw, the building will explode, scattering **Crystal Shards** all over the landscape. Pick them up to receive a host of new jobs for your characters.

New jobs gained from Crystals on Fire Ship

Name	Vigor	Speed	Stamina	Mag.Pwr
Trainer	+21	-5	+25	-23
Geomancer	+4	+2	+4	+24
Ninja	+15	+14	+3	-10

TOWN OF KARNAK REVISITED

Checklist

- [ ] Rest and stock up
- [ ] Talk to Cid

Cid

On your return trip to the Town of Karnak, you'll discover that some of the shops are offering new items and weapons for sale. Pick up the **Fire Rod** located in the barrel at the front edge of the town wall. Now that the fire blocking the staircase leading up to it has been extinguished, you'll have no trouble reaching it.

Weapons Shop

(guy between shop owners)

Mythril Pike	790
Ninja Knife	600
Whip	1100
Monster Bell	500

Cid is on the second floor of the Pub. Unfortunately, he has lost his will to help out in your quest to find the remaining Crystal, and you have no way to get around without a ship or Dragon.

Now that the blockade obstructing the path to the Library of Ancients has been destroyed, stock up and prepare for the trip down to the southwest.

NOTE

Watch out for the Quadrharpy lurking in the desert areas south of Karnak. With its powerful AquaRake spell, it can quickly wipe out your party. If you're willing, have a Blue Mage learn the AquaRake spell from it.

Enemies
Biblos (Boss)
Ifrit (Boss)
Items
Ether (1)
Ninja Suit (2)
Phoenix Down (3)

LIBRARY OF ANCIENTS

Checklist

- [ ] Find and fight Ifrit (Boss)
- [ ] Fight Biblos (Boss)
- [ ] Find Mid

The Scholars

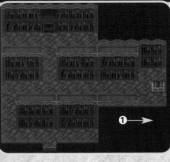

The Library of Ancients is located in a forest to the far southwest of the Town of Karnak. Inside, examine the urn in the lower left corner of the second floor. It will replenish your HP and MP completely!

The scholars in the library inform you that the lower levels of the building are overrun with monster books. They also tell you that Mid, Cid's grandson, is located somewhere below. It's your job to find him.

The Roof

If you stop by the roof of the Library, you'll discover that some scholars are burning a few possessed books. If you want, try to read each of the three books lined up below the furnace. Two of them contain general clues about the game, while the far right one contains monsters!

Finding Mid

To get through the Library of Ancients, enter through the door on the lower level near the entrance to the building. Inside the maze, you must shift bookcases and find secret passages by either examining holes in the bookshelves, or pushing up against the actual bookshelves.

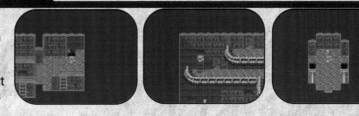

After weaving your way through the stacks of books, you'll eventually reach the room harboring Ifrit.

Ifrit

LV: 22
HP: 3000

Suggested Level: 13
Weakness: Ice
Item Won: Ifrit Summon

If you have at least three Red or Black Mages in your party, Ifrit is easy to destroy by using Ice magic. After getting hit with Ifrit's Fire2 spell, you must heal immediately in order to survive. Continue to use Ice magic and heal party members with Cure or Cure2.

You can also defeat Ifrit by summoning Shiva using a Summoner. After the battle, Ifrit will become Summon Magic for a Summoner.

Biblos

LV: 24
HP: 3600

Suggested Level: 15
Weakness: Fire
Items Won: Hard Body

Before you reach the small room where Mid is researching books, you must first fight past Biblos. Since you just captured Ifrit, summon it with a Summoner in your party. Biblos is immune to all magic except Fire spells, so keep this in mind.

To quickly end the fight, have a Blue Mage cast Doom Claw, which you learned from the Iron Claw Boss at Karnak Castle.

Mid

After the fight, Mid will escort you back to the surface of the Library and will listen to your story. At this point, he promptly takes off for Karnak without you. Exit the Library and return to the Town of Karnak.

See...with this book we should be able to repower the Fire Ship!

Reunion

Once you arrive in Karnak again, return to the second floor of the Pub and speak with Cid. Mid will interrupt and they will both take off to repair the Fire Ship. Follow them and they'll let you use the ship to sail to the Town of Crescent to the far southeast of Karnak.

Cid: Ouch! Knock it off, Mid!

Why don't you rest below until we get her started?!

Enemies
None
Items
None

JACHOL VILLAGE (OPTIONAL)

Checklist

☐ Learn about the Jachol Caves

☐ Play Piano #4

The Cave of Ancients

Jachol Village is located at the southern tip of the western continent, nestled between two mountain ridges. While in town, you will hear talk of the caves to the east. Apparently, these caves harbor treasures of the ancient civilization before them.

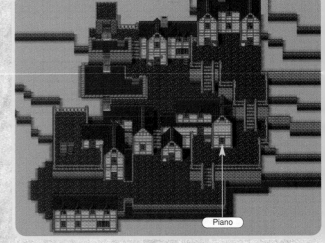

Piano

The stores sell weapons and tools that were discovered in a cave up north...

Item Shop

Tonic	40
Antidote	30
Eye Drop	20
Maiden's Kiss	60
Cornucopia	50
Soft	150
Phoenix Down	1000
Tent	250

Weapon Shop

Cleaver	3200
Coral Sword	2800
Mage Slasher	900
Trident	2700
Katana	5800
Silver Bow	1500

Magic Shop

(White Magic)	
Cure2	620
Raise	700
Muddle	650
Mute	280
Protes	280
Cure	180
Scan	80
Antdot	90

Armor Shop

Green Beret	2500
Ninja Suit	3000
Poet Robe	1000

Enemies
Nut Eater
Skull Eater

Items
Shuriken (1)
Tent (2)
Shock Whip (3)
(or Note if you released were-
wolf from jail)

JACHOL CAVE

Checklist

☐ Collect items

Chests Galore

There's not much to do in Jachol Cave aside from getting items. You must press switches on the wall to shift
passageways so that you can find your way through to
the main section of the caves.
When you're done plundering all
the chests, exit this area and head
for Crescent.

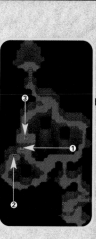

Enemies
Biosoldier
Doublizard
Crescent

Items
Piano #5

CRESCENT TOWN

Checklist

☐ Capture Black Chocobo from Black Chocobo Forest

☐ Get Crystal Shards

☐ Play Piano #5

Item Shop

Tonic	40
Antidote	30
Eye Drop	20
Maiden's Kiss	60
Cornucopia	50
Soft	150
Phoenix Down	1000
Tent	250

Magic Shop

(Black Magic)	
Fire2	600
Ice2	600
Bolt2	600
Poison	290
Sleep	300
Fire	150
Ice	150
Bolt	150

Armor Shop

Plumed Hat	350
Poet Robe	1000

Weapon Shop

Fire Bow	2500
Ice Bow	2500
Lightning Bow	2500
Silver Harp	800

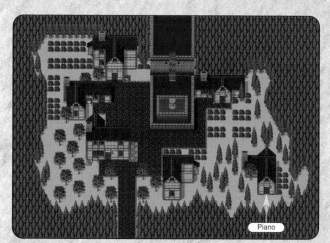

Piano

NOTE

If you're lucky, you may receive a Death Sickle after a fight with a Crescent.

NOTE

At the Minstrel's House, play the piano and then speak with him. By doing so, you'll learn the Strength Song for a Bard in your party.

The Black Chocobo

In Crescent, you discover that the Fire Ship has been sucked underwater by a large whirlpool that was triggered by an earthquake! Speak with all of the villagers to learn about a forest to the south. This is where you'll learn about the legendary Black Chocobo!

After tracking the Black Chocobo down, you'll discover that two **Crystal Shards** are hidden in the Chocobo's feathers. After capturing the Black Chocobo, you can use it to fly anywhere in the world. However, you can only land it in a forested area. Ride the Chocobo back to the Library of Ancients to speak with Cid and Mid.

The Crystal Shards

New jobs gained from Crystals in Chocobo Forest

Name	Vigor	Speed	Stamina	Mag.Pwr
Bard	-8	+8	-9	+11
Hunter	+16	+12	+1	-5

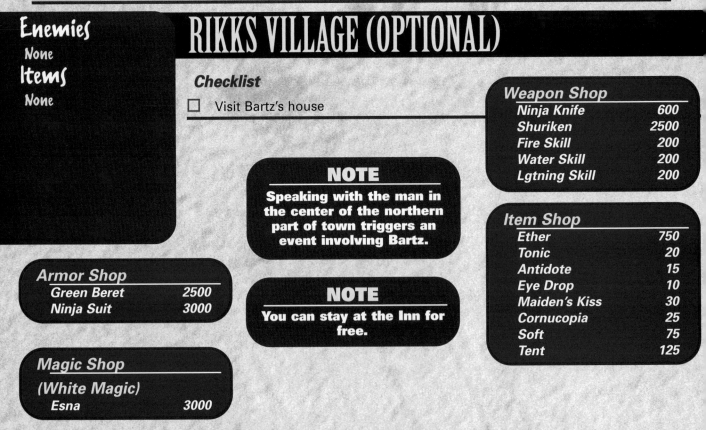

Enemies
None

Items
None

RIKKS VILLAGE (OPTIONAL)

Checklist

☐ Visit Bartz's house

NOTE

Speaking with the man in the center of the northern part of town triggers an event involving Bartz.

NOTE

You can stay at the Inn for free.

Weapon Shop

Ninja Knife	600
Shuriken	2500
Fire Skill	200
Water Skill	200
Lgtning Skill	200

Item Shop

Ether	750
Tonic	20
Antidote	15
Eye Drop	10
Maiden's Kiss	30
Cornucopia	25
Soft	75
Tent	125

Armor Shop

Green Beret	2500
Ninja Suit	3000

Magic Shop

(White Magic)

Esna	3000

Memories

Visit the Bard staying at Bartz's old house. After examining the music box on the table in the back of the house, Bartz will have a flashback of his parents. Afterwards, speak with the Bard again to learn the **Temptation Song**.

Enemies
None

Items
None

EASTERLY VILLAGE (OPTIONAL)

Checklist

- [ ] Get Ramuh summon
- [ ] Learn Toad
- [ ] Learn the Love Song

Relics

Fire Ring	50000
Coral Ring	50000
Angel Ring	50000

Finding Ramuh

To the far northeast of Karnak and the Library of Ancients, you'll find the isolated village of Easterly. When you reach the town, one of the villagers mentions an old man wandering the eastern woods with powerful thunder spells.

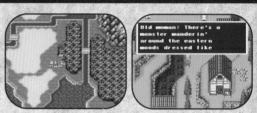

Exit the town and head east across the bridge. Wander around until you finally run into Ramuh.

Magic Shop

(Time Magic)

Demi	620
Stop	580
Haste	320
Mute	320
Slow	80
Regen	100

Item Shop

Tonic	40
Antidote	30
Eye Drop	20
Maiden's Kiss	60
Cornucopia	50
Soft	150
Phoenix Down	1000
Tent	250

Ramuh

LV: 21
HP: 4000

Suggested Level: 19
Weakness: Summon magic
Item Won: Ramuh Summon magic

The fight against Ramuh can be difficult if you're at a low level. Ramuh's Bolt spells are incredibly strong, so make sure you have a White Mage in your party for healing purposes.

*Use Summoners to cast **Shiva** or **Ifrit** on Ramuh. A quick way to defeat Ramuh is to create a party of Ninjas and throw Water Skills that can be purchased in Rikks Village. After causing enough damage, you'll hear the voice of Ifrit and the fight will be over.*

The Sleepy Toad

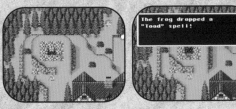

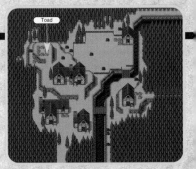

Check out the small square of flowers along the western edge of town. Step on the lower, right-hand flower and press the [X] button to cause a hole in the ground to open. The sleepy toad that the old man told you about will hop out and drop the **Toad** magic for a Black Mage to cast in battle.

Learning the Love Song

Walk over to the small pen of sheep at the back of town, and attempt to examine the sheep in the upper left-hand corner near the fence. It will get annoyed with you, and kick you over the fence near a wandering Minstrel. After speaking to the Minstrel, you'll learn the **Love Song** for any Bard in your party.

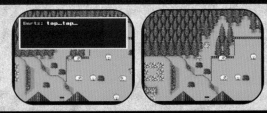

Enemies
None

Items
None

LIBRARY OF ANCIENTS

Checklist

☐ Speak with Cid and Mid

To the Desert!

Cid and Mid tell you about an ancient city of ruins located to the far south, past the impassable desert. They're convinced that you have what it takes to get past the dunes in the desert and reach the ruins. Heal your party and head to the west of the Library to find the entrance to the Sand Tides.

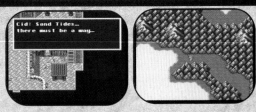

Enemies
SandKille
Sandboi
SandBear

Items
None

SAND TIDES DESERT

Checklist

☐ Fight the SandWorm

☐ Get through the Sand Tides

Building a Bridge

When you arrive at the Sand Tides, you discover that there is no way to cross the zig-zagging rivers of sand. Cid and Mid arrive shortly after to tell you their plan. All you need to do is destroy the SandWorms, which will create a bridge past the entrance.

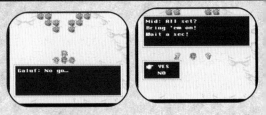

When you're ready, let Mid use his whistle to call forth the SandWorm!

SandWorm

LV: 18
HP: 3000

Suggested Level: 18
Weakness: Water
Items Won: None

*When fighting the SandWorm, you must hit it at the appropriate hole in the ground. It will continue to move, so carefully take aim. Also, if you cast magic or attack an empty hole, the SandWorm will always counter with a **Demi** spell, depleting half of your party's HP.*

*SandWorm can also cast **Quicksand**, which will inflict plenty of damage to your entire party and temporarily poison them. If you have a Blue Mage who has learned **AquaRake**, use it on the SandWorm to quickly end the fight. If you don't have AquaRake, then use **Waterskill** with a Ninja's throw ability, or simply continue to bombard it with physical attacks.*

Survive the Desert

You can now pass through the desert by riding along the different sand dune tides. Keep heading south until you pass through and exit on the south end of the Sand Tides.

NOTE

Using a Thief, try to steal a Javelin from the Sand Bears in the desert.

Enemies

None

Items

None

TOWN OF GORN

Checklist

☐ Find King Tycoon

The Elusive King

The moment you walk into the legendary Town of Ruins, also known as the Town of Gorn, you discover that you are not alone. You'll find that King Tycoon is shifting amongst the rubble, but you can't quite catch him. Follow him as best as you can, and then head north to the central building in the ruins.

As you approach King Tycoon, a trap door will suck you underground and deposit you in a strange, mechanical structure.

Enemies
ClayClaw (Boss)

Items
Shurikens (1 & 2)
"Mini" (3)

Checklist
☐ Find the exit

☐ Defeat ClayClaw (Boss)

A Strange New World

After landing, follow the path to reach an area with an exit to the south and a locked door to the north. Don't press the switch on the north wall just yet; instead, head south through the opening.

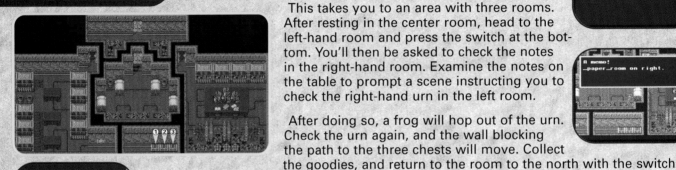

This takes you to an area with three rooms. After resting in the center room, head to the left-hand room and press the switch at the bottom. You'll then be asked to check the notes in the right-hand room. Examine the notes on the table to prompt a scene instructing you to check the right-hand urn in the left room.

After doing so, a frog will hop out of the urn. Check the urn again, and the wall blocking the path to the three chests will move. Collect the goodies, and return to the room to the north with the switch and locked door.

After pressing the switch, Cid and Mid will drop through a hole in the ground in the Black Chocobo Forest. Head through the doorway to see two ships in a dock.

Cid and Mid will join you on the Airship. After some repairs, you can use the Airship to fly anywhere. However, shortly after taking flight, a Boss comes seeking a fight!

ClayClaw

LV: 43
HP: 2000

Suggested Level: 20
Weakness: Bolt
Items Won: IceBow

ClayClaw has some tough attacks, however, you can counter them by using Ramuh or a Red/Black Mage's Bolt2 spells. If you have a Ninja in your party, use Shurikens to quickly destroy ClayClaw in about two rounds. After the fight, you'll dock again and Cid and Mid will urge you on to the Town of Gorn.

The Town of Gorn Revisited

As you approach the Town of Gorn, the ruins will suddenly disappear, only to be replaced by a large floating fortress! Return to the Airship Base to speak with Cid and Mid.

Enemies
Adamantaim (Boss)
Items
Adamantite

RETURN TO TYCOON METEOR

Checklist

☐ Get Adamantite

☐ Defeat Adamantaim (Boss)

Getting Adamantite

When you return to the Airship Base, Cid and Mid ask you to retrieve some Adamantite in order to make the ship fly higher. This is the only way to reach the floating fortress that emerged from the Gorn ruins.

Mid: Adamantite! If we reinforce the ship with this, it will fly higher!

Received "Adamantite!"

Take the Airship and fly back to the Tycoon Meteor. Once inside, pick up the **Adamantite** from the back wall of the small cavern. However, when you try to exit, a Boss confronts you.

LV: 20
HP: 2000

Suggested Level: 21
Weakness: Ice
Items Won: Turtle Shell

Adamantaim

There are a few ways to destroy the Boss, but it all depends on the types of party members you have with you. You can use a Blue Mage's ability to cast **L5 Doom**, *which you may have learned in the Library of Ancients, or you can use* **Shurikens** *if you have a Ninja in your party.*

If neither of these are viable options, simply whittle down the Boss' health using lots of **Ice** *magic.*

Enemies

La Mage
RonkaKnigt
Fan Wizard
Lamia
StonedMask
Archeoavis (Boss)

Items

Gold Armor (1)
Elixir (2)
Phoenix Down (3)
Gold Shield (4)
Potion (5)
5000 GP (6)
Shuriken (7)
AncientSword (8)
Moonring (9)
Power Wrist (10)
Cottage (11)
Ether (12)

Checklist

☐ Defeat the Sub-Bosses to enter

☐ Find the Earth Crystal

☐ Defeat Archeoavis (Boss)

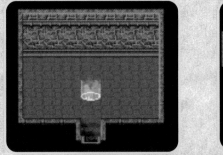

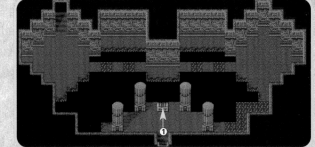

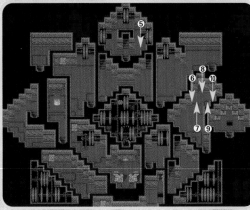

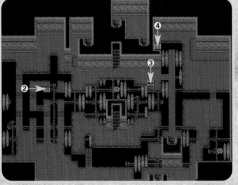

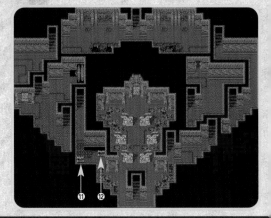

Reaching the Floating Ruins

When you're ready, head out in the Airship and press the [X] button. Choose the arrow pointing up when prompted, and you'll come face to face with the gunship exterior of the Floating Ruins.

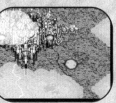

To coax out the Soul Gun Launcher, you must destroy the two guns on either side of the Floating Ruins. At any time between fights, you can rest up or restock by flying the Airship off the screen to the south. When you're ready, confront the guns on either the left or right side of the ship.

Sub-Boss: Rocket Guns
(Flamethrowers, Missile Launchers)

Suggested Level: 20
Weakness: Bolt
Item Won: Speed Drink, Hard Body

*Each fight against the Rocket Guns features a pair of them. It's best to have a Ninja in your party so you can throw **Lightningskill** in succession. Two hits from the Lightningskill will wipe out the Rocket Guns. You can buy this item from the Weapons Shop in Rikks Village. If you have a Blue Mage in your party, you can learn **Ray Burn** from the flamethrowing Rocket Guns.*

After destroying each of the four pairs of Rocket Guns, the main Soul Gun Launcher will emerge from the center of the floating ruins. You can save your game, rest, or restock by flying off-screen, and then return.

Soul Gun Launcher

Suggested Level: 20
Weakness: Bolt
Item Won: Dark Matter, Potion (x2)

Soul Gun/Sol Cannon
LV: 36   HP: 22500

Launcher
LV: 50   HP: 10800

*This fight can really test your mettle if you're unprepared. If you have a Blue Mage who has learned **L5 Doom**, then use it to quickly destroy the Gun Launcher. If not, use **Bolt2** and **LightningSkill** to inflict lots of damage. It's also a good idea to have a Monk, who can cause big damage to this Boss.*

Entering the Ruins

 After defeating the Soul Gun Launcher, you can enter the interior maze of the Ruins of Ronka. You have to cross lots of invisible bridges in the floor for the first part of the maze. In the second part, you must explore a series of rooms containing staircases and doorways to reach the Save Point and, ultimately, open the door to the central room. Now it's time, however, to prepare to fight the Boss.

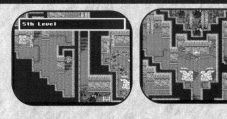

NOTE
Try stealing Lamia's Tiara from the Lamia enemy inside the Ronka Ruins.

LV: 19
HP: 6400

2nd form
LV: 20
HP: 2500

Suggested Level: 21
Weakness: Variable
Item Won: Hero Drink

Archeoavis

Archeoavis presents the toughest battle in World 1. It's weaknesses constantly change, so it's difficult to use magic to win this battle. To defeat Archeoavis without sustaining too much damage, change all your party members into Monks and rely on their increased physical attack power. Also, you should have one of the Monks equip !White as his or her second ability so that he/she can cast Cure2 when needed.

After causing enough damage to Archeoavis, it will revive itself in a weaker form. Its attacks will still be strong, however, its HP will be greatly reduced. Keep hitting it with physical attacks, and you'll easily win this battle. For a quick kill, use L5 Death on Archeoavis' second form.

Krile and King Tycoon

After defeating Archeoavis, follow King Tycoon into the Crystal Room. Then Galuf's granddaughter appears and knocks some sense into King Tycoon. In addition, Krile helps Galuf recover his memory. Once the King comes to, he is reunited with his daughters.

The Crystal is abruptly destroyed by X-Death, who dares Galuf to follow him to his home planet before it is also destroyed. At the expense of his life, King Tycoon manages to purge the evil that X-Death has endowed into the Crystal Shards.

After picking up the Crystal Shards, the Floating Ruins will start to self-destruct.

New jobs gained from Crystals in Earth Shrine

Name	Vigor	Speed	Stamina	Mag.Pwr
Samurai	+19	+2	+19	-12
Lancer	+18	+5	+15	-12
Dancer	+5	+5	-10	-5
Chemist	+2	+3	+6	-4

Enemies
None

Items
None

AIRSHIP BASE & TYCOON METEOR

Checklist

☐ Find Cid and Mid

Where's Cid?

When you return to the Airship Base, head to the room to the right of the resting area inside the base. There's a letter on the table from Cid informing you that he and Mid have returned to the Tycoon Meteor so they can replace the Adamantite.

Using the Airship, head to the Tycoon Meteor. When you arrive, you discover that Cid and Mid have returned the Adamantite. Also, you learn that it might power up the meteors enough to enable your party to travel to Galuf's world. They immediately head for the next meteor: Karnak.

NOTE

Now's a good time to revisit North Mountain. Make one of the characters a Trainer, and find a fight with a GhilCat. Take control of it, and cast Float on your party. Don't heal your party until after the fight against Titan.

Enemies
Titan (Boss)

Items
None

KARNAK METEOR (2ND TRIP)

Checklist

☐ Fight Titan (Boss)

A Den of Monsters!

When you arrive at Karnak Meteor, Cid and Mid discover a monster guarding the warp tile inside. You must enter and defeat it for them.

LV: 1
HP: 2500

Suggested Level: 21
Weakness: None
Item Won: Titan
Summon Magic

Titan

If your party is floating during the battle, this fight is easy. Float ensures that you won't sustain any damage from Titan's powerful Earth Shaker spell. Simply pound the Boss with physical hits, and heal your party with items, the Healing Rod, or Cure 2.

If your party isn't floating, make sure you keep your party's health at a maximum, because Titan will cast Earth Shaker right before it expires.

WALZ METEOR

Checklist

☐ Fight Byurobolos (Boss)

Attacked!

Cid and Mid are anxiously awaiting your arrival at the Walz Meteor. They successfully replace the Adamantite, but as soon as they do, a flurry of monsters attack.

LV: 22
HP: 2200

Suggested Level: 21
Weakness: None
Item Won: None

Byurobolos

The quickest way to defeat this group of monsters is to use a Ninja and throw Lightningskill or Waterskill, which affects all the enemies.

The Byurobolos will cast Arise to resurrect the dead members of its group, so cast Mute to keep them from returning. This fight isn't too tough, but make sure your party members are at full HP because these enemies may cast Exploder for over 400 points of damage to one party member before they die.

GORN METEOR

Checklist

☐ Fight KimaBrain (Boss)

The Last Meteor

When you arrive at the Gorn Meteor, you're greeted once again by Cid and Mid. This time, however, they disappear inside the meteor but don't come out. You must head inside to investigate. Once you enter the meteor, you're in for a surprise!

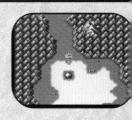

KimaBrain

LV: 19
HP: 3300

Suggested Level: 21
Weakness: None
Item Won: Phoenix
Down

KimaBrain's toughest attack is the Blaze spell, which will cause approximately 250 points of damage to your entire party. Simply heal your party with Cure2 after it casts Blaze, and counterattack with the Samurai's Coin Toss ability or the Ninja's Shuriken throwing talents. Three hits from a Shuriken should finish off KimaBrain.

Enemies
None

Items
None

THE WARP ZONE

Checklist

☐ Reaching Galuf's planet

Warp Speed

Stock up and buy all the necessary goodies you need before heading to the Warp Zone. When you're ready, take your Airship and fly over to the point on the map where all the rays emitting from the four meteors converge.

It's time to head to World 2!

NEW WORLD

Checklist

☐ Fight Abductor (Boss)

Abducted!

When you finally reach the new world, pitch a tent in the forest on the small island. During the night, some monsters crash your campsite and abduct Reina and Faris forcing Bartz to fight the Boss.

The best attack to use against Abductor is **Doom Claw** (if you have it). If not, make sure you have **Cure2** and hit the Boss with your most devastating physical attacks. A good job ability to use is Monk with the secondary ability of **!White**. It should also be noted that losing the fight to Abductor does *not* change the storyline.

Enemies
Shell Bear
MotorDrive
Hypnot
BlueDragon
A amngolem
ReflectMage
BlindWolf
TwinLizard
YellowDragon
A Rage
MagicDragon
BlakWarlock
Harpy
Red Harpy
Imp
Abductor
Gilgamesh (Boss)
Items
C   Shards

X-DEATH'S CASTLE

Checklist

☐ Save Bartz, Reina and Faris

☐ Fight Gilgamesh (Boss)

☐ Escape the Castle

NOTE
You can steal a Spear from the Shell Bear enemies.

Rescue Your Friends!

When the scene shifts to X-Death's Castle, you'll learn about X-Death's plan to wipe out Galuf and his army. He uses your party as hostages to discourage Galuf from attacking the castle.

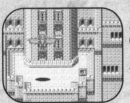

Galuf ignores the warning and sneaks in anyway. He'll automatically pick up the **Crystal Shards** from a treasure chest in the main hall. Now you must find the dungeon and free your friends.

From the location of the Crystal Shards, there's a Save Point through the upper left-hand doorway. In the save room, head up one more room to the north so you can use the **Recovery Pools** on either side to restore your HP/MP completely.

The dungeons are a few more floors down. Head there to meet up with Gilgamesh.

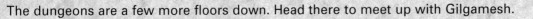

Gilgamesh

LV: ??
HP: ????

Suggested Level: 21
Weakness: None
Item Won: None

Choose Monk as Galuf's job ability in this fight, and use !Guard as your third slot ability. The Monk's counterattack ability is especially helpful, because all of Gilgamesh's attacks are physical hits. You should also cast some defensive magic, like Protes, when the fight begins. After causing enough damage to Gilgamesh, he will escape from battle.

You can now free Bartz, Faris and Reina. Do so and exit the castle, but make sure you save your game before you head through the double doors.

Enemies

LilChariot
Wingkiller
Neogarula
Fishite
Gilgamesh (Boss)

Items

None

BIG BRIDGE

Checklist

☐ Escape from the Bridge

☐ Fight Gilgamesh (Boss)

☐ Reach Krile

A Bridge Too Far

Upon exiting the castle, you discover that you must trek across the Big Bridge to reach Krile and Galuf's backup military. The only problem is that the bridge is completely overrun with X-Death's goons.

When you reach the second lookout room on the bridge, prepare to battle against Gilgamesh once again.

Gilgamesh

LV: ??
HP: ????

Suggested Level: 21
Weakness: None
Item Won: None

The second fight with Gilgamesh is a little tougher than the first. This time he'll cast protective spells, such as Shell and Protes, to weaken your party's attacks. To counter this, cast Mute at the start of the battle. You can also have a Time Mage cast Slow to keep Gilgamesh from getting more than one turn per round.

Simply keep hitting Gilgamesh, and eventually you'll cause this Boss to run away yet again!

The Barrier

After the fight, battle through the remainder of the Big Bridge. You'll eventually reach Krile, who's waiting on the other side. Unfortunately, the reunion is short-lived as X-Death activates a massive, magical barrier around the entire castle grounds. The effects of the barrier tosses your entire party off into a different corner of the world before you can get through the door that Krile is holding open for you.

Krile: GRANDPA, the barrier!!

Enemies
None

Items
Piano #6

LUGOR BORDERTOWN

Checklist

- [ ] Rest and stock up
- [ ] Stay at the Inn
- [ ] Play Piano #6

NOTE
Dancing on stage will get you 100 GP (in Pub).

Armor Shop

Gold Shield	3000
Gold Helmet	3500
Green Beret	2500
Wizard Hat	1500
Gold Armor	4000
Ninja Suit	3000
Earth Robe	2000

Weapon Shop

HalcyonBlade	3400
War Hammer	6400
Katana	5800
Half Moon	5600
Wind Lance	5400
Dark Bow	3800
Dream Harp	1600
Chain Whip	3300

Magic Shop

(Black Magic)

Drain	3000
Break	3000
Bio	3000

(White Magic)

Blink	3000
Shell	3000
Esna	3000

(Time Magic)

Comet	3000
Slow2	3000
Return	3000

Item Shop

(Left)

Potion	360
Tonic	40
Phoenix Down	1000
Soft	150
Maiden's Kiss	60
Cornucopia	50
Eye Drop	20
Antidote	30

(Right)

Ether	1500
Holy Water	150
Cottage	600
Giant Drink	110
Power Drink	110
Speed Drink	110
Hard Body	110
Hero Drink	110

Lugor Bordertown

Check the World Map, and head toward the flashing light to the east. When you arrive, restock your supplies and check out the items around town.

Some of the villagers mention a cursed castle to the south, while others talk about Moogles living in the forest. However, before you wander off, check in at the town Inn.

Wow! What a surprise...customers! Tonight's on the house!

After your much needed rest, head to the south from Lugor.

Piano

Enemies
None
Items
None

MOOGLE FOREST

Checklist
☐ Find the Moogle

Kupo

The Moogle Forest is to the far southeast of Lugor Bordertown. You must wind through the mudlands onto a small peninsula jutting north at the tip of the continent. A small patch of forest conceals a lone Moogle.

 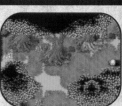

Speaking to the Moogle startles it, causing it to run off and fall through a hole in the ground. Follow it down the hole and drop into a set of underground caverns.

Enemies
Mogeater
Acrophis
BloodSlime
Freeziabat
Tyrannosaurus (Boss)
Items
4400 GP (1)
Phoenix Down (2)

UNDERGROUND RIVER

Checklist
☐ Find the Moogle
☐ Fight Tyrannosaurus (Boss)

Waterways

After dropping into the Underground River caverns, you must ride the waterways to get from platform to platform. Don't forget to pick up the items in the chests along the way and save a Phoenix Down for later!

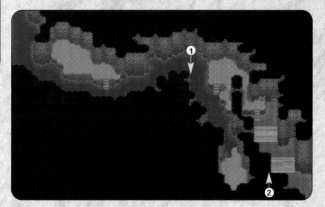 

Moogle Spotted!

When you reach the outlet of the cavern, you'll spot Moogle sparring with what looks like a dinosaur's skeleton. Prepare to fight!

49

LV: 29
HP: 5000

Suggested Level: 21
Weakness: Cure,
Phoenix Down
Item Won: None

Tyrannosaurus

This fight is ridiculously easy if you're prepared. Because this Boss is an undead creature, all you need to do is use a Phoenix Down on it to send it to a more restful afterlife. If, however, you don't have a Phoenix Down, you should explore the caverns some more, because there's a Phoenix Down in a chest near the fight site. Otherwise, you must use healing items, normal attacks, and Cure2 spells to whittle down this Boss' health.

Enemies

None

Items

Elf Cloak (1)
Ether (2)
Phoenix Down (3)
10,000 GP (4)
1 GP (5)
Dancing Dirk (6)
Cottage (7)

MOOGLE VILLAGE

Checklist

☐ Find the rescued Moogle

☐ Reunite with Krile

A Moogle's Reward

After the Boss fight, the Moogle will show you the way to its village. When it's your turn, follow the directions carefully. You'll also notice that there are no enemies in this area as long as you avoid stepping on the desert areas.

NOTE

Stepping on the desert sand while following the Moogle's directions will usually result in a fight with a SandCrawler. This is a tough fight, and you can't escape from the battle either. Avoid it at all costs!

When you reach the forest, search around below and to the left of the trees to find the village. Upon entering, the dancing Moogles will scatter in a fright. None of them will talk to you except for the one you rescued, which is standing beside the locked hut to the far right.

This time the Moogle will lead you inside its hut to reward you with the contents of six chests. Indulge yourself, and then exit the hut.

NOTE

Before speaking to the Moogle on the roof, take a moment to enter the center hut and grab the Moogle costume. Put it on and enter the left hut to speak with the Moogle inside. It will offer to let you take the Elf's Cloak from the chest.

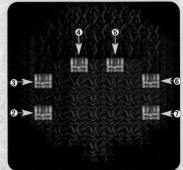

Dragon's Flight

After an event involving Krile and her Dragon, the pair will land in Moogle Village to return you to Galuf's home. Now it's time to head to Val Castle.

Enemies

(Basement)
Rockstatue

Items
Hero Drink (1)
Telepo (2)
Angel Robe (3)
Lamia's Harp (4)
Great Sword/Regal
 Cutlass (5)

VAL CASTLE

Checklist

- [ ] Rest and stock up
- [ ] Speak with Krile

King Galuf?

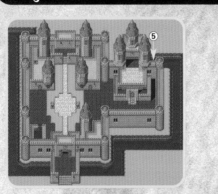

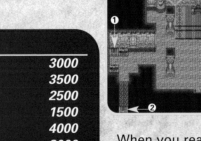

When you reach Val Castle, you'll discover that Galuf is actually a King! Take a moment to roam the castle so you can collect items, rest, and stock up.

Make sure you pick up the **Hero Drink** and **Telepo** spell from the chests in the lower left-hand corner of King's Hall. You'll find the various shops and the Inn located in the castle's courtyard.

Magic Shop

(Black Magic)
Drain	3000
Break	3000
Bio	3000

(White Magic)
Blink	3000
Shell	3000
Esna	3000

(Time Magic)
Comet	3000
Slow2	3000
Return	3000

Item Shop

(Left)
Potion	360
Tonic	40
Phoenix Down	1000
Soft	150
Maiden's Kiss	60
Cornucopia	50
Eye Drop	20
Antidote	30

(Right)
Ether	1500
Holy Water	150
Cottage	600
Giant Drink	110
Power Drink	110
Speed Drink	110
Hard Body	110
Hero Drink	110

Armor Shop

Gold Shield	3000
Gold Helmet	3500
Green Beret	2500
Wizard Hat	1500
Gold Armor	4000
Ninja Suit	3000
Earth Robe	2000
Gauntlet	3000

Weapon Shop

HalcyonBlade	3400
War Hammer	6400
Katana	5800
Half Moon	5600
Wind Lance	5400
Dark Bow	3800
Dream Harp	1600
Chain Whip	3300

Learned "Telepo!"

The Great Sword

Are you in need of some new weapons? Head to the front of the courtyard, and enter the small Water Pool in the lower left-hand corner of the yard. You'll get sucked through an underground waterway until you reach the outside moat. Follow the moat to the back of the castle on the far right side. Now examine the dead end to receive the **Great Sword**. When you check your inventory, you'll discover that the Great Sword is actually the **Regal Cutlass**.

When you want to return to the castle, simply pull the switch near the location where the whirlpool dumped you (left-hand portion near the back of the castle moat). This takes you back to the courtyard through the underground canal.

Merchant Secrets

Before you leave, explore the merchant building to the right in the castle courtyard. Make sure you fetch the **Angel Robe** from the chest behind the Armor/Weapons Shop. While you're still in this same room, examine the south wall separating you from the Armor/Weapons Shop. Specifically, if you examine the wall directly above the small handle placed on the wall on the opposite side, you'll trigger a *Secret Door*. Enter the shop and the

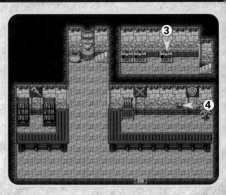

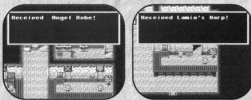

merchants will scold you for hopping behind the counter. One of them will give you **Lamia'sHarp** just to make you leave!

Krile's Request

Krile is on the roof of Val Castle, crying next to the Dragon. She informs you that the Dragon is dying, and that it was only pretending to be better when it took her to Moogle Village. Reina offers to get the Dragon some Dragon Grass, and Galuf mentions that there is some at the Valley of Dragons to the far north.

Stock up and prepare to leave the castle. Talk to the guards at the gate to leave.

Enemies
Weresnake
Kornago
Ridicule

Items
Kornago's Gourd (1)

KELB VILLAGE

Checklist
☐ Speak with Kelga
☐ Get Kornago's Gourd
☐ Learn Requiem

Armor Shop

(Left)

RopeHeadband	3500
Power Tasuki	4500
Power Wrist	2500

(Right)

Gold Shield	3000
Gold Helmet	3500
Green Beret	2500

Wizard Hat	1500
Gold Armor	4000
Ninja Suit	3000
Earth Robe	2000
Gauntlet	3000

Weapon Shop

(Left)

Cluster	5100
Crossbow	5000
Poison Rod	1500
Shuriken	2500
Fire Skill	200
Water Skill	200
LgtningSkill	200

(Right)

HalcyonBlade	3400
War Hammer	6400
Katana	5800
Half Moon	5600
Wind Lance	5400
Dark Bow	3800
Dream Harp	1600
Chain Whip	3300

Magic Shop

(Black Magic)

Drain	3000
Break	3000
Bio	3000

(White Magic)

Blink	3000
Shell	3000
Esna	3000

(Time Magic)

Comet	3000
Slow2	3000
Return	3000

Item Shop

(Top)

Potion	360
Tonic	40
Phoenix Down	1000
Soft	150
Maiden's Kiss	60
Cornucopia	50
Eye Drop	20
Antidote	30

(Right)

Ether	1500
Holy Water	150
Cottage	600
Giant Drink	110
Power Drink	110
Speed Drink	110
Hard Body	110
Hero Drink	110

The Dawn Warriors

After exiting Val Castle, head directly north along the row of mountains to find Kelb Village nestled in the mountain range. Upon entering, you'll notice that all of the buildings are locked and no one is outside walking around.

Enter the only open building in the village to the north. However, while inside, you'll mistakenly get attacked by the village soldiers, who think you're enemies. You then meet Kelga, one of the four Dawn Warriors who sealed away X-Death 30 years ago.

You also discover that Bartz's father, Drogan, was also one of the four original Dawn Warriors. It's because of this fact that Kelga enables you to pass through the north gate to reach the Valley of Dragons.

Getting Kornago's Gourd

As you explore the town, a mage will appear and ask for a "frog." You must catch a Kornago frog on the World Map in battle (using the **Trainer's** ability) and return it to him. He'll offer to give you the **Kornago's Gourd** accessory if you give him the frog and 10,000 GP.

NOTE

Speak to the Werewolf at the Inn, and then sit next to him. He'll restore your HP and MP for free, and then give you eight Tonics. You can do this up to three separate times.

Learning Requiem

To learn the Bard's song, **Requiem**, talk to one of the werewolf children in the back of the town. It's important that you learn this song before you head to the Valley of Dragons.

Enemies

Drippy
DragonZombie
Skelesaur
PoisonEagle
Grimalkin
Golem
Dragongrass (Boss)
Dragonbulbs (Boss)

Items

5000 GP (1)
Cottage (2)
Bonemail (3)
7000 GP (4)
Coronet (5)
Wind Sword (6)
Phoenix Down (7)

VALLEY OF DRAGONS

Checklist

☐ Obtain Dragon Grass

☐ Fight Dragongrass & Dragonbulbs (Bosses)

Navigating the Valley of Dragons

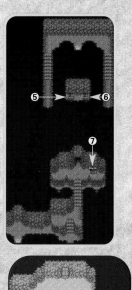

The Valley of Dragons is at the foot of the large mountain directly north of Kelb Village. When you enter, you'll discover that you must weave in and out of the mountain through caves and the mountainside to get to the top to retrieve the **Dragon Grass**.

You won't meet any resistance until you get past the rope bridge. Just past the scattered dragon bones, you'll find a sealed door and an unreachable switch. Simply walk to the right of the sealed door, and you will fall through a hidden hole in the ground.

Helping Golem

When you reach the scattered dragon bones, you'll most likely run into Golem. However, at this point, Golem is flying solo and usually attacks a party member shortly before escaping in one turn.

Don't bother tracking Golem at this point; instead wait until you reach the highest part of the mountain. Before encountering the **Dragon Grass**, wander along the mountainside until you see Golem fighting a DragonZombie and a Skelesaur.

You need to help Golem without attacking it. To do this, use the Bard's **Sing** ability and cast **Requiem** to damage the undead enemies, which won't hurt Golem. If you win the fight without hurting Golem, it becomes Summon Magic for your party.

NOTE

After clearing the Rope Bridge, do *NOT* use a Berserker in your party. You will lose the chance to obtain the Golem Summon Magic.

LV: 29
HP: 12,000

Suggested Level: 24
Weakness: None
(Dragonbulbs resistant to Fire)
Item Won: Dragon Grass, Elixir

Dragongrass & Dragonbulbs

If you picked up Golem, then this fight is easy. Simply use a Summoner to cast Golem at the beginning of the fight to nullify the poisonous Pollen attacks. Dragonbulbs' physical attacks are weak, but they will regenerate after they are destroyed. Simply keep plugging away at the main blade of Dragongrass to whittle down its HP.

If you don't have Golem, cast Esna from a White or Red Mage to cure poisoned party members, and hit the Dragongrass until the fight ends.

NOTE

To avoid fighting all the way down to the exit of the Valley of Dragons, simply have a Time Mage cast Telepo to return to the entrance of the maze.

Enemies
(Basement)
Rock Statue

Items
None

RETURN TO VAL CASTLE

Checklist
☐ Talk to Krile
☐ Give Dragon Grass to the Dragon

Gill's Calling

When you return to Val Castle, you learn that Krile has become ill. When you visit her, she tells you that a sage named Gill has requested that you immediately visit him at his island cave. After the conversation, head to the roof with the Dragon Grass.

Treating the Dragon

After Reina feeds the sick Dragon the Dragon Grass, Krile joins you on the rooftop and urges you to continue the quest. You can now use the Dragon to reach Gill's Shrine.

GILL'S SHRINE

Checklist

☐ Find the Shrine

Heading North

From the castle, head to the north past Kelb Village, and then take a right at the Valley of Dragons through the narrow canyon. Then exit into the open skies by passing through the opening to the far, upper-right of the continent.

Gill's Shrine is a small, rocky hole in the ground on a tiny island to the north of the opening. However, upon entering the Shrine, it begins to quake. It's so severe, in fact, that you must leave the Shrine and return to the Dragon. After the island sinks, head west to the nearby castle.

SURGATE CASTLE

Checklist

☐ Find all the items

☐ Learn about Zeza

Getting In

When you reach the castle gates, use the lever to the left of the doors to open the gate. A soldier will escort you to the main throne room, and ask that you take anything you need from the castle.

Zeza has taken his naval fleet to X-Death's Castle in hopes to attack, so take some time to explore the castle.

The Song of Speed

Make sure you visit the King's Chamber's and read the red book on top of his desk. After doing so, you can learn the **Song of Speed** for a Bard in your party.

Armor Shop

Gold Shield	3000
Gold Helmet	3500
RopeHeadband	3500
Wizard Hat	1500
Gold Armor	4000
Power Tasuki	4500
Earth Robe	2000
Gauntlet	3000

Weapon Shop

Regal Cutlass	8400
Short Spear	8100
Bizen's Pride	8800
Poison Axe	9600

Magic Shop

(Black Magic)

Drain	3000
Break	3000
Bio	3000

(White Magic)

Blink	3000
Shell	3000
Esna	3000

(Time Magic)

Comet	3000
Slow2	3000
Return	3000

Item Shop

(Top)

Potion	360
Tonic	40
Phoenix Down	1000
Soft	150
Maiden's Kiss	60
Cornucopia	50
Eye Drop	20
Antidote	30

(Bottom)

Ether	1500
Holy Water	150
Cottage	600
Giant Drink	110
Power Drink	110
Speed Drink	110
Hard Body	110
Hero Drink	110

The Library

As you pass through the castle, you'll eventually find a large library with several shelves arranged in alphabetical order. Speak with the man standing near the long desk, and he'll ask you to help him put back all the books.

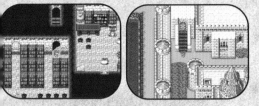

Nearby are three books; examine the far right book of the three. You'll discover the title of the book is "Weird Ronka." Place it on the center left shelf on the bottom row of books. Next, pick up "Register of Monsters" and place it on the far right shelf in the middle row. The last book, "Forbidden Book," belongs on the center left shelf of the top row of shelves.

When finished, the man will leave the library through a hidden door. Follow him and take the staircase to the next room. You'll eventually end up in a room with a bunch of chests. Pick up **5000 GP** from the only unopened chest, and then continue outside into the small garden and cross to the right beneath the tower walkway above. Enter the far right room and learn the **"Float"** spell!

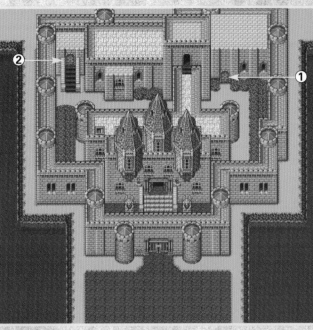

Enemies

BlakGoblins
Gilgamesh (Boss)
Enkidoh (Boss)

Items

None

ZEZA'S SHIP

Checklist

☐ Rest in the chambers

☐ Fight Gilgamesh & Enkidoh (Bosses)

☐ Access the submarine

The Royal Fleet

Zeza's fleet is located to the east of X-Death's castle continent. Land on the largest ship, which is Zeza's boat. After a greeting, he asks that you rest in the chambers below deck. After doing so, you'll awake in the middle of the night as some monsters attack the ship!

Monsters!

When you head to the deck, you'll see the crew getting attacked. Head straight for the Boss (the red monster) at the south end of the boat. You'll need to fight one monster to get there, and once again it's Gilgamesh!

Gilgamesh	Enkidoh
LV: ??	LV: 29
HP: ????	HP: 4000

Suggested Level: 25
Weakness: None
Items Won: Gold Shield
(Gilgamesh)

Gilgamesh & Enkidoh

Enkidoh joins Gilgamesh later in this fight, and heals both itself and Gilgamesh for over 4000 HPs. The best way to defeat this duo is to keep Enkidoh from healing Gilgamesh. Then hit Gilgamesh with Titan summon spells, Monk critical attacks, and the Golem summon spell to tighten up your defenses.

With Gilgamesh out of the way, concentrate on Enkidoh with plenty of tough physical attacks.

NOTE

It's possible to steal a Genji Glove from Gilgamesh during the fight. This is a very rare item, so don't pass it up.

Enemies

Neon
Traveler
ReflectKnigt
LvlTripper
Gravidead
Magnities
Ultragigas
Atomos (Boss)

Items

9000 GP (1)
Monsters! /Blood Sword (2)
18,000 GP (3)
Monsters! /HairOrnament (4)

SHIELD GENERATOR

Checklist

☐ Receive Whisper Grass

☐ Reach the top of the tower

☐ Fight Atomos (Boss)

Using the Submarine

After the Boss fight, Zeza will reveal a secret passage below deck that leads to a submarine. The submarine travels through a tunnel that accesses the Barrier Tower of X-Death's Castle.

You can rest in the quarters below the pilot room of the sub, and then when you're ready, exit through the door behind the sub controls. If you need some items, examine the sub controls and return the sub to Zeza's ship. You can then use the Dragon to fly anywhere you want.

Getting the Whisper Grass

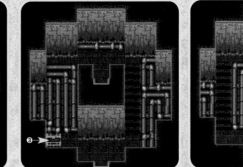

To tower; left stairs to Hair Ornament, right stairs to top of tower

When you enter the Barrier Tower, Zeza will hand over a blade of **Whisper Grass**, which resembles a walkie-talkie. You must head to the top of the tower to take out the antenna, while Zeza will head to the basement to turn off the power. After he leaves, head to the door on the upper-left so you can save your game.

Ascension

As you head up the tower, pick up as many items as possible. Be careful though, because some of the chests contain Red Dragons, which are tough to defeat.

When you reach the top of the tower, save your game and approach the antenna. Zeza will contact you and ask you to destroy it. Upon doing so, you get attacked.

LV: 41
HP: 19,997

Suggested Level: 27
Weakness: None
Item Won: Dark Matter

Atomos

This Boss fight is tough, no matter how you look at it. You should use a few Monks and Samurai to make things easier. Atomos' most devastating attack is its Comet spell, which can wipe out a single party member each time it's cast. When this occurs, avoid reviving your character unless it's absolutely necessary. If you do revive them, Atomos will simply cast Comet again, probably knocking out the character again.

If you leave the character knocked out, he/she will slowly begin to get sucked into Atomos' "Wormhole" and won't return until the end of the fight. When this occurs, start hitting Atomos with physical attacks from your Monks and use $Toss attacks from the Samurais.

Farewell

After the Boss fight, you discover that Zeza is trapped in the tower's basement. With no way to reach him and the building falling down around you, you have no choice but to leave courtesy of the Dragon.

Galuf gives a tearful farewell to his friend, and insists on waiting for him in the cave below. But after a few seconds, he regains his senses and rejoins you in the submarine.

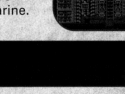

Enemies

Radiator
Metamorpha

Items

None

GILL'S SHRINE

Checklist

☐ Find the Shrine

☐ Speak with Gill

☐ Get the Elder Branch

The Sunken Island

Galuf suggests that you find Gill using the submarine. Locate the blinking dot on the map in the middle of the north ocean. Head there in your sub, and descend deep into the cave at the blinking dot's location.

The Chest and Stone Puzzle

When you reach the heart of Gill's Shrine, you'll find several chests in a circle and several doors lining the walls that are blocked for the time being. The center chest is the only one with anything in it, so open it to remove the **Stone** inside. Now your objective is to place the Stone in the appropriate open chest to unlock one of the blocked doorways.

You first need to place the Stone in the upper-left chest to open the right door above. Enter the doorway and flip the switch in the passageway. This will clear a walkway in another cave nearby. Return to the chest room, and remove the Stone from the chest, and place it in the bottom-left chest to open the next door. Now you can head down the passage to the main area of the Shrine.

NOTE

If you're lucky, you may receive the Lumino-Staff after a fight against Metamorpha.

Meeting Gill

When you finally meet up with Gill, he'll ask you to go to Moore Forest. Apparently, X-Death has some interest in something in the forest, so head there immediately.

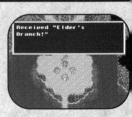

Gill warns that the forest is magical, and will attack anyone who tries to enter. Therefore, he hands over the **Elder's Branch**, which will allow you passage into the forest, however, you'll have to deal with the monsters inside. Return to the submarine, and begin your journey north to Moore Village.

Enemies

Iron Dress
Bald Money
LandTurtle
Cure Beast
Druid

Items

None

Checklist

☐ Find the island

☐ Find and fight Shoat

The Secret Island

On your way to Moore Village, access the World Map while underwater and you'll see a white dot to the far north. Note that you won't see it unless you're submerged in the sub. There's an opening underwater leading into an underground tunnel.

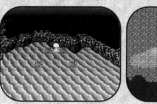

Finding Shoat

Go through the tunnel until you emerge on a small, heavily wooded area with a small lake. You may want to stop in at the isolated forest to the southeast to find a female Chocobo, but your main objective here is to find Shoat.

Wander around the wooded area, and you'll eventually find an enemy by the name of Shoat. Prepare yourself for one tough battle!

LV: 38
HP: 5000

Suggested Level: 26
Weakness: None
Item Won: Shoat Summon Magic

Secret Boss: Shoat

Before the fight, equip the ability EqupRibbon or make one of your characters into a Dancer. By doing so, you can equip a Ribbon for protection against Shoat's powerful Devil's Eye spell. The moment it connects, it turns a character into stone unless you have the Ribbon equipped.

During this fight, you'll use plenty of Softs and lots of MP casting Cure2 and Esna. Have the Dancer or the character wearing the Ribbon as the main character cast Soft, while using the other characters to plug away at Shoat until it's destroyed.

Enemies
None

Items
HuntingKnife (1)

Checklist
- [ ] Rest and stock up
- [ ] Speak with villagers about Moore Forest
- [ ] Play Piano #7

Talk of the Town

The only way to reach Moore Village is by using the submarine to navigate the narrow, underwater passages. Check the World Map, and locate the blinking dot on the northern tip of the western continent. If you're coming from Chocobo Island, then Moore Village is located on the peninsula directly to the south.

When you surface in the small lake outside the village, make sure you save your game. In the village, you'll discover that most people know about Moore Forest and will offer lots of information about how to get around in it.

Item Shop
(Right)
Potion	360
Tonic	40
Phoenix Down	1000
Soft	150
Maiden's Kiss	60
Cornucopia	50
Eye Drop	20
Antidote	30

(Left)
Ether	1500
Holy Water	150
Cottage	600
Giant Drink	110
Power Drink	110
Speed Drink	110
Hard Body	110
Hero Drink	110

Armor Shop
DiamndShield	6000
DiamondHelmt	7000
Tiger Mask	5000
Poet Cap	3000
DiamondArmor	8000
DiamondPlate	6000
LuminousRobe	4000
DimndArmBand	4000

Weapon Shop
Air Lancet	6800
Elf Bow	7500

Magic Shop
(Black Magic)
Fire3	6000
Ice3	6000
Bolt3	6000
Drain	3000
Break	3000
Bio	3000

(White Magic)
Cure3	6000
Rflect	6000
Bersrk	6000
Blink	3000
Shell	3000
Esna	3000

(Time Magic)
Demi2	6000
Haste2	6000
Old	6000
Comet	3000
Slow2	3000
Return	3000

Piano

No one can enter
Moore Forest east
of here.

Stock up on plenty of **Ethers**, **Cottages**, and **Potions**. Moore Forest is really tough, and you can't use Telepo to exit if you run out of items. When you're ready, exit the town and head to the east across the wooden bridge.

MOORE FOREST

Enemies

Galacjelly
MiniMage
Imp
Mamon
Succubus
Seal Guardians (Boss)

Items

2500 GP (1)
Ether (2)
4900 GP (3)
Phoenix Down (4)
9500 GP (5)
Cottage (6)
Giant Drink (7)
Elixir (8)
Mace (9)
Aegis Shield (10)
Ash (11)
Flame Saber (12)

Checklist

☐ Find the Wood Sprites

☐ Find the Moogle

☐ Reach the Elder's Tree and fight the Seal Guardians (Boss)

NOTE

If you don't pick up the Aegis Shield until *after* the Moogle takes you underground, it turns into a Flame Shield.

Surviving the Forest

Moore Forest has some tricky paths, so look for tree trunks with small black holes in their base. This indicates that a Wood Sprite lives inside. After examining a hole, a tunnel will be created for you to pass through to the next area.

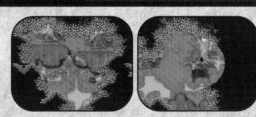

From the entrance, find the Wood Sprite to the upper-right. The next Wood Sprite is a little to the left of center north. In the next area, there's a Save Point but no Wood Sprite.

Heal and save your game, and then head up and to the left from the Save Point.

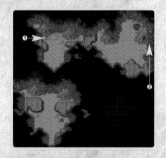

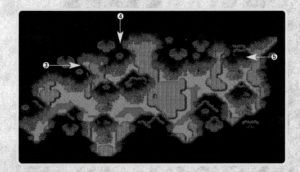

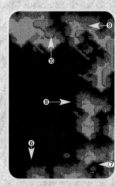

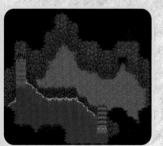

Flame shield (if Aegis Shield isn't picked up)

Fire!

At some point in the forest, you discover that X-Death has set the forest ablaze! With the flames rising around your party, pick up the **Aegis Shield**, and then wait a while in the same area.

Bartz: It can't be...
X-Death is setting the forest on fire!

The Moogle

Before long, a Moogle appears. It panics because of the encroaching flames, so it creates a hole in the ground and plunges through. You have no choice but to follow.

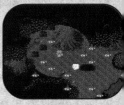

While in the underground cave, use the Recovery Spring to replenish your party members' HP and MP. After speaking with the Moogle, it will let you pass through to the surface.

From the Moogle's underground spring, head to the left and pick up the remaining items from the chests. In the left-hand area, head to the north to enter the Elder's Tree. Now it's time to confront the Boss lurking inside.

Seal Guardians

LV: 77
HP: 7777

Suggested Level: 31
Weakness: Variable
Item Won: None

This is by far the toughest battle yet. You should ensure that most—if not all—of your party have the ability to cast Cure3. Start the fight by casting Float on your party to avoid the Earth Shaker attacks.

There are four different Boss creatures, each with its own element: Bolt, Fire, Ice, and Earth. They also have some powerful magic spells that can wipe out your entire party in one hit. If you can, have each character summon Titan during your first turn. If you're lucky, you'll wipe out three of the Bosses. If this doesn't work, then you're history! When one of the Bosses nears its death, it will cast all of its attacks at once. However, if you eliminate three of them during your first turn, then you'll be left with the Earth Boss, which is good because your party is floating.

However, if you can't summon Titan four times on your first turn, then try knocking out one Boss at a time instead. It's wise to have a high level White Mage, Black Mage, Summoner, and Ninja or Samurai. The $Toss is probably the best ability, if you have the GP to spare.

Galuf to the Rescue

After the fight, X-Death appears and attacks your party with the power of the Crystals. Back at Val Castle, Krile senses her grandfather's danger and rushes off to help. During the struggle, Krile gets captured, forcing Galuf to save her. He fights X-Death alone, and the outcome of the battle is the same. Even if you reach zero HP, you'll continue to fight until you've inflicted enough damage to X-Death to end the fight.

After the battle, Krile agrees to join your party in Galuf's place. It's time to follow X-Death to the castle!

Enemies

Groundworm
Gilgame

Items

Lots of GP

GILGAME'S CAVE (OPTIONAL)

Checklist

☐ Gather GP and build levels

Nest of Monsters and Money!

Gilgame's Cave is to the west of the Big Bridge, through a cave opening along the mountain ridge. This is a particularly tough place to scout for some extra GP, but it's worth it.

Simply check behind every door inside the cave, and you'll find increasingly large stashes of money. The enemies are incredibly difficult, but not impossible. You'll even notice that you'll run into Gilgame rather frequently.

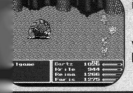

Gilgame has a lot of HP, but if you use a lot of Ice magic (**Shiva**, **Ice2-3**, etc.) you'll do fine. You can also change each party member into a Bard and use the **Hide** ability while Gilgame uses Turtle twice.

Enemies

Twinlizard
Blind Wolf
A Rage
ReflectMage
Dragon
BlakWarlock
Adamngolem
Hypnot
Motordrive
Blue Dragon
Red Dragon
Yellow Dragon
Gilgames (Boss)
X-Death (Boss)

Items

DiamondShield (1)
Ether (2)
Ice Shield (3)
Ether (4)
(5)
Bow (6)
Kotetsu (7)
Blizzard (8)
Elixir (9)
9900 GP (10)
8000 GP (11)
Double   (12)
Partisan (13)
Magishuriken (14)

X-DEATH'S CASTLE REVISITED

Checklist

☐ Navigate the Castle maze

☐ Find and fight Carbuncle

☐ Fight Gilgamesh

☐ Fight X-Death

NOTE

With a Thief in your party, try to pick up the Judge-Staff from the BlackWarlock.

Surviving X-Death's Maze

NOTE

Place a Geomancer in your party to determine where the location of traps are in the floor. In addition, this will cancel out the effect of damage floors.

You must climb to the 13th floor to meet up with X-Death. However, along the way, you must clear the first few floors to reveal the true vision of X-Death's maze.

You can heal and save on the 1st floor of the castle, but on the 3rd floor make sure you enter the center room. If you backtrack a few steps, you can disable X-Death's spell of illusion and reveal the maze for what it really is.

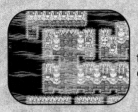

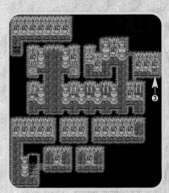

On the 4th floor, press the switch in the room to the left through the upper-right. Exit to the next floor through the door to the left.

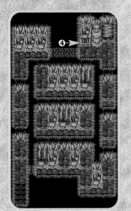

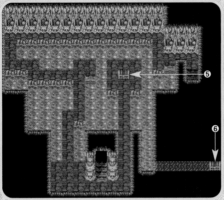

On the 5th floor, head through the odd-looking door to the right to reach the 6th floor. Now head up the center staircase to continue, but make sure you hit the hidden paths to retrieve the items in the chests.

The 7th floor harbors a skull switch and a moving platform. You can activate the platform by stepping on the switch, but you must press the ⬤ button to stop the platform at the right position. Get it to stop in the center; your reward is a Save Point in the next area.

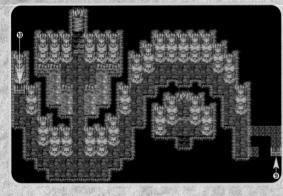

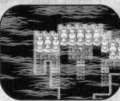

Head straight through the 8th floor, picking up items along the way. When you reach the 9th floor, follow the path to the south to reach the next screen. Proceed up the stairs to the next level.

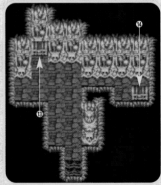

On the 10th floor, you'll meet Carbuncle. Walk slowly and have a Geomancer scan the floor to reveal any traps. You must walk along the skull blocks to the far end to find Carbuncle.

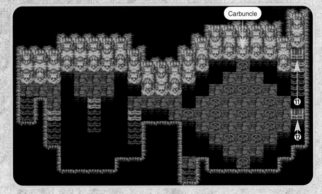

Carbuncle

Secret Boss: Carbuncle

LV: 44
HP: 15,000

Suggested Level: 30
Weakness: None
Item Won: Carbuncle
Summon Magic

To defeat Carbuncle, summon Shoat enough times so that you can eventually defeat it in one attack. This will take some time, but it's the most painless way to win. Otherwise, have a mage cast Rflect on each party member to deflect Carbuncle's spells. You can even equip Wall Rings to register the same effect.

NOTE
You can steal a Wall Ring from Carbuncle if you have the Steal ability.

Finding Gilgamesh

After the fight with Carbuncle, warp back to the 9th floor and then return to the 10th floor. Instead of heading to the uppermost block, go to the bottom one. This creates a path to a staircase on the left side. The next room contains a Save Point, so when you're ready, it's time to confront Gilgamesh!

NOTE
To reach the chest in the upper right-hand corner of the 10th floor, return to the 9th floor and go to the upper right-hand section of the room. You can climb the stairs to reach the chest.

Sub-Boss: Gilgamesh

LV: ??
HP: ????

Suggested Level: 30
Weakness: None
Item Won: Excalipur

Gilgamesh is a cake-walk compared to Carbuncle or X-Death. Have one party member skilled in White Magic so you can cast

Cure3, Esna, and Protes on your entire party. Have a Ninja throw some Shurikens, and the $Toss ability for a Samurai can't hurt either (if you have plenty of GP).

Continue to punish Gilgamesh with lots of powerful attacks, and it will run off again.

NOTE
Try to steal the Genji Helmet from Gilgamesh.

X-Death

LV: 66
HP: 32,768

Suggested Level: 32
Weakness: Holy
Item Won: None

At the start of this fight, you should cast Haste2, Shell, and Protes. You should also summon Golem to protect your party from physical attacks. To attack X-Death, make sure that you have plenty of MP for spells like Bolt3 as well as Carbuncle. The Blue Mage's White Wind spell is the most effective HP restoring method.

Attack X-Death by throwing Shurikens, as well as the Samurai's $Toss ability. Both are really potent against X-Death. Also, make sure you have a character who can Raise unconscious party members at any time. Good luck!

Enemies
None
Items
None

A NEW BEGINNING?

Checklist
☐ Get Krile to join your party

The Return

Make your way up to Tycoon Castle. When you arrive, head inside to speak with the Chancellor. He'll greet Reina and Faris with open arms and announce a large celebration.

Princess Salsa

Head out to the balcony to speak with Krile, who joins your party. Then leave the castle and visit the basement to speak with Jenica. He'll tell you a little about Salsa/Faris and her childhood.

When you're ready, leave the castle and head to the cave to the far west.

BOKO

Checklist
☐ Get Boko

Getting Boko

Boko, your Chocobo, is alive and well so ride it across the World Map. Boko can cross shallow lakes and rivers, so it's time to head to Gill's Shrine.

Enemies
Sleepy
Cowpoke
Hedgehog
Python
Shadow
Neogigas
Desertorpedo
Baretta
Antolyon (Boss)
Items
None

GILL'S SHRINE REVISITED

Checklist
☐ Fight Antolyon (Boss)
☐ Faris rejoins the party
☐ Speak with Gill

On the Way to the Shrine

Now that you have Boko, return to Tycoon Castle and head to the far north. From there, cross the long river and head southwest through the canyon, and then turn north towards Tule Village. As you approach the small valley near Gill's Shrine, a hole opens up in the ground and sucks you under!

When you come to, you discover that you're not alone in the small, dark cave!

69

Antolyon

Watch out for Antolyon's Dischord spell, which halves your levels if it connects. Simply use strong physical attacks on it, and when you've caused enough damage, it will escape.

Faris Returns

To exit the cave, grab the rope dangling down the hole. When you finally get out of the hole, you're rejoined by Faris, who has followed you from Tycoon Castle.

Now head to the south, and then to the west to find the cave entrance to Gill's Shrine.

The Emergence of the Void

Find Gill inside the cave, and he'll tell you that X-Death is planning to revive N-Zone, a black, void world filled with evil from 1000 years ago.

You'll then meet X-Death, who tells you his plans for destroying the world.

Enemies
None

Items
Sealed Book (receive from Scholars)

LIBRARY OF THE ANCIENTS

Checklist

☐ Learn about the Legendary Weapons

☐ Get the Sealed Book

☐ Learn the Song of Magic

The Legendary Weapons

Gill will lead your party to the Library of Ancients, and inform you of your new quest. Your job is to unlock each of the four different legendary Lithographs scattered throughout the world. This will enable you to pick up all of the Legendary Weapons sealed within the Sealed Castle of Kuza.

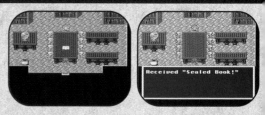

The Scholars will give you the **Sealed Book,** which you can use to access some of the dungeons and mazes that you previously couldn't access.

Learn the Song of Magic

After your meeting with Gill, revisit the roof of the Library of Ancients and speak with the Scholar standing to the right of the furnace. He will teach you the **Song of Magic** for a Bard job class. Exit the Library of Ancients, and head west through the mountains to reach the Pyramid.

Elder's Tree

As you pass through the canyon, you'll stumble across the Elder's Tree in the newly relocated Moore Forest. Continue to the west to reach the Desert.

Bartz: Elder's Tree...
Faris: Moore Forest is beginning to revive...

Enemies

BrandLamia
Nile
Archosaur(?)
Th_Damned
ZejaZone
MechaHead
Archaosaur
A_Guard
Bludgeoner
RockStatue
_midia
_dDragon
BlueDragon
YellowDragon
Gargoyles (Bosses)

Items

Monsters! /Ice Shield (1)
Hex Ring (2)

(3rd floor)
Monsters! and Flame
Shield (3)
Monsters! and Dark
Matter (4)
Monsters! and White
Robes (5)

(_th floor)
_ (6)
Elixir (7)
Monsters! and Black
Robes (8)
Thornlet (9)

(5th floor)
Monsters! and Dark
Matter (10)
Monsters! and Black
Costume (11)

(6th floor)
Monsters! and Dark
Matter (12)
Monsters! and
Crystalmail (13)
Items (7th floor)
Monsters! and Dark
Matter (14)
Monsters! and Dark
Matter (15)
9000 GP (16)
8000 GP (17)
Elixir (18)
10,000 GP (19)
Cottage (20)
Monsters! and Earth
Hammer (21)
12,000 GP (22)
Monsters! and Dark
Matter (23)
Elixir (24)
Monsters! and Dark
Matter (25)

(8th floor)
Ribbon (26)
Protect Ring (27)
HairOrnament (28)
Lithograph (29)

PYRAMID

Checklist

- [ ] Open the entrance
- [ ] Fight the Gargoyles (Bosses)
- [ ] Get the Lithograph

NOTE
A Bard with Requiem will make life much easier through the Pyramid.

NOTE
To get to the 5th floor, you must fall down from the 6th floor or use the secret passage.

NOTE
To reach the 6th floor, use the top center stairs on the 5th floor.

Entering the Pyramid

As you approach the Desert, you discover that the Sand Tides are no longer functioning. Cross the sands to the Pyramid and approach the entrance.

Bartz: The Sand Tides have stopped.

Use the **Sealed Book** to enter. Upon doing so, the two Gargoyles guarding the gate will come to life and attack you!

Gargoyles

Suggested Level: 32
Weakness: None
Item Won: None

It's best to attack the Gargoyles with a balanced attack of strong physical hits and magic. If you kill one Gargoyle, the remaining one will revive it if you don't act quickly. The best way to take them out is to have a Summoner cast Titan, or have a Black Mage cause some damage with Bolt3. After the fight, you can enter the Pyramid.

Tricks and Traps of the Pyramid

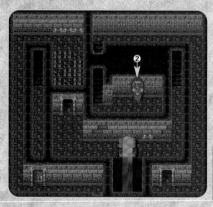

All eight floors of the Pyramid are filled with tough enemies and tricky traps. It's wise to have someone equipped with the Thief's Secret ability to spot hidden passages in the walls. It's also wise to have either a Bard or someone with the Sing ability to use Requiem on most of the enemies. Some monsters, like Nile or Zefa Zone, are immune to Requiem, but the rest of the enemies will take 1500 points of damage if used correctly.

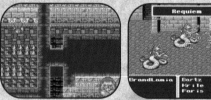

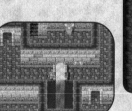

Always avoid stepping on the spikes, because they will poison your party. You can usually shift the spikes by pressing a blue switch on the wall.

The MechaHeads

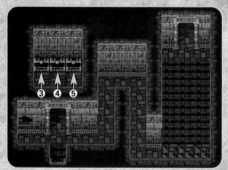

On the 4th floor, you'll enter a sand-filled room with a few Auspices and several MechaHeads. You have no choice but to fight your way through each and every one of the enemies in this room.

The MechaHeads are incredibly tough, but they're no match against **Bolt3** or **Water/LightningSkill**.

The Mummy

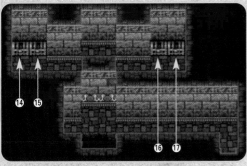

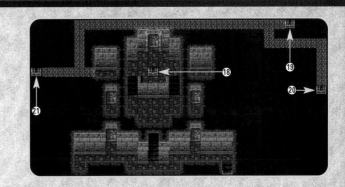

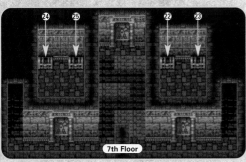

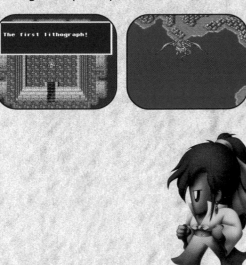

7th Floor

Make sure you check out all of the coffins. They contain passages and items, however, you must first fight the Mummy trapped inside. You can quickly dispose of the Mummies by using the **Requiem** song.

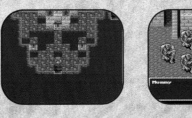

Disappearing Floor

On the 8th floor, there's a room with some tricky flooring. Make sure you watch which sections of the floor do not move, and then carefully WALK—don't dash—onto them. Then, when the time is right, you can proceed to the chests or the two staircases on either side of the room.

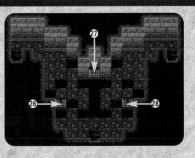

Getting the Lithograph

You'll find the **Lithograph** on the center pedestal on the top floor. With the Lithograph, your party can retrieve three of the 12 Legendary Weapons from Kuza Castle.

The first lithograph!

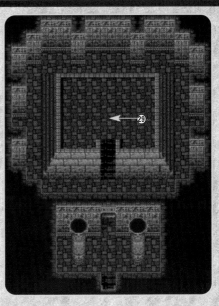

73

Enemies

Slug
Gloomwidow
Bewitcin
Mellusion (Boss)

Items

None

ELDER'S TREE REVISITED

Checklist

☐ Fight Mellusion (Boss)

☐ Reina rejoins your party

X-Death!

After leaving the Pyramid, pitch a Tent or Cottage to heal your party, and then save your game. Now head back east and go through the Elder's Forest.

You'll discover that Reina is unconscious on the ground in Elder's Forest, and it appears that she has been possessed. Now it's time for yet another Boss fight!

LV: 29-33
HP: 20,000
Suggested Level:26
Weakness: Variable
Item Won: None

Mellusion

Mellusion has shifting elemental weaknesses. When the Boss casts Wall Change, note that it's changing its weakness. It's best to fight Mellusion by hitting it with your most powerful physical attacks, or use a Black or Red Mage to test the Boss' weakness by casting a low level Bolt, Fire or Ice spell. Then hit the Boss with whichever spell doesn't heal it. Also, Aero works well against Mellusion.

Reina Rejoins

When Reina rejoins your party, use a Phoenix Down to revive her and replenish your party's HP and MP using a Tent or Cottage. Now it's time to reclaim the Airship from the eastern shore.

X-Death Strikes!

After boarding the Airship, fly around the globe and find where some of the towns have relocated to.

When you're finished exploring, set your craft down outside the Sealed Castle to the northeast of Tule Village.

Enemies
XDeathSoul (Boss)
ShieldDragon (Boss)

Items
3 Legendary Weapons
(basement)

THE SEALED CASTLE

Checklist

☐ Fight ShieldDragon (Boss)

☐ Get three Legendary Weapons

☐ Fight XDeathSoul (Boss)

Entering the Castle

When you arrive, the Chancellor will offer to read the Sealed Book for you. Also, make sure you speak with the Scholar to the right of the entrance to access some magical Spring Water. Enter the great hall to the north, but prepare for another battle.

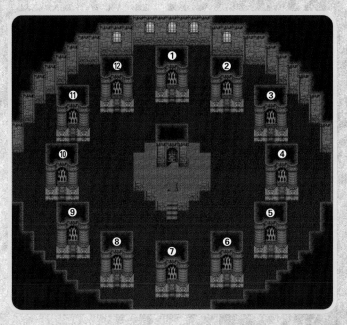

Sub-Boss: ShieldDragon

LV: 29
HP: 19,999

Suggested Level: 34
Weakness: None
Item Won: None

At the start of the fight, this Boss will have Reflct enabled, so don't cast any elemental magic or it will hit your party instead.

Its main attacks are ZombieBreath, and some very lethal critical attacks. It's best to use the Trainer's Control ability to get the dragon to cast Flame on itself. You may also want to use a Bard's Sing ability to use Requiem. If you don't inflict enough damage in a set amount of turns, the dragon may escape!

Claiming Your Weapons

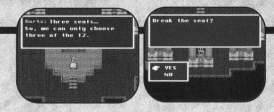

When you reach Kuza Castle's basement, you can choose from 12 different, but very powerful, weapons. Below is a list of the Legendary Weapons and their details. Note that you can only choose three at this point, so pick carefully.

Name	Description
Masamune	First attack in battle
Rune Axe	MP used for critical attacks
Holy Lance	Fortified with Holy
Ninja Blade	Increases Evade rate
Excalibur	Fortified with Holy
Earth Bell	Randomly casts Quake
Apolon Harp	Critical hits increased vs. Dragons
Magnus Rod	Fortified with all elements; high Mag attack
Yoichi's Bow	Increases critical hits
Fire Bute	Randomly casts Fire3
Sage Staff	Increases Holy damage
Assassin Dagger	Instantly kills random targets

After making your choices, exit the basement and return to the entrance. However, on your way, you'll get attacked by XDeathSoul!

Sub-Boss: XDeathSoul

Suggested Level: 34
Weakness: None
Item Won: None

This Boss is similar to X-Death in every aspect, including tough physical hits, a huge inventory of powerful spells and good defense.

Fight this Boss by using high level magic and Earth Magic. This fight is tough, so keep in mind that you can escape if you're low on items and MP.

NOTE

In Lugor Bordertown, a female merchant at the Armor and Weapon shop will give you a Ribbon if you get between the counters.

Enemies
None

Items
Tent (1)
Ether (2)
300 GP (3)

PIRATE'S COVE (OPTIONAL)

Checklist

☐ Get Hydra Summon Magic

Hydra

Take your Airship to Pirate's Cove, and return to the secret docks deep inside. With Faris and Reina in your party, you'll be able to see a short event involving Faris and her dearly departed Hydra. Afterwards, you'll be awarded the **Hydra Summon Magic**. This is powerful stuff, so make sure you pick it up.

Enemies
Rock Statue
Nut Eater
Skulleater
Odin (Boss)

Items
Odin Summon Magic

VAL CASTLE BASEMENT (OPTIONAL)

Checklist

☐ Get Odin Summon Magic

Getting Past the Gates

If you check the basement of Val Castle, you'll find that the doors are still locked. How do you get inside? Now that Jachol and the Jachol Caves have moved nearby, you can enter the basement through the caves.

Enter the cave opening to the west and press the bottom left switch to open a passage revealing many switches. Wait a few seconds for the fake switches to disapper, and then press the remaining switch. This will open another passage to the ornate door inside. To unlock the door, check the chest to the upper-left.

Continue to follow the path until you reach a dead end. Now just climb the vines to reach the basement of Val Castle! Make your way to the top of the room and examine the glowing green orb to summon Odin!

Secret Boss: Odin

LV: 2
HP: 17,000

Suggested Level: 37
Weakness: Break
Item won: Odin
Summon Magic

The toughest part of this battle is that you must defeat Odin in less than one minute. You must hit Odin with everything you have, while keeping every party member alive.

It's wise to bring a Black Mage for the Break spell, and a Summoner for Hydra. You'll definitely want to reserve plenty of MP for Raise and Cure3, because Odin casts spells that affect the entire party.

If you manage to defeat Odin within the allotted time, you receive it as a Summon Magic! If you fail, then the game will reset, forcing you to start over from your last Save Point.

NOTE

If you're lucky, you can steal a Protect Ring from Odin.

Enemies

None

Items

Brave Blade/Chicken Knife (hidden spot in forest)

MOORE VILLAGE (OPTIONAL)

Checklist

☐ Find the hidden sword

Proving Your Bravery

If you want, visit the small shed at the bottom-left of town. You can now pass through it and go into the forest below. Keep pushing through the trees (the path is obscured) until you reach a wizard guarding two boxes. The box on the left contains a Brave Blade, while the box on the right contains a Chicken Knife.

Translated, the mage's riddle means that the Brave Blade will weaken in power the more you run from battle, while the Chicken Knife increases in strength the more you escape combat. This number includes the amount of times you've run throughout the entire game, even leading up to this event!

Enemies
None
Items
None

THE TOWN OF CRESCENT

Checklist

☐ Get information on Mirage Village

The Legendary Village

You'll find the Town of Crescent on an island to the far southeast. When you talk to the villagers wandering the streets, some of them will mention that a "mirage" has appeared in the forest to the far south of their town. Could they mean the ancient village of Mirage?

They say a village appeared in the forest, like a mirage. Think it's true?

NOTE

Learn the "Power Song" from the Minstrel in the Minstel's House in the bottom right of town.

Enemies
None
Items
Thief's Knife (1)

MIRAGE VILLAGE

Checklist

☐ Final Piano (hidden passage near Black Chocobo area)

☐ Thief's Knife (barrel behind bar counter)

Weapon Shop (2nd Dealer)

MagiShuriken	25,000
Shuriken	2500
Double Lance	10,800
Moonring	1100
Fire Skill	200
Water Skill	200
LgtningSkill	200

Item Shop

(Bottom)

Elixir	50000
Ether	1500
Holy Water	150
Giant Drink	110
Power Drink	110
Speed Drink	110
Hard Body	110
Hero Drink	110

(Top)

Tonic	40
Potion	360
Phoenix Down	1000
Maiden's Kiss	60
Antidote	30
Eye Drop	20
Soft	150
Cornucopia	50

Armor Shop

CrystlShield	9000
CrystalHelmt	10,500
Black Hood	6500
Circlet	4500
CrystalMail	12,000
BlackCostume	9000
Black Robe	8000
White Robe	8000

Armor Shop (2nd Dealer)

Winged Shoes	50,000
Angel Ring	50,000
Fire Ring	50,000
Coral Ring	50,000
Lamia'sTiara	2500
Angel Robe	3000

Weapon Shop

Flame Saber	10,000
Blizzard	11,000
Earth Hammer	12,800
Mace	7800
Magic Bow	10,000
Ichimonji	14,800
Partisan	10,200

Magic Shop

(White Magic)

Mini	300

(Black Magic)

Toad	300

(Time Magic)

Speed	30
Float	300
Telepo	600

(Summon Magic)

Chocobo	300
Sylph	350
Remora	250

Magic Shop (2nd Dealer)

(White Magic)

Arise	10,000
Dispel	10,000

(Black Magic)

Doom	10000
Asper	1000

(Time Magic)

Quick	1000
X-zone	10000

The Mirage

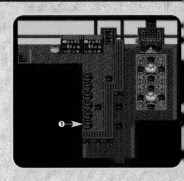

Head to the southwest along the narrow strip of land until you reach a small forest. Inside the forest, you'll find Mirage Village!

While there's nothing particularly special about the town, you will find the most powerful weaponry (excluding the Legendary Weapons), armor, items, and magic for sale at a fairly hefty price.

It's a good idea to equip the **Secret** ability from the Thief job to uncover all the hidden passages in every building. There are a lot of them, and if you want to find all the different merchants, this is important.

The Black Chocobo

Although the Black Chocobo isn't necessary for the remainder of your quest, you will need it to access North Mountain and Phoenix Tower in the desert far to the north. The Black Chocobo is the only available transport that can land in the forest near the desert.

The Magic Lamp

In the Tavern, you'll run into a man who offers you a gift if you actually ride a Chocobo all the way around the world. Take his challenge, and return to Boko (if you don't remember, check your map; it will appear as a small, yellow bird symbol). Ride Boko all the way to the northwest along the rivers leading to Easterly Falls.

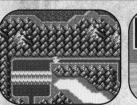

When you approach the falls, you can pick up the **Magic Lamp** from the edge of the water!

The Piano Master!

The final **Piano** is hidden in the building at the south of the village. Using a Thief's **Secret** ability, check the walls to find a path leading straight to a small room containing the last Piano! Play it and return to Crescent, and then speak with the Minstrel. He'll teach you the **LVL Song** as a reward for your skills!

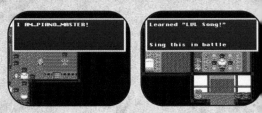

Enemies

Tote Avis
Slownin
Invisible
Druid
ShadeDancr
The Damned
Red Harpy
Imp
Prototype
Stoker (Boss)

Items

12,000 GP (1)
Monsters! and Razor
  Ring (2)
9000 GP (3)
Elixir (4),
  Monsters! and Protect
  Ring (5)
CrystalHelmt (6)
Ether (7)
Beast Killer (8)
Ether (9)
Dragon Fang (10)
Circlet (11)
Dark Matter (12)
Lithograph (13)

ISLAND SHRINE

Checklist

☐ Defeat the Gargoyles

☐ Get the Lithograph

☐ Fight Stoker (Boss)

More Gargoyles

You'll find the Island Shrine at the center of two long bridges to the northeast of Val Castle. When you approach the gates, you'll have to fight another pair of Gargoyles before you can enter.

After the fight, your must climb the shrine to the top to get the second **Lithograph**.

Riding the Pipes

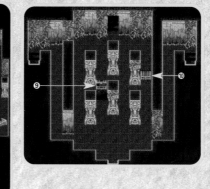

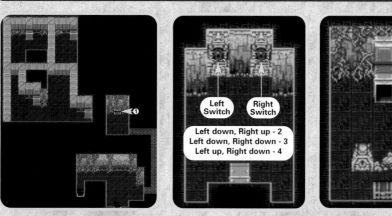

Left Switch   Right Switch

Left down, Right up - 2
Left down, Right down - 3
Left up, Right down - 4

To Save Point

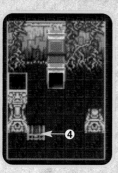

To Level 3

The only real puzzle inside the Island Shrine is the first one you stumble across. You must enter the heart of the shrine through an air duct that will deposit you in a room with two switches. Now, to travel around and find the door to the rest of the shrine, you must play with the switches. Any of the remaining end locations of the air ducts will dump you in a room with treasure, so it's not too tough.

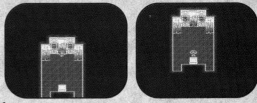

To find the next doorway, make sure the right switch is up and the left switch is down. Then you're free to continue.

The Second Lithograph

When you reach the top floor of the Island Shrine, you'll find the **Lithograph** on a pedestal at the north end of the room. However, the moment you pick it up, another Boss will show up to challenge you.

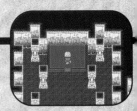

Stoker

LV: 7
HP: 20,000

Suggested Level: 34
Weakness: None
Item Won: None

When the fight begins, Stoker will morph into four different images. Only one of the images is real, meaning it takes damage. Its level is relatively low, but you must determine if you're hitting the correct image before you can inflict any damage. In addition, each time you damage Stoker's real image, it will shift and change positions, meaning you must start over again.

Refrain from casting any spell that affects the entire group of four images. Doing so will cause the Boss to counterattack with Blaze—four times!. Stick to physical attacks from a distance, and remember to summon Golem to keep your party from sustaining too much damage.

NOTE
You can steal Dark Matter from Stoker!

Fork Tower Revealed!

After the fight, the tower to the west of Crescent opens up for business. This is just one part of the double-sided Fork Tower. You learn that you must defeat and destroy each of the two Fork Towers (magic and strength) to keep X-Death at bay. Exit the Island Shrine and rest your party.

Enemies

Tiny[....]e
RicardMage
Flare
Deemaster
Berserkr
DualKnight
Iron
Minitaurus (Boss)
Omniscient (Boss)

Items

(Power Tower)

Potion (1)
Defender (2)

(Magic Tower)

Ether (3)
Wonder Wand (4)

FORK TOWER

Checklist

- [ ] Divide your party up into two groups
- [ ] Climb the tower
- [ ] Defeat the Minitaurus (Boss)
- [ ] Defeat Omniscient (Boss)

Splitting Up

The Magic Tower is to the west of Crescent. Stock up on everything, including **Potions**, **Ethers**, and **Shurikens**, from either Mirage Village or Crescent.

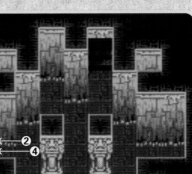

Magic Tower → ← Power Tower

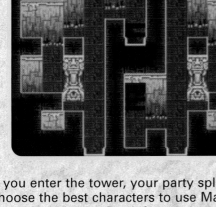

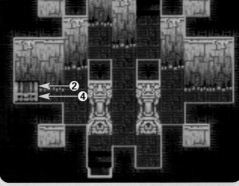

When you enter the tower, your party splits into two groups of two characters. Choose the best characters to use Magic, while the other two should have strong physical attacks. Don't forget to equip them and choose their classes accordingly.

It's recommended that Summoners with Black Mage abilities or White Mage abilities head to the Magic Tower (left), while strong fighters, like Monks, Ninjas or Samurai, head to Strength Tower (right).

Both towers are identical in structure, but they harbor different items and enemies. You must first lead the Magic group up to the Boss' chambers, followed by the Strength group.

When the Strength group reaches the Boss room, you'll begin the long fight!

Minitaurus

LV: 37
HP: 19,850

Suggested Level: 35
Weakness: None
Item Won: White Magic "Holy!"

There are multiple ways to handle this fight. First, your magic abilities will be null, therefore you must rely upon Potions and other healing items to replenish HP. Minitaurus only attacks with strong physical hits (600+ HP of damage).

Create two Monks with the Level2 Knight ability, Guard, so you can choose to Guard each turn and rely on the Monk ability to counterattack when Minitaurus makes its move. This strategy is slow and sometimes unreliable, but it usually works with little effort.

You can also have a Ninja and Samurai both equipped with Legendary Weapons. Have the Ninja also equip the Double Lance (which attacks twice), and use the ability Sshot! (Level 4 Hunter).

NOTE
Avoid equipping a weapon fortified with Holy, like Excalibur or the Holy Lance. This will heal Minitaurus instead of damage it!

Omniscient

LV: 53
HP: 16,999

Suggested Level: 35
Weakness: Wind
Item Won: Black Magic "Flare!"

Now it's the Magic group's turn to fight! This fight won't be easier; in most ways, it's even more difficult.

First, summon Carbuncle repeatedly throughout the battle to maintain your Reflect shield. This will prevent any elemental spells cast by the Boss (including its death spell, Flare) from having an effect on your party, and in turn will damage Omniscient.

Rely on Bolt3 (Black Mage) and Hydra (Summoner). If you must heal your party, use items and not Magic because you will reflect the Cure spell to the Boss. If the Boss casts Reflect on itself, and then use Dispel to counter it.

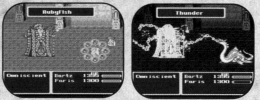

The Submersible Airship!

After the fight, you will once again gain access to the Airship Base. Rest and save, and then take the Airship down below.

After Cid modifies the Airship, explore the underwater regions of the strange new world. Prepare to dive deep to find the third dungeon containing the third Lithograph.

With it we can convert an air-ship into a submarine...
Hero: That's great!

Enemies

Unknown
Green Slime
Spore
Skeleton
Worm
Nergade (Boss)
Phobos (Boss)
Triton (Boss)

Items

Water Skill (1)
Dragon Fang (2)
Fire Ring (3)
Phoenix Down (4)
Ether (5)
KaiserKnuckle (6)
Lithograph (7)

GREAT SEA TRENCH

Checklist

☐ Find the Lithograph

☐ Defeat Nergade, Phobos, and Triton (Bosses)

Into the Deep

Sail or fly over to the south-eastern corner of the map, and dive deep into the water. Check the World Map and you should see a white dot just off the coast of the nearest continent.

When you find the location, head down into a large crevice.

Things to Know about the Great Sea Trench

You should equip one of your characters with the Geomancer ability **AntiTrap**. There's plenty of molten lava that you must walk through to reach the core room.

You may also want to equip the **Sing** ability or create some Bards in your party. All of the enemies in the Great Sea Trench are undead; therefore, singing **Requiem** will cause heavy damage to these creatures.

Armor Shop

CrystalShield	9000
CrystalHelmet	10,500
Black Hood	6500
Circlet	4500
CrystalMail	12,000
BlackCostume	9000
Black Robe	8000
White Robe	8000

Weapon Shop

Earth Hammer	12,800
Mace	7800
Magic Bow	10,000
Ichimonji	14,800

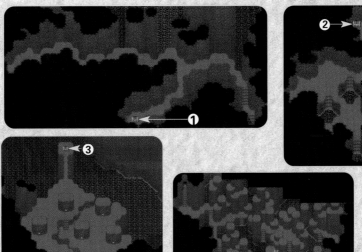

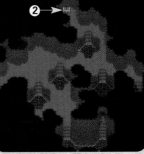

Also, there are lots of switches along the walls. When there's more than one in an area, they usually only lead to more treasure chests. There are also two Save Points along the way.

Dwarf Village

When you reach the 7th floor, stock up on weapons and armor (if you need to) and save your game. You'll notice one of the dwarves is digging a tunnel that ends up directly beneath Mirage Village, as well.

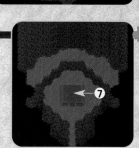

Finding the Lithograph

When you're ready, head through the south exit and through the next water-filled room to reach the entrance to the Boss area. You must press all the switches in the room (the three lower ones) to stop the lava flow in the center wall of the cave. Examine the chest to open the doorway to the room holding the **Lithograph**.

Unfortunately, three of X-Death's goons crash the party. Prepare to fight!

Suggested Level: 37
Weakness: Cure, Bolt
Item Won: Meteo Magic

Nergade (Blue), Phobos (Green), Triton (Red)

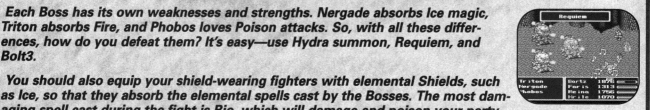

Negrade	Phobos	Triton
LV: 20	LV: 39	LV: 37
HP: 13,333	HP: 13,333	HP: 13,333

Each Boss has its own weaknesses and strengths. Nergade absorbs Ice magic, Triton absorbs Fire, and Phobos loves Poison attacks. So, with all these differences, how do you defeat them? It's easy—use Hydra summon, Requiem, and Bolt3.

You should also equip your shield-wearing fighters with elemental Shields, such as Ice, so that they absorb the elemental spells cast by the Bosses. The most damaging spell cast during the fight is Bio, which will damage and poison your party.

Simply keep casting Cure3, and have your other characters continue casting magic and singing. Also, note that if a Boss goes under while the other two are still fighting, it will revive!

After the fight, you'll receive Meteo magic for a Time Mage. Grab the Lithograph and hightail it out of the Great Sea Trench.

Sealed Castle of Kuza

Return to the Castle of Kuza to pick up three more of the Legendary Weapons. Only three more remain! However, before you head off to find the remaining Lithograph, take a few minutes to find out what else is open to you.

Enemies
None
Items
Air (1)
Mimic Crystal Shard

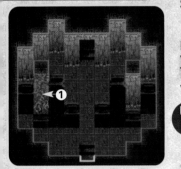

SUNKEN TOWER OF WALZ (OPTIONAL)

Checklist
☐ Find Gogo under the time limit

☐ Escape Walz Tower

Underwater

Using your boat, cruise the inner sea south of the Phoenix Tower Desert. While underwater, you'll discover the Sunken Tower of Walz lying right next to the coast. Swim over it and enter.

The entire building is completely submerged, and you'll only have seven minutes to complete your task, or run the risk of drowning. Therefore, make sure you have a Thief in your party with the Caution ability equipped. With this ability, you can dash, escape from battle quickly, and prevent rear attacks.

The Missing Crystal Shard

Remember that solitary Crystal Shard in the Tower of Walz? Make your way to the lowest level of the Tower, and you'll find it lying on the walkway.

This crystal shard gives me great power... now back off while you still can!

► YES
   NO

The moment you examine it, however, a voice will challenge you to a fight.

Secret Boss: Gogo

Suggested Level: None
Weakness: None
Item Won: Mimic Job

When you begin this fight, there should be plenty of time on the clock. He'll talk for a good portion of the battle and drop hints about how to handle the fight. Don't attack Gogo at all, or else Gogo will return the favor in kind. Once Gogo realizes that you understand his nature, then the fight ends and he'll reward you with the Mimic Job and 50 ABP!

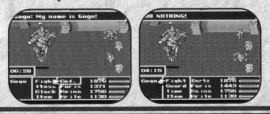

NOTE

On the surface of the water near the Sunken Tower of Walz, fight the Stingray and use a Trainer to control it. You'll want a Blue Mage to learn its Guardian spell. Also, you can steal a Rune Edge from it. Lastly, it will sometimes drop the Dragon Beard, which is an extremely rare item.

Enemies
Ghilacat
Rockcutter
Bahamut (Boss)

Items
Bahamut Summon Magic

NORTH MOUNTAIN (OPTIONAL)

Checklist

☐ Find Bahamut

☐ Defeat Bahamut (Boss)

Finding and Fighting Bahamut

Now that you have some time on your hands, get the Black Chocobo from Mirage Village. You can use it to fly to the forest in the desert area housing the Phoenix Tower and North Mountain.

Enter North Mountain and make your way to the top, avoiding the familiar purple flowers along the mountainside. When you reach the top, Bahamut will fly down and challenge you to a very tough fight.

LV: 99
HP: 40,000

Suggested Level: 37
Weakness: None
Item Won: Bahamut
Summon Magic

Bahamut

To defeat Bahamut, equip your party with elemental armor (Ice Shield, Flame Ring) so they will absorb some of Bahamut's attacks. Bahamut packs the MegaFlare spell, which will cause 2000 points of damage to your entire party! To win, you must cast Slow or Stop, while pummeling it with your most powerful spells (Flare, Holy, Odin).

Enemies
Serpentina
LiquidFlame
MagicPot
Sherry
Soul Cannon
Disabler
Negot

Items
5000 GP (1)
Magic Pot (2)
10,000 GP (3)
15,000 GP (4)
Magic Pot (5)
Magic Pot (6)
20,000 GP (7)
25,000 GP (8)
Magic Pot (9)

PHOENIX TOWER (OPTIONAL)

Checklist

☐ Reach the top

☐ Find Phoenix

A Word to the Wise

There are 30 floors in Phoenix Tower, full of incredibly tough enemies. Most of the enemies will also cast abnormal status spells, so prepare accordingly. Also, there is NO Save Point inside the Tower, but you can use the **Telepo** spell to return to the Tower's base.

NOTE

You can steal a Prism Dress from Serpentina, and Red Shoes from Sherry.

The Magic Pots

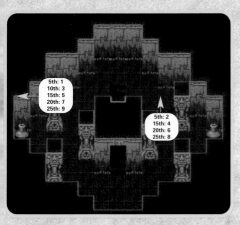

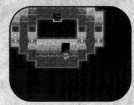

When you reach certain floors in the Phoenix Tower, you can examine two Magic Pots on either side of the room. One Pot will contain an item or GP, while the other will contain monsters. However, there's something special about this monster. You can't cause any damage to it, but it will keep asking for Elixir.

Go ahead and use an Elixir on it. You may have to use more than one to make it finally escape from the fight. When it does, you'll receive 100 ABP.

A Cheater's Guide to Phoenix Tower

The following is a quick reference guide that explains how to reach the top of the Phoenix Tower.

Floor	Directions
1st	Explore the path to the left of the center to find the hidden stairway.
2nd	Take the staircase.
3rd	Take the hidden staircase to the left.
4th	Go through the left door (hidden) and fight to continue.
5th	Give both Magic Pots Elixirs to get 100 ABP, then use the stairs.
6th	Go up the stairs.
7th	Head through the right door, then fight to continue.
8th	Go through the right door, then fight to continue.
9th	Go through the left door, then fight to continue.
10th	Give both Magic Pots Elixirs to get 100 ABP, then use the stairs.
11th	Use the stairs.
12th	Take the left door.
13th	Head through the right door, then fight to continue.
14th	Go through the right door.
15th	Check the two Magic Pots, then take the stairs.
16th	Use the staircase.
17th	Take the left door.
18th	Take the left door.
19th	Take the right door.
20th	Check the two Magic Pots, then head up.
21st	Take the staircase.
22nd	Go through the left door, then fight to continue.
23rd	Use the left door.
24th	Use the right door.
25th	Check the two Magic Pots, then climb up.
26th	Take the right door, then fight to continue.
27th	Take the right door, then fight to continue.
28th	Go through the right door.
29th	Go through the center door.
30th	Find the Dragon.

Getting Phoenix

When you reach the top of the Tower, you'll spot a Dragon. Afterwards, you're asked if you want to "cut the Dragon's tongue". If you reply "yes," you won't receive the **Phoenix Summon Magic**, so reply "no." You'll then receive the Summon Magic, and will be free to **Telepo** out of the Tower.

Enemies

Aquagel
MercuryBat
Corral
F????uard
Alcumia
Leviathan (Boss)

Items

Ether (1)
Turtle Shell (2)
Air Lancet (3)
Giant Drink (4)
Rune Edge (5)
Protect Ring (6)
Phoenix Down (7)
Wall Ring (8)
Enchanter (9)
Artemis (Artemis Bow) (10)
12,000 GP (11)
???ple Ax (12)
Aegis Shield (13)
Magishuriken (14)

EASTERLY FALLS

Checklist

☐ Find the Lithograph

☐ Defeat Leviathan (Boss)

Finding Easterly Village Falls

You must use the submarine to explore the upper-left section of the World Map. If you check your map while underwater, you'll spot the opening of a cave along the coastline of the northwestern continent.

Enter the cave and continue until you surface once again. Now head straight into the waterfalls to enter the caves of Easterly Village Falls.

Those Wacky Gargoyles

Use your strength and magic skills to take out the gargoyles. Only then can you enter the falls.

Using Dash

When you reach B2F, you must equip a character with the **Dash** ability to clear the waterfall and grab the **Protect Ring** from the chest inside. But first you must press the switch, and then run!

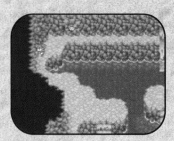

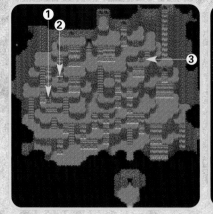

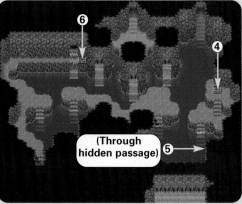

(Through hidden passage)

Dinglberry!

If you meet this creature on your journey, prepare for a tough battle. You should try to destroy it before it reaches your party. If not, the unlucky target of its attack may receive the **Cooking Sword** attack.

If you choose to fight it, use spells like **Break**, **Odin**, or **Shoat** to try to take out Dinglberry quickly.

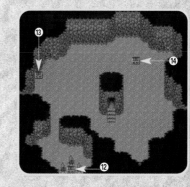

Falling Down

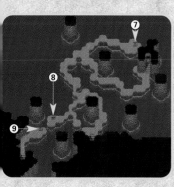

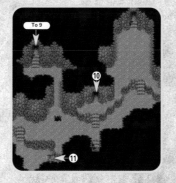

When you reach a certain level of the caves, you'll discover that the floor is riddled with traps that will drop you to the lowest level. Use the switches along the wall to reveal some of the spikes in the ground, as well as some of the holes.

After collecting the treasures, your objective is to fall down a specific hole so you can find the lowest room, which contains the **Lithograph**. This hole is on **B4 Floor** in the lower, left-hand corner of the room. Press the switch near the chest to reveal holes. Drop down either hole to fall into the Lithograph room!

LV: 37
HP: 40,000

Suggested Level: 36
Weakness: Bolt
Item Won: Leviathan Summon Magic, Wall Ring

Leviathan

The best way to defeat Leviathan is costly, but worth it. Invest in four Coral Rings from Mirage Village. This will enable you to absorb the Boss' Tidal Wave attack. Also, bring along some Black Mage abilities so you can cast Bolt3. For a final touch, summon Odin to finish off the Boss. To protect your party from the Boss' physical hits, summon Golem; however, this is not entirely necessary because you'll heal each time it casts Tidal Wave.

After the fight, you can use Leviathan as a Summon Magic spell and you'll also have access to the final three Legendary Weapons at Kuza Castle!

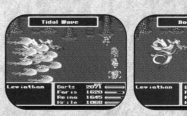

NOTE
You can steal an Elixir from Leviathan.

N-ZONE

KUZA CASTLE

After leaving Easterly Village Falls, it's time to claim the last three of the Legendary Weapons. Pick them up, and then prepare for your long journey into the Void.

Checking Your Progress

Before you head into the N-Zone, make a pit stop beneath the waters to visit a man claiming to be your "psychic friend."

His cave is located deep below the ocean surface, just off the coast of the Town of Karnak. When you enter, speak with the man and he'll tell you the number of times you've fought, how many monsters you've destroyed, your percentage of collected treasures, your average EXP, and the number of times you've run from fights.

The Guardian Spell

As you sail your ship around the coast near the Sunken Tower of Walz, you'll meet several interesting monsters. However, the most prized monster is the Stingray, which resembles a blue bat. Make sure you have a Trainer and a Blue Mage in your group (or characters equipped with **Learning** and **!Cntrl**).

When you encounter the Stingray, control it and have it cast Guardian on your party repeatedly. This spell will cast Float, Shell, Protes, and a bunch of other defensive spells on your entire party, significantly reducing damage during a long fight. Only then should you destroy the Stingray. It's important to learn **Guardian** before you warp to the N-Zone, because success in many of the Boss fights depend on it during battle.

Easter Island?

If you want, you can check out the sunken Moai off the northern coast from the desert area where Northern Mountain is located. Head north from the Sunken Tower of Walz, and continue until you reach the north ocean, and then take the plunge. Continue north and you'll come across a familiar face on the ocean floor.

Preparing for the End

Make sure you have a complete stock of **Elixirs**, **Ethers**, **Potions**, and **Cottages** before you enter the N-Zone. There are only a few Save Points from this point forward, and there are NO SHOPS! The enemies are also extremely tough, so build levels and master jobs BEFORE going in.

The best place to do this is in the desert, the Phoenix Tower, or on the open sea. Some enemies in these locations will reward you with lots of GP, and more than a few ABP to help boost your stats!

Enemies

Quadraharpy
Landquid
Centipeelr
SandBear

Items

None

N-ZONE ENTRANCE: DESERT

Heading in

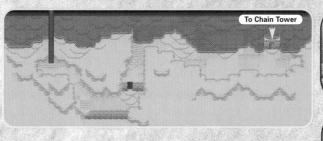

To Chain Tower

Once X-Death obtains The Void, our new world will emerge...one of darkness.

Take your Airship to the N-Zone black hole, which is located near where Tycoon Village was located. Upon arrival, you'll get taken to the edge of the Void.

You must now cross the sands of the small desert heading east until you reach the stone doors leading further inside. Some monsters will be there to greet you, but you won't have to fight them now.

Enemies

Grenade
DeathDealer
Aquaus
Cycloskull
LevelChecker

Items

Ether (1)
Cottage (2)
Dark Matter (3)
Elixir (4)
Elixir (5)
Blood Sword (6)

CHAIN TOWER

Riding the Ropes

NOTE

If any party member has a level divisible by 5, give them a Wall Ring to prevent the LevelCheckers from hiting them with L5 Doom.

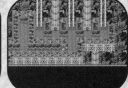

The first section of the dungeon is fairly straightforward. Connected by conveyor chains, press the ⊗ button when facing them to ride to the other side. Simply follow the path to go to the secret basement of Mirage Village!

The Frozen Mirage!

NOTE

The Cycloskull will sometimes drop a Rune Chime.

You'll emerge from the only door in the secret area of Mirage Village.

With all of the townspeople frozen in place and nothing else to do, exit the area to enter the next area of the dungeon.

FOREST OF N-ZONE

Journey through the Woods

As you exit Mirage Village, you'll end up in the forest. There are no tricks to getting through the woods, so fight a lot of enemies to build up your levels before the Boss fight.

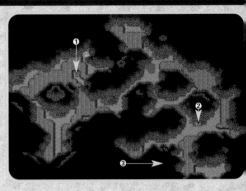

To find the Boss, head to the southeastern corner of the forest and examine the tree. There's a large hole in it, and a Wood Sprite will open the tunnel below. A fight ensues as you attempt to enter it.

WoodSprite

Suggested Level: 38
Weakness: None
Item Won: None

Bring along as many Summoners as possible, as well as a few characters with the White Mage ability. The main part of WoodSprite's attack is its defense, which is Reflect. Because of this, avoid casting any elemental Black magic, unless you cast Dispel on it.

Otherwise, use Summon Magic like Leviathan or Black magic like Flare. WoodSprite usually doesn't attack, so this fight will be fairly easy.

NOTE

You can steal a Plumed Hat from WoodSprite during this fight.

Enemies

Oculus
Dragon Great
Omega
Sybaritic
Metamorpha
Omega (Boss-Optional)
Apprehender (Boss)

Items

Coral Ring (1)
Angel Ring (2)

WATER FALLS OF N-ZONE

Down the Falls

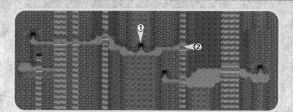

The Water Fall area is incredibly straightforward, plus it also contains the first Save Point. Just outside the Save Point, you'll see a weird-looking robot. This robot is called Omega, and you'll want to avoid it all costs.

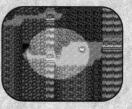

If you encounter difficulties, simply inch up close to it near the cliff, and then dash through when it moves closer to the wall. The next room contains the Boss of the falls.

Omega (Optional)

Suggested Level: 50+
Weakness: Bolt
Item Won: None

Omega is one of the two "optional" Boss fights that you will encounter in N-Zone. Fighting this Boss is only recommended for those who have truly mastered the game and have several different jobs mastered for each character.

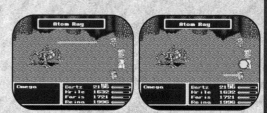

The most important jobs to have mastered are Sorcerer, Hunter and Ninja. Sorcerers can use Magic Sword attacks, the Hunter will have the !Sshot ability, while the Ninja can equip two swords.

With these classes mastered, you must then have four Fire Rings in your inventory to equip on all the characters. This will protect you from some of Omega's nastier attacks, like Atom Ray and Burn Ray. You should also equip the three non-Mimes with two swords apiece. Then make three of your characters "Bare" and the fourth into Mime. The Bare characters should have !Sword and !Sshot as their two chosen abilities, and the Mime should have !Time Lv.5 and !White Lv. 5.

Now that you're set, start the fight and immediately have all the Bare fighters cast Bolt3 to their swords, followed by the Mime casting Haste2 on the party. During the next round, have all the Bare fighters use !Sshot, while the Mime should concentrate on healing.

Apprehender

To defeat Apprehender, bring along your toughest Black Magic and repeatedly cast Fire3. To avoid wasting MP, bring a quick Black Mage and three Mimes to do the work. The Boss is weak against Fire, but don't summon Ifrit or it will heal it. You should also summon Golem to guard against Apprehender's physical hits.

NOTE

If you have a character with the Steal ability in your party, you can steal Ash from Apprehender.

Enemies

Ninja
DragonAvis
SwordDancer
Iron Giant
Death Claw
Yojimbo
YellowDragon
MithrilDragon
Fury
Azulmagia (Boss)
Alte Roit/
  Jura Avis (Boss)
Catastroph (Boss)
Halycanos (Boss)
Twin Tania (Boss)

Items

Winged Shoes (1)
Thor's Hammer (2)
Red Shoes (3)
P___ Dress (4)
Man Eater (5)

THE TOWER OF N-ZONE

Up the Tower

After the Boss fight, read the book on the desk, after which you'll see a flash. This signifies that once you exit the room, you'll end up above the clouds in a spectral tower.

If you need to see the invisible tower paths that follow, place a Thief with the Secret ability in your party, but this isn't entirely necessary. The road to the main tower is fairly easy enough to follow.

To Final Maze

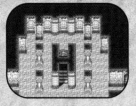

When you enter the tower, pick up the treasures on either side in the small turrets, and then head through the lower, left-hand doorway to reach the prison area.

You must fight a string of Bosses in all of the occupied cells. The order that follows indicates the best order, because after you destroy Azulmagia, you'll get a Save Point. To fight any of the Bosses, go up to the cell bars.

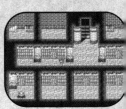

The following are the locations of each Boss:

Far left (bottom):	Azulmagia
Center right (top):	Alte Roit/Jura Avis (3)
Far right (bottom):	Alte Roit/Jura Avis (3)
Far right (top):	Catastroph

Azulmagia

Suggested Level: 37
Weakness: Poison
Item Won: None

Tell Azulmagia that you are the ones with the Crystal Shards. Make sure you have a Sorcerer in your party so you can cast Bio on his/her sword. You can even have three Mimes mimic the attack as well. If you continue to hit Azulmagia with Bio and Bio Sword magic, you'll have no problems. Also, you can quickly defeat it by having !Sshot for your Sorcerer. This will hit the Boss four times for each character with Mimic.

NOTE
You can steal a Giant'sGlove from Azulmagia.

Alte Roit/Jura Avis

Suggested Level: 37
Weakness: None
Item Won: Dragon Fang

Against any of the six Alte Roit Bosses, you'll definitely want a party member who can cast Return (Time Mage) at any given time. At the start of the battle, cast Holy or Demi2 on your weapons. Alte Roit isn't very powerful, but it can cast Encircle to erase one of your party members. If this happens, use Return to start the battle over again.

After causing about 5000 to 6000 points of damage to Alte Roit, it will transform into its "true form," Jura Avis. A big dragon with the ability to cast Air Wing among other spells, you can dispose of it by using elemental spells like Bolt, Fire, or Ice. Rely on your Summon magic to win this battle.

Catastroph

The battle against Catastroph can be one of the easiest Boss fights in the entire game—if you come prepared. First, cast Float on each party member, and then equip at least one character with a Wall Ring.

Catastroph will use its Gravity100 spell to ground the floating party members not equipped with a Wall Ring. However, since one character is still floating, Catastroph will continually cast Gravity100 throughout the entire battle. The spell causes no damage, so you're free to attack it with all you've got.

The Imprisoned Woman

After clearing the dungeon, you'll notice a woman standing in the far, upper-right cell. Follow her up the staircase.

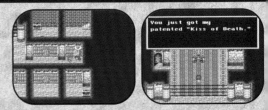

Save your game and follow her up the small set of steps to reach the top of the tower. Enter the center door and head up to the throne. If you try to enter the small door to the left a few times, you'll finally get pushed away and the woman will find you again.

This time, however, she's not looking for a date. She transforms into the "King of Dimension Castle, Lord Halycanos" and challenges you to a fight!

Halycanos

Halycanos starts the battle by turning your entire party into frogs! Make sure you have a Sorcerer in your party, along with a White Mage. Use Maiden's Kiss to restore everyone, and then use Mute Sword magic to silence and attack Halycanos repeatedly. This will silence its magic spells, but don't forget about its physical attack, which can cause up to 5000 points of damage to a single character.

Try casting Mini on Halycanos, as well as spells like Slow2 or Demi2. Also, you can summon Golem to protect your party from the Boss' physical hits.

NOTE
You can steal a Lumino-Staff from Halycanos.

Yojimbo!

As you head up the tower, you'll undoubtedly come across an enemy called Yojimbo (it resembles a dressed-down samurai). If you can withstand its Squeeze attacks and high power, you should try to steal items from it. Usually, it will only have **Cottages**, but on a rare occasion you can obtain a **Stratos** weapon by using your Thief's **Mug** ability. The Stratos is the most powerful Katana in the game, and even surpasses the Masamune in strength.

Suggested Level: 39
Weakness: Water, Holy
Item Won: Tinkerbell
(randomly)

Twin Tania

For this fight, make sure you have one of the four classes: Summoners, White Mages, Blue Mages, Time Mages, and Sorcerers. Also, equip Coral Rings on everybody so you can absorb Twin Tania's lethal Tidal Wave attack. If you have a Time Mage in your party, start the fight by casting Slow2. This Boss moves fast, so any help you can get is a plus. Next, cast Guardian on your party using a Blue Mage. Then cast Golem to avoid physical damage. Now you can throw Leviathan and Holy at it. Use Cure3 whenever you need to, and try to stay at max HP at all times to avoid getting wiped out by Twin Tania's Gigaflare attack.

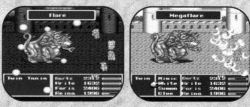

An easier and quicker way to destroy Twin Tania is to wait for the message that indicates that it's gathering power. When you see it, immediately attack it with Odin. This is its most vulnerable moment, causing it to go down easy.

Enemies

- BehemothKing
- Belfagel
- Maximus
- Mind Flare
- Crystelle
- Necromancer
- Mover
- Gilgamesh (Sub-Boss)
- Shinryu (Secret Boss-Optional)
- Necrophobe (Sub-Boss)
- X-Death (Boss)
- Neo-X-Deth (Boss)

Items

- Magishuriken (1)
- Magishuriken (2)
- Elixir (3)
- Monsters!/Dragon Seal/Ragnarok (4)
- Magishuriken (5)

THE FINAL MAZE

Warping to the Final Dimension

After the fight with Twin Tania, climb the stairs to the top platform to warp to the final area of the N-Zone dungeon. You must make your way through each of the following areas to the warp, which will then take you to the next part of the maze.

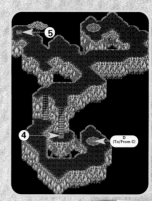

From the entrance warp, head to the next one to the south. Here you'll find a familiar face—it's Gilgamesh, fully transformed!

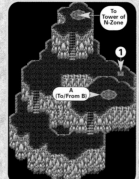

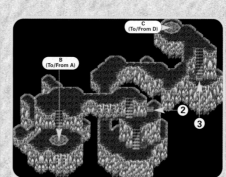

Sub-Boss: Gilgamesh

Suggested Level: N/A
Weakness: None
Item Won: None

Start the fight by casting Golem to protect your party from Gilgamesh's sword hits, and then pound the Boss with your most powerful attacks. After a few rounds, Gilgamesh will ask that you help him find a way out and tells you that he'll meet you on the other side.

Gilgamesh will then escape, giving you access to the next warp point.

NOTE
You can steal a Genji Shield during the fight against Gilgamesh.

Secret Boss: Shinryu (Optional)

Suggested Level: Very high
Weakness: None
Item Won: Dragon Seal

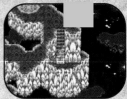

After clearing the third warp (entrance warp, Gilgamesh warp, Warp #2, Warp #3), you'll spot a chest at the bottom of a staircase. DON'T open it unless you're prepared! Inside, you'll have to fight Shinryu—an incredibly brutal Boss, even tougher than X-Death.

To defeat this Boss, you need four Coral Rings, eight Dragon Lances, and everyone must have mastered the Ninja class, learned the Thief's Mug ability, and learned the Lancer's Jump ability.

You can only get the Dragon Lances by mugging a monster called the CrystalDragon in the N-Zone. This is the only weapon that will inflict critical damage against Shinryu and is necessary to defeat it.

Make each of your characters Bare, and then equip them with two Dragon Lances apiece. Also, stick Jump in as one of their abilities. When the fight begins, Shinryu will cast Tidal Wave, which you should be able to absorb with your Coral Rings, and then JUMP!

When each character comes down, you'll cause enough critical damage that Shinryu will go down immediately! You'll then be able to get the Dragon Seal and Ragnarok!

Finding NecroPhobe

When you reach the second to the last warp, explore the far, upper-left area of the platform. You should spot a glowing green orb. Heal up, and then examine it to fight the Sub-Boss, Necrophobe! If you defeat it, you'll gain access to the all-important final Save Point.

Sub-Boss: NecroPhobe

Suggested Level: N/A
Weakness: Holy
Item Won: None

If your levels and HP are high enough, this fight shouldn't be too tough. Necrophobe has four barriers surrounding it that will protect it from any attacks. When the fight begins, each barrier will cast Flare to each of your characters. Avoid using Black Magic at this point, because each of the barriers has Reflect enabled.

Summon Golem to defend against Necrophobe's powerful physical hits, and then cast as many "all party" Summon spells as possible. Try using Leviathan, Bahamut, or Odin from all your party members (it's smart to bring some Mimes), and the barriers should go down after only four or five rounds. The Samurai's $Toss ability is also very helpful for taking care of the barriers. To finish off NecroPhobe, summon Odin, which has a high attack rate using VengSwrd against this particular Boss.

NOTE
You can steal an Elixir or a Thief'sGlove from Necrophobe.

Secret: Gilgamesh's Farewell!

To see Gilgamesh's goodbye speech, you must avoid killing Necrophobe after destroying all four barriers. Keep at the Boss, but don't kill it. After you whittle down its HP to around 10% (about 5000 HP), a visitor stops by: Gilgamesh!

You won't need to do any more fighting when this happens, because Gilgamesh will take care of NecroPhobe for you. But do try stealing a **Genji Glove** from Gilgamesh for old time's sake.

Mastering Jobs

Now that you've found a Save Point and you hopefully have a Cottage and a few Tents to heal your party, fight lots of the monsters wandering the final dungeon.

Most fights will net you around 25 to 30 ABP, and if you can find and defeat the Mover enemies, you'll receive a whopping 199 ABP and at least 100,000 GP! It's important to max out your jobs, so that you are prepared to face X-Death.

What to Bring to the Final Fight

Classes

Bare	Bartz
Mimes	Reina, Krile, Faris

Jobs Mastered

Bartz:	Knight, Monk, Thief, Samurai, Chemist
Reina:	Monk, White Mage, Black Mage, Time Mage, Red Mage
Faris:	Monk, Thief, Samurai, Summoner, Mime
Krile:	Monk, White Mage, Black Mage, Blue Mage, Red Mage

Abilities

Bartz:	$Toss, !Mix
Reina:	Redx2, !White (Level 6), !Time (Level 6)
Faris:	$Toss, Summon, Item
Krile:	Redx2, !Black, !Blue

The Final Fight with X-Death

When the battle begins, cast Guardian, !Mix, Golem, and Haste2 on your entire party. Then pummel X-Death with everything you have: Holy, Leviathan, Bahamut, Flare, Meteor—these all work wonders against it.

Watch out for X-Death's White Ball attack, which will petrify and kill one party member. You must use Raise and Soft or Esna to cure them.

After this fight, prepare for the ultimate battle against X-Death's new form: Neo X-Deth!

Fighting Neo X-Deth: Helpful Fighting Hints

Before fighting Neo X-Deth, check out the following hints to ensure an easier fight.

- Bring along plenty of **Esna** and **Arise**
- Avoid bringing Summon spells
- Make sure that Golem was cast to your entire party
- Use the **$Toss** ability

The Endings

For each character that is still alive at the end of the battle with Neo X-Deth, you'll see an event involving their ending. So, if all four party members are still alive (wounded, petrified, or zombie don't count), you'll get to watch all four endings. Enjoy the show and congratulations on a job well done!

For more detailed information on how to defeat the final Boss, check out our website at www.bradygames.com.

Bestiary

Bestiary Legend

Abbrev.	What It Means
HP	Hit Points
MP	Magic Points
LV	Level
AT	Strength of a direct attack the creature inflicts on a target
DF	Defense against attacks received from an opponent
SP	Indicates the speed at which it rotates through the attack order; the higher the number, the faster it rotates
EV	Indicates chance of evading an attack from an opponent (expressed as a percentage)
MD	Creature's amount of defense against Magic; the higher the number, the lower the damage
GIL	Amount of money received after defeating creature in battle
EXP	Amount of experience points received after defeating creature in battle
STEAL	Item received when using the "Steal" command as a Thief
DROP	Item dropped by creature after defeating it

NAME	HP	MP	LV	AT	DF	SP	EV	MD	GIL	EXP	STEAL	DROP
A Rage	1050	100	34	49	5	30	10	5	366	750	Tonic	Phoenix Down
Acrophis	900	0	30	36	20	25	0	20	267	410	Tonic	N/A
Adamngolem	3650	0	37	62	10	35	0	5	378	1100	Tonic	Potion
Alcumia	4500	3900	47	70	10	35	50	10	546	1000	Maiden'sKiss	Elixir
Aquazone	800	100	31	39	0	30	0	5	279	490	Tonic	Antidote
Aquagel	3300	100	46	67	20	22	0	0	540	1268	Tonic	Speed Drink
Archeosaurus	9960	1000	35	67	20	33	0	5	444	1800	N/A	Dragon Fang
Archeotoad	800	100	25	34	0	25	0	0	213	390	N/A	N/A
Armon	1500	300	25	90	35	25	0	0	740	0	Antidote	Potion
Auspices	1280	50	35	57	20	42	10	20	0	800	Antidote	Antidote
Bald Money	1300	0	35	43	0	30	10	5	339	660	N/A	Holy Water
Baretta	1000	0	41	61	55	21	0	20	429	1050	Tonic	Potion
BehemoKing	18,000	300	82	95	15	25	0	0	1000	0	Phoenix Down	Double Lance
Belfagel	6000	500	55	73	30	40	15	10	950	0	Moonring	Ice Shield
Berserker	2140	0	44	77	5	20	0	0	495	1000	Speed Drink	Death Sickle
Bewitchin	2000	200	42	65	10	25	0	5	459	1200	Silk Robe	LuminousRobe

NAME	HP	MP	LV	AT	DF	SP	EV	MD	GIL	EXP	STEAL	DROP
BigButrfly	9000	500	29	75	20	55	5	10	5000	0	Potion	Giant Drink
Big Horn	90	0	8	10	0	20	0	5	50	40	N/A	Tonic
BioSoldier	540	500	18	30	0	15	10	5	168	320	Battle Ax	Antidote
BlackFlame	220	100	22	28	0	20	50	25	174	290	N/A	Speed Drink
BlakGoblin	20	0	7	5	0	10	0	5	21	20	Tonic	LeatherShoes
BlakWarlok	1999	500	36	50	10	30	0	5	375	950	Poison Rod	Power Staff
Blind Wolf	900	0	33	54	5	25	20	5	363	500	N/A	Eye Drop
Blizzard	2300	0	45	77	10	20	0	5	510	1200	N/A	Potion
Blockhead	600	100	26	37	0	30	0	5	228	330	N/A	N/A
BloodSlime	600	100	29	36	39	25	0	0	264	365	Holy Water	Holy Water
BlueDragon	6900	1000	38	64	10	35	20	5	500	2500	Dragon Fang	Dragon Fang
Bludgeoner	6000	0	41	70	10	43	0	5	10	3	Potion	Crystalmail
Bndrsnatch	120	0	9	14	0	15	10	5	100	60	Tonic	Tonic
Bomb	440	50	21	29	0	15	0	5	162	230	Tonic	Tonic
BrandLamia	2100	60	40	54	10	27	0	5	435	700	Maiden'sKiss	Lamia'sTiara
Cactus	1000	50	29	37	0	25	0	5	255	419	Tonic	N/A
Centipeelr	2780	100	48	75	10	25	0	0	570	1250	Tonic	Potion
Cockataur	100	0	12	15	0	15	30	5	75	55	Soft	N/A
Cool Dust	240	100	17	21	0	15	0	5	120	130	Tonic	Dark Matter
Corbett	2800	0	29	40	0	35	0	25	1000	0	N/A	Potion
Corral	2150	100	46	66	20	25	0	0	534	1268	Tonic	N/A
Cowpoke	2200	100	37	52	5	35	0	5	399	825	Power Drink	Speed Drink
Crescent	580	0	22	30	0	20	0	5	171	300	Silver Bow	Death Sickle
Crystelle	3	500	52	100	50	20	50	0	800	0	Ether	CrystalHelmt
CrystlDrgn	17,500	10,000	62	128	40	50	0	20	10,000	0	Elixir	Crystalmail
CrystSlugs	75	50	10	8	0	15	0	5	60	38	Tonic	Elixir
Cure Beast	1000	100	34	42	0	35	10	5	333	620	N/A	Elixir
Cybis	25	100	19	30	10	50	90	35	100	200	N/A	Soft
Cycloskull	3000	100	48	75	10	25	0	0	564	1380	Turtle Shell	Rune Chime
Death Claw	4000	200	51	70	29	25	0	0	600	1700	Hero Drink	Soft
DeemMaster	2600	1000	43	82	45	20	20	0	480	900	Tonic	Potion
Defeater	260	100	18	22	0	20	0	0	129	150	Tonic	Speed Drink
Desertorpedo	2150	0	40	59	10	22	0	5	426	900	Tonic	Dark Matter
DethDealer	3000	100	63	75	10	25	0	0	567	1400	Holy Water	Phoenix Down
Devourer	1000	100	28	37	0	25	0	5	246	385	N/A	N/A
Diablo	16	0	3	4	3	7	0	5	20	7	N/A	N/A
Dinglberry	39,393	100	46	119	10	49	30	0	537	1268	Plumed Hat	Mirage Vest

NAME	HP	MP	LV	AT	DF	SP	EV	MD	GIL	EXP	STEAL	DROP
Disabler	3800	300	49	77	30	20	10	10	579	1500	Wall Ring	Lamia'sHarp
Doublizard	700	0	21	29	20	15	0	5	165	260	N/A	Tonic
DrgnZombie	4590	0	24	46	10	29	0	5	500	1650	N/A	Dragon Fang
DragonAvis	7000	1000	49	100	15	22	0	15	618	2020	Trident	Dragon Fang
Drippy	900	100	32	35	5	35	0	5	294	540	MythrilHammr	Tent
Drgn Great	10,000	1000	51	100	20	20	0	20	615	1900	Dragon Fang	Dragon Fang
Druid	2200	900	44	60	10	30	0	5	501	1500	Tonic	Phoenix Down
DualKnight	2140	0	44	78	5	1	0	0	489	1100	Power Drink	Power Drink
Elf Toad	160	50	13	15	0	10	0	5	81	65	N/A	Tonic
Executor	2000	10,000	42	52	10	35	0	0	462	1300	N/A	DimndArmBand
Fall Guard	4000	100	47	60	30	20	0	0	543	1335	RopeHeadband	KaisrKnuckle
Fan Wizard	1000	200	24	35	2	30	0	0	207	470	Tonic	Dark Bow
Ferry Walk	1000	1000	28	36	0	25	0	5	243	385	Holy Water	Potion
Fins	550	10	20	27	0	26	0	5	100	180	Tonic	Tonic
Fishite	400	0	25	40	0	25	0	0	200	300	N/A	Tonic
Flare	3000	1000	44	89	35	21	0	0	486	1100	Elixir	Poet Cap
Freeziabat	2300	200	32	42	30	39	0	15	273	888	Potion	Potion
Fury	5000	1000	50	80	20	20	0	0	630	2250	Wall Ring	Black Robe
Galacjelly	75	100	34	45	20	25	50	0	348	750	Eye Drop	Ether
Garula	500	0	9	12	5	10	0	5	0	0	Maiden'sKiss	N/A
Gatlings	80	0	7	9	0	20	0	5	42	30	N/A	Soft
GhilaCat	100	20	12	12	0	15	15	0	72	55	Tonic	N/A
Gigas	760	35	19	28	0	20	0	0	144	350	Elixir	Giant Drink
Glastos	250	0	15	20	11	10	0	4	100	230	N/A	Turtle Shell
GloomWidow	1820	0	42	60	10	20	0	5	456	1100	Tonic	N/A
Goblin	16	3	6	5	0	10	0	5	20	10	Tonic	Leather Cap
GrandMummy	6000	300	0	55	30	34	10	10	0	0	Potion	Potion
Gravidead	1800	200	34	38	20	35	10	10	327	720	N/A	Earth Robe
Grenade	3000	500	47	75	10	25	0	0	558	1100	Potion	Potion
Grimalkin	500	0	32	36	5	30	0	0	200	300	N/A	Holy Water
Groundpede	1450	200	24	42	5	30	0	0	291	520	N/A	Hard Body
Harpy	666	5000	14	50	50	35	50	50	93	100	Hard Body	Phoenix Down
Hedgehog	1000	0	37	54	25	38	0	5	402	850	Soft	Soft
Hydra	3000	1000	26	42	20	50	10	5	219	3108	N/A	Phoenix Down
Hypnot	2600	100	37	59	5	35	0	5	381	1150	N/A	Phoenix Down
Hyudra	2000	1000	25	38	10	45	0	5	216	1800	Ether	Dragon Fang
IceSoldier	160	20	13	17	0	15	0	5	84	65	MythrilSword	Tonic

NAME	HP	MP	LV	AT	DF	SP	EV	MD	GIL	EXP	STEAL	DROP
Imp	2000	200	36	90	5	30	30	5	354	840	Tonic	DmndArmBand
Invisible	7000	1000	52	90	10	47	25	10	0	0	Ninja Suit	N/A
Iron	2140	0	44	80	25	20	0	0	492	1200	Giant Drink	Giant Drink
Iron Dress	2200	0	44	70	50	30	10	15	504	1300	Tonic	Tent
Iron Giant	18,000	10,000	61	100	50	55	0	0	597	10,000	Iron Helmet	Giant Drink
Jestrex	2580	485	48	90	15	25	20	0	606	1390	Speed Drink	Eye Drop
Karnak	140	0	19	20	0	10	10	0	141	140	Tonic	N/A
Kestrel	19,000	10,000	27	77	40	59	40	30	10,000	0	Maiden'sKiss	Angel Ring
Killer Bee	20	0	1	5	0	10	10	5	20	15	N/A	N/A
Kornago	1000	300	31	38	0	30	0	5	285	512	Tonic	Eye Drop
Kuzer	5000	1000	28	45	10	35	0	0	1000	1000	N/A	Elixir
La Mage	760	200	19	25	0	25	0	0	198	370	Poet Robe	Elixir
Lamia	900	100	24	35	0	35	0	3	210	490	Maiden'sKiss	N/A
Landcrawler	22,000	500	48	100	20	25	0	5	576	3270	AncientSword	Elixir
Landsquid	2780	500	48	71	10	25	0	0	576	3270	Potion	Holy Water
LandTurtle	1300	0	34	42	30	25	0	15	336	790	Tonic	Turtle Shell
Landwort	180	0	14	19	0	15	0	5	99	120	Tonic	N/A
LevelChekr	5000	500	54	90	20	20	0	0	624	1520	Tonic	Elixir
LilChariot	480	100	8	40	0	25	0	0	200	300	N/A	Potion
LumbrBeast	130	0	11	10	1	20	0	5	63	46	Tonic	Elixirl
MagicDragon	2900	300	36	58	10	27	0	5	372	1200	Tonic	Elixir
Magnities	1200	100	33	43	10	35	40	5	315	610	N/A	Potion
Mamon	1700	100	35	46	5	30	0	5	351	700	N/A	Potion
Mandrake	1000	100	28	36	0	25	0	5	249	385	Eye Drop	N/A
Mauldwin	20	5	1	5	0	10	0	5	27	20	N/A	Elixir
Maximus	10,000	1000	51	100	15	20	0	0	900	0	Potion	Circlet
MechaHead	7210	5000	37	59	28	37	10	18	0	0	Ether	Speed Drink
Mercury Bat	500	500	46	65	10	20	50	0	531	1020	Tonic	Potion
Metamorpha	7000	10,000	43	40	10	33	0	5	777	20	Staff	Lumino-Staff
Mind Flare	4700	500	53	90	20	20	0	0	800	0	Green Beret	White Robe
MiniDragon	1000	100	22	30	30	20	30	50	180	900	N/A	N/A
MiniMage	1100	10	11	30	5	30	0	0	345	600	N/A	Wizard Hat
MithrlDrgn	600	200	16	28	15	15	0	20	114	270	Tonic	MythrilGlove
Mog Eater	1000	50	23	39	5	30	0	5	270	665	N/A	N/A
Money Mage	20	7	5	5	0	7	0	5	30	20	Tonic	Rod
MossFungus	5000	200	48	75	15	25	0	0	591	1520	Potion	Antidote
MotorDrive	3300	0	38	63	15	32	20	15	384	1300	Tonic	Hero Drink

NAME	HP	MP	LV	AT	DF	SP	EV	MD	GIL	EXP	STEAL	DROP
Mottletrap	240	100	17	24	10	20	0	0	126	150	Ether	N/A
Mover	10,000	500	52	128	40	35	0	0	50,000	0	Fire Skill	LgtningSkill
Mummy	2900	50	27	48	25	50	10	20	500	0	Tonic	Holy Water
Neo Garula	980	1000	27	40	0	25	0	0	500	300	N/A	Water Skill
Necromancer	6900	300	54	79	15	27	0	30	1000	0	Holy Water	Holy Water
Neogigas	4170	5000	39	62	5	37	20	30	411	810	N/A	Giant Drink
Neon	700	100	33	44	5	25	20	5	312	600	Speed Drink	Speed Drink
Nile	1200	10	38	51	35	21	0	6	441	480	N/A	Hard Body
Ninja	5000	200	52	90	15	26	70	0	612	1800	Shuriken	Magishuriken
Nut Eater	20	0	1	5	0	10	0	5	20	10	Tonic	Tonic
Octofist	60	0	7	8	0	20	0	5	45	21	N/A	Tonic
Oculus	2100	0	49	75	33	22	0	16	594	1350	Dark Matter	Phoenix Down
PaddleThru	280	50	14	19	0	15	0	5	93	100	Tonic	N/A
Page 32	480	500	19	27	0	30	0	5	147	180	Tonic	Tonic
Page 64	500	500	20	27	1	35	0	5	150	200	Tonic	Phoenix Down
Page 128	700	500	20	28	0	35	0	5	153	190	Ether	Tonic
Page 256	900	500	21	29	0	35	10	5	156	210	Potion	MythrlShield
Pantera	18,000	1000	42	61	5	30	10	15	0	0	Phoenix Down	N/A
Pao	500	0	27	40	0	20	0	0	0	0	Tonic	Tent
PoisnEagle	100	0	32	37	0	35	50	0	303	500	N/A	Antidote
Poltrgeist	240	100	17	21	0	20	10	5	123	135	Potion	N/A
Prototype	5000	1000	23	33	100	20	0	100	0	2000	Ether	Dark Matter
PsychoHeds	90	100	11	9	0	10	0	5	66	46	N/A	Fire Skill
Pyramidia	2200	1000	41	61	10	26	0	5	438	800	Power Drink	Tonic
Python	1800	0	39	49	5	24	0	5	405	680	Antidote	Eye Drop
Quadrharpy	1000	150	23	50	20	40	0	20	186	1000	N/A	Phoenix Down
Radiator	900	1000	40	47	30	5	0	20	417	800	N/A	Tonic
Red Dragon	7500	1000	30	65	12	34	0	8	500	3000	Potion	Elixir
Red Harpy	1900	100	43	60	10	24	0	5	465	1250	Potion	Holy Water
RflecKnigt	1600	200	33	47	30	30	0	0	318	700	War Hammer	Wall Ring
RflecMage	1300	100		36AT	52	5	28	0	5	0	369	900	N/A Ether
RicardMage	100	70	10	17	0	15	0	5	87	75	Rod	Fire Rod
Ridicule	1380	200	31	41	5	35	0	0	288	900	Maiden'sKiss	Hero Drink
RockStatue	3300	20	45	76	20	26	0	5	507	100	Potion	Soft
RockCutter	120	0	11	13	0	10	0	5	69	46	Tonic	N/A
RonkaKnigt	860	0	24	36	20	25	20	10	201	380	Potion	MythrlShield
Sand Bear	1000	0	24	36	10	35	0	10	195	360	N/A	N/A

NAME	HP	MP	LV	AT	DF	SP	EV	MD	GIL	EXP	STEAL	DROP
Sandboil	420	0	23	33	5	20	0	5	189	260	Tonic	Tonic
Sandcrawlr	15,000	1000	29	45	10	35	0	5	1000	1000	N/A	Power Drink
SandKiller	620	0	23	34	0	20	0	5	192	300	N/A	Antidote
Sea Devil	5000	1000	30	71	15	20	0	10	3000	0	Potion	Turtle Shell
Sergeant	400	100	0	25	0	20	0	0	132	160	Tonic	Silver Plate
Serpentina	3900	300	49	76	30	20	10	5	582	1500	Prism Dress	HairOrnament
ShadeDancr	4480	100	43	75	10	30	20	5	468	1550	Power Wrist	Cornucopia
Shadow	1000	0	40	57	25	26	30	5	408	880	N/A	Holy Water
Shell Fish	1000	0	28	0	0	30	0	0	540	0	Tonic	Potion
Shell Bear	380	0	27	37	0	20	0	0	334	89	N/A	Potion
Sherry	4000	300	49	78	30	20	10	0	585	1500	Red Shoes	Winged Shoes
ShieldDrgn	19,999	20,000	29	40	40	40	0	25	1000	10,000	MythrlShield	Gold Shield
Shoat	5000	500	38	55	20	45	0	10	0	0	N/A	N/A
Silent Bee	220	50	16	20	0	15	0	5	111	120	N/A	Soft
Skelesaur	2590	10,000	32	39	10	28	0	5	300	890	Soft	Ether
Skeleton	70	0	10	8	0	15	0	5	57	38	N/A	Dirk
Skull Eater	1	100	32	50	90	50	90	90	100	300	Tent	Elixir
Sleepy	1600	100	36	50	5	30	10	5	396	700	N/A	Leather Cap
Slownin	2400	0	43	81	10	35	30	5	474	1400	Katana	Kotetsu
Slug	1820	100	42	62	10	20	10	5	453	1100	Tonic	N/A
Soccer	50	0	6	7	0	20	0	5	40	21	N/A	Tonic
Sorcerer	350	500	18	20	0	20	0	0	138	180	Mage Slasher	Ether
Sizzoner	2300	0	39	71	10	20	0	0	516	1250	Tonic	Tonic
Steel Bat	20	10,000	2	3	0	5	0	5	20	9	N/A	N/A
Stingray	30,000	1000	93	66	60	70	40	20	0	0	Dark Matter	Dragon Beard
Stone	50	0	12	13	8	10	0	5	78	55	SilvrGlasses	N/A
Stone Golem	1000	0	22	32	20	20	0	50	177	550	Soft	Potion
Stoned Mask	450	20	24	34	20	25	0	0	204	320	Soft	N/A
Stray Cat	20	0	2	5	0	10	0	5	20	15	N/A	N/A
Stroper	20	0	3	4	0	7	0	5	20	8	Tonic	N/A
Subterran	1000	100	27	36	0	30	0	5	237	353	N/A	N/A
Succubus	2700	100	36	55	20	35	20	5	357	2200	Antidote	Dragon Fang
SwrdDancer	3000	0	48	75	15	25	0	0	561	2400	MythrilHelmt	Blizzard
Sybaritic	3200	0	52	100	70	20	70	0	642	1480	Turtle Shell	Elixir
Tarantula	200	0	27	35	0	20	0	0	231	88	N/A	Tonic
Tattoo	100	0	8	11	30	20	10	10	70	50	N/A	Tent
The Damned	1980	0	44	65	10	20	0	5	471	1200	N/A	Holy Water

NAME	HP	MP	LV	AT	DF	SP	EV	MD	GIL	EXP	STEAL	DROP
Thunderpit	600	100	21	27	0	25	0	5	100	160	Tonic	LgtningSkill
Tiny Mage	1540	500	43	80	40	20	15	0	477	780	N/A	Tonic
Tote Avis	33,090	1000	47	70	10	50	20	10	0	0	Ab Splitter	Ab Splitter
Traveler	1400	100	33	40	0	35	20	5	321	580	N/A	Dream Harp
Trent	700	50	26	36	0	25	0	5	225	330	Potion	Tonic
Tripper	1300	100	34	41	10	30	10	5	324	710	Tonic	Potion
TwinLizard	1500	0	33	54	10	35	0	5	360	720	N/A	Tonic
T-Wrecks	2300	0	45	85	30	25	20	30	513	2000	Antidote	Dragon Fang
Unknown (Green Slime)	3500	500	47	61	40	20	0	0	519	1080	Tonic	Giant Drink
Unknown (Spore)	2500	500	41	60	25	20	0	0	525	1200	Tonic	Speed Drink
Unknown (Skeleton)	6500	500	47	67	35	20	0	0	528	2000	Tonic	Hard Body
Unknown (Worm)	2500	500	46	62	30	20	0	0	522	1350	Tonic	Power Drink
Ultragigas	2420	500	34	49	20	31	10	10	330	1200	N/A	Giant Drink
Verminator	1000	500	27	35	0	25	0	5	240	353	Tonic	Ether
Water Bus	600	50	26	37	0	25	0	5	222	330	N/A	N/A
WaterScorp	500	0	26	59	20	35	80	0	680	0	Tonic	Tonic
Weresnake	900	20	31	40	0	30	10	5	282	490	Tonic	Potion
WhiteFlame	1600	100	49	65	50	25	33	25	588	1430	Eye Drop	Ether
White Snake	25	0	4	5	0	10	0	5	24	20	N/A	N/A
Wild Dog	95	100	15	20	0	10	0	10	125	70	Tonic	N/A
WingKiller	300	0	26	40	0	28	0	0	200	300	N/A	Antidote
X-DethSoul	20,000	20,000	1	77	40	40	50	45	0	0	N/A	Dark Matter
Y Burn	200	0	14	17	0	18	0	5	90	160	MythrilKnife	Tonic
YellowDrgn	8500	1000	38	65	10	35	0	5	500	2600	LightningRod	Coral Ring
Yojimbo	3690	0	52	109	5	20	10	0	645	2000	Cottage	Power Tasuki
Zefa Zone	3780	5000	53	55	25	30	30	30	500	2000	Tonic	Elixir
Zuu	850	0	15	22	0	15	0	5	150	360	N/A	Elixir

Weapons

NOTE

"2-hand" means the weapon does not require two hands, but can be used that way for extra damage.

Weapons in bold indicate the 12 legendary sealed weapons.

Name	Use	Function
Broadsword	Bat.Pwr +12	Throw in battle, can use Magic Sword, "2-hand"
Long Sword	Bat.Pwr +19	Throw in battle, can use Magic Sword, "2-hand"
MythrilSword	Bat.Pwr +28	Throw in battle, can use Magic Sword, "2-hand"
Coral Sword	Bat.Pwr +34	Throw in battle, can use Magic Sword, "2-hand"
AncientSword	Bat.Pwr +40	Throw in battle, can use Magic Sword, "2-hand," casts Old after some hits
Half Moon	Bat.Pwr +46	Throw in battle, can use Magic Sword, "2-hand," casts Sleep after some hits
RegalCutlass	Bat.Pwr +54	Throw in battle, can use Magic Sword, "2-hand"
Blood Sword	Mag.Pwr +5, Bat. Pwr +81	Casts "Red Feast" on some hits
Flame Saber	Bat.Pwr +60	Can use Magic Sword, "2-hand"
Blizzard	Bat.Pwr +62	N/A
Excalipur	Bat.Pwr +97	Throw in battle, cursed to rarely hit, causes no damage
(*)Brave Blade	Vigor +5, Bat.Pwr + 0	N/A
(**)ChickenKnife	Speed +5, Bat.Pwr + 0	Can use Magic Sword
Defender	Bat.Pwr +96	Throw in battle, defends against random attacks
Enchanter	Mag.Pwr +3, Bat.Pwr +99	Can use Magic Sword, "2-hand"
Rune Edge	Bat.Pwr +57	Can do 2-handed critical hit using MP
Ragnarok	Bat.Pwr +137	Throw in battle, can use Magic Sword, "2-hand"
Excalibur	**Vigor +5, Bat.Pwr +107**	**Throw in battle, can use Magic Sword, "2-hand," imbued with Holy**
Katana	Bat.Pwr +39	Throw in battle, "2-hand"
Bizen'sPride	Bat.Pwr +48	Throw in battle, "2-hand"
Wind Sword	Bat.Pwr +41	Throw in battle, "2-hand"
Kotetsu	Bat.Pwr +55	Throw in battle, "2-hand"
Ichimonji	Bat.Pwr +84	Throw in battle, "2-hand"
MonsterKillr	Bat.Pwr +94	Throw in battle, "2-hand"
Strato	Bat.Pwr +117	Throw in battle, "2-hand"
Masamune	**Bat.Pwr +104**	**Throw in battle, "2-hand," always strike first**
Knife	Bat.Pwr +4	Throw in battle, can use Magic Sword
Dirk	Bat.Pwr +11	Throw in battle, can use Magic Sword
MythrilKnife	Bat.Pwr +20	Throw in battle, can use Magic Sword
Ninja Knife	Speed +1, Bat.Pwr +26	Throw in battle, can use Magic Sword
HuntingKnife	Bat.Pwr +33	Throw in battle, parries some attacks
Mage Slasher	Bat.Pwr +28, Mag.Pwr +1	Throw in battle, casts Mute after some hits

Cluster	Speed +1, Bat.Pwr +43	Throw in battle, can use Magic Sword
HalcyonBlade	Bat.Pwr +38	Throw in battle, can use Magic Sword
Dancing Dirk	Speed +1, Mag.Pwr +1, Bat.Pwr +48	Can use Magic Sword, sometimes random dance attacks instead of Dirk attack
Air Lancet	Bat.Pwr +53	Throw in battle, can use Magic Sword
Thief Knife	Speed +1, Bat.Pwr +63	Can use Magic Sword, sometimes does Mug attack
Sasuke	**Speed +1, Bat.Pwr +96**	**Throw in battle, can use Magic Sword**
Man-Eater	Vigor +2, Speed +2, Stamina +2, Mag.Pwr +2, Bat.Pwr +86	
Assassin	**Speed +1, Bat.Pwr +78**	**Throw in battle, can use Magic sword, some hits cast Doom**
Battle Ax	Bat.Pwr +20	Throw in battle, can use "2-hand"
MythrilHammer	Bat.Pwr +25	Can use "2-hand"
Cleaver	Bat.Pwr +30	Can use "2-hand"
Death Sickle	Bat.Pwr +40	Can use "2-hand", casts Doom on some hits
War Hammer	Bat.Pwr +35	Throw in battle, can use "2-hand"
Poison Ax	Bat.Pwr +45	Throw in battle, can use "2-hand"
Double Ax	Bat.Pwr +88	Can use "2 hand"
Earth Hammer	Bat.Pwr +55	Throw in battle, can use "2-hand," casts Earthquake on some misses
Thor'sHammer	Bat.Pwr +78	Attack from back row, "2-hand"
Rune Ax	**Mag.Pwr +3, Bat.Pwr +68**	**Throw in battle, can do 2-handed critical hit using MP**
Mythril Pike	Bat.Pwr +27	Throw in battle, 2X jump attacks
Spear	Speed +1, Bat.Pwr +	2X jump attacks
Javelin	Vigor +1, Bat.Pwr +52	Throw in battle, 2X jump attacks
Trident	Bat.Pwr +35	Throw in battle, 2X jump attacks
Wind Lance	Bat.Pwr +44	Throw in battle, 2X jump attacks
Short Spear	Bat.Pwr +51	Throw in battle
Partisan	Bat.Pwr +59	Throw in battle, 2X jump attacks
Dragon Lance	Bat.Pwr +116	Throw in battle, 2X jump attacks
Holy Lance	**Vigor +3, Bat.Pwr +106**	**Throw in battle, 2X jump attacks, Imbued with Holy**
Silver Bow	Bat.Pwr +35	2 handed weapon, attack from back row
Fire Bow	Bat Pwr. +36	2-handed weapon, attack from back row
Ice Bow	Bat Pwr. +36	2-handed weapon, attack from back row
LightningBow	Bat Pwr. +36	2-handed weapon, attack from back row
Dark Bow	Bat.Pwr +40	2-handed weapon, attack from back row
Crossbow	Bat.Pwr +49	2-handed weapon, attack from back row, critical hit is an instant kill
Elfin Bow	Bat.Pwr+53	2-handed weapon, attack from back row
Gale Bow	Bat. Pwr +66	2-handed weapon, attack from back row, sometimes does Sshot attack
Magic Bow	Bat.Pwr -3	2-handed weapon, attack from back row
Ab Splitter	Bat.Pwr +89	2-handed weapon, attack from back row
Artemis	Bat.Pwr +108	2-handed weapon, attack from back row
Yoichi's Bow	**Vigor +3, Speed +3, Bat.Pwr +98**	**2-handed weapon, attack from back row**
Moonring	Bat.Pwr +32	Attack from back row
Razor Ring	Bat.Pwr +68	Attack from back row
Double Lance	Bat.Pwr +61	Throw in battle
Staff	Bat.Pwr +6	N/A
HealingStaff	Mag.Pwr + 37	Cure spell & removes some effects

Power Staff	Vigor +5, Bat.Pwr -3	N/A
Lumino-Staff	Mag.Pwr +2, Bat.Pwr +42	N/A
Judge-Staff	Mag.Pwr +3, Bat.Pwr +57	Imbued with Holy
Sage Staff	**Bat.Pwr +50**	**Raise power for Holy**
Flail	Bat. Pwr +13	Can use "2-hand," attack from back row
Mace	Bat.Pwr +47	Can use "2-hand," attack from back row
Wooden Rod	Bat.Pwr +5, Mag.Pwr +1	Attack from back row
Ice Rod	Bat.Pwr +13	Increases Ice magic attack, attack from back row
Fire Rod	Bat.Pwr +13	Increases Fire magic attack, attack from back row
LightningRod	Bat.Pwr +13	Increases Bolt magic attack, attack from back row
Poison Rod	Bat.Pwr +29	Increases Poison magic
Power Rod	Mag.Pwr +3, Bat.Pwr +27	Attack from back row
Wonder Wand	Mag.Pwr +2, Bat.Pwr -3	Attack from back row, casts Return if used as an item
Magus Rod	**Bat.Pwr +37**	**Power for Fire/Spirit/Bolt/Poison/ Earth magic**
Monster Bell	Bat.Pwr +21	Attack from back row
Rune Chime	Bat.Pwr +42	Attack from back row, critical hits using MP
Tinkerbell	Bat.Pwr +52	Attack from back row
Earth Bell	**Bat.Pwr +32**	**Attack from back row**
Whip	Bat.Pwr +23	Attack from back row, sometimes paralyzes after hit
Shock Whip	Bat.Pwr +39	Attack from back row, sometimes casts Bolt after hit
Chain Whip	Bat.Pwr +49	Attack from back row, sometimes paralyzes after hit
Beast Killer	Bat.Pwr +69	Attack from back row, sometimes paralyzes after hit
Dragon Beard	Bat.Pwr +89	Attack from back row
Fire Bute	**Vigor +2, Speed +2, Bat.Pwr +79**	**Attack from back row**
Silver Harp	Bat.Pwr +12	2-handed attack from back row
Dream Harp	Bat.Pwr +22	2-handed attack from back row
Lamia's Harp	Bat.Pwr +32	2-handed attack from back row, same as TemptSong
Apollo Harp	**Bat.Pwr +42**	**2-handed, attack from back row, vs. Dragons**
Shuriken	No effect	Throw in battle, damage one enemy
MagiShuriken	No effect	Throw in battle, damage one enemy
LgtningSkill	No effect	Throw in battle, damage all enemies
Water Skill	No effect	Throw in battle, damage all enemies
Fire Skill	No effect	Throw in battle, damage all enemies
Ash	No effect	Throw in battle, damage one enemy

**(*) Indicates that the blade's Bat.Pwr will decrease if party runs away from fights.
(**) Indicates that the blade's Bat.Pwr is determined by number of fights party ran away from before getting blade.**

Armor

Head Armor

Name	Effect	Notes
Leather Cap	Defense +1, Mag.Def +1, Weight 1	
BronzeHelmet	Defense +2, Mag.Def +2, Weight 4	
Iron Helmet	Defense +4, Mag.Def +2, Weight 4	
MythrilHelmt	Defense +6, Mag.Def +2, Weight 4	
Gold Helmet	Defense +8, Mag.Def +2, Weight 4	
DiamondHelmt	Defense +10, Mag.Def +2, Weight 4	
CrystlHelmt	Defense +13, Mag.Def +2, Weight 4	
Genji Helmet	Defense +15, Mag.Def +2, Weight 5	
Plumed Hat	Defense +2, Mag.Def +2, Weight 2	
Poet Cap	Mag.Pwr +2, Defense +6, Mag.Def +2, Weight 2	
Green Beret	Vigor +1, Speed +1, Defense +3, Mag.Def +2, Weight 2	
RopeHeadband	Vigor +3, Defense +6, Weight 2	
Wizard Hat	Mag.Pwr +1, Defense +4, Mag.Def +2, Weight 2	
Coronet	Mag.Pwr +1, Defense +5, Mag.Def +4, Weight 8	Raises "control" attacks
HairOrnament	Mag.Def +2, Weight 2	Halves MP use in battle
Tiger Mask	Defense +9, Mag.Def +2, Weight 2	
Lamia'sTiara	Mag.Pwr +3, Defense +3, Mag.Def +7, Weight 2	
Ribbon	Vigor +5, Speed +5, Stamina +5, Mag.Pwr +5, Defense +12,	Cures most status effects
Thornlet	Defense +20, Mag.Def +5, Weight 4	HP gradually decreases
Black Hood	Speed +2, Defense +12, Mag.Def +2	
Circlet	Mag.Pwr +3, Defense +10, Mag.Def +2	

Body Armor

Name	Effect	Notes
LeatherArmor	Defense +1, Mag.Def +1, Weight 2	
Bronze Armor	Defense +4, Mag.Def +2, Weight 8	
Bronze Plate	Defense +3, Mag.Def +2, Weight 4	
Iron Armor	Defense +6, Mag.Def +2, Weight 8	
Silver Plate	Defense +7, Mag.Def +2	
MythrilArmor	Defense +9, Mag.Def +2, Weight 8	
Gold Armor	Defense +12, Mag.Def +2, Weight 8	
DiamondArmor	Defense +15, Mag.Def +2, Weight 8	
DiamondPlate	Defense +13, Mag.Def +2, Weight 4	
Bonemail	Defense +30, Mag.Def +5, Weight 3	Wearer reacts to spells as if undead
Crystalmail	Defense +20, Mag.Def +2, Weight 8	
Genji Armor	Defense +22, Mag.Def +2, Weight 9	
Cotton Robe	Defense +2, Mag.Def +4, Weight 2	
Silk Robe	Defense +4, Mag.Def +6, Weight 2	
Poet Robe	Defense +6, Mag.Def +8, Weight 2	
Earth Robe	Defense +8, Mag.Def +10, Weight 2	
LuminousRobe	Mag.Pwr +2, Defense +11, Mag.Def +12, Weight 2	
Angel Robe	Stamina +5, Defense +10, Mag.Def +11, Weight 2	
White Robe	Stamina +3, Mag.Pwr +3, Defense +14, Mag.Def + 14, Weight 2	
Black Robe	Mag.Pwr +5, Defense +14, Mag.Def +14, Weight 2	
Kung-fu Suit	Vigor +1, Defense +5, Mag.Def +2, Weight 3	
Ninja Suit	Speed +1, Defense +9, Mag.Def +2, Weight 3	
Power Tasuki	Vigor +3, Defense +11, Weight 0	
BlackCostume	Vigor +1, Speed +1, Defense +17, Mag.Def +2, Weight 3	
Mirage Vest	Defense +14, Mag.Def +4, Weight 3	Acts like "Twin" (ninja) ability, forces first physical attack to miss
Prism Dress	Defense +15, Mag.Def +3, Weight	Raises chance of performing "Sword Dance"

Hand Armor

Name	Effect	Notes
LetherShield	Evade 10%, Weight 2	
BronzeShield	Defense +1, Evade 15%, Weight 5	
Iron Shield	Defense +2, Evade 20%, Weight 5	
MythrlShield	Defense +3, Evade 25%, Weight 5	
Gold Shield	Defense +4, Evade 30%, Weight 5	
DiamndShield	Defense +6, Evade 35%, Weight 5	
Aegis Shield	Mag.Pwr +1, Defense +5, Evade 33%, Weight 4	Blocks random magic attacks
Ice Shield	Defense +7, Evade 40%, Mag.Def +5, Weight 5	Absorbs ice attacks and uses it to heal
Flame Shield	Defense +7, Evade 40%, Mag.Def +5, Weight 5	Absorbs flame attacks and uses it to heal
CrystlShield	Defense +8, Evade 45%, Weight 5	
Genji Shield	Defense +9, Evade 50%, Mag.Def +1, Weight 6	

Relics

Name	Effect	Notes
Leather Shoes	Defense +2, Mag.Def +1, Weight 1	
Winged Shoes	Mag.Def +3	Casts Haste on wearer
Red Shoes	Defense +11, Mag.Def +2, Weight 1	Increases chance of "Sword Dance"
SilvrGlasses	Defense +1, Mag.Def +1, Weight 1	Defend vs. Flash
SilvrArmBand	Defense +2, Mag.Def +3, Weight 3	
Elf Cloak	Speed +1, Mag.Pwr +1, Mag.Def + 3, Weight 1	Avoids some attacks
MythrilGlove	Defense +3, Weight 5	
Thief'sGlove	Speed +1, Defense +4, Weight 1	Increases chance of Steal
Power Wrist	Vigor +3, Defense +3, Weight 0	
Gauntlet	Defense +6, Mag.Def +1, Weight 5	
Giant'sGlove	Vigor +5, Speed –5, Stamina +5, Mag.Pwr –5, Defense +9, Mag.Def +1, Weight 14	
KornagoGourd	Weight 15	Makes monsters easier to catch (1/2 HP instead of 1/8)
Fire Ring	Defense +5, Mag.Def +5, Weight 1	Absorbs flame, protects vs. cold, weak vs. water
Coral Ring	Defense +5, Mag.Def +5, Weight 1	Absorbs water, protects vs. fire, weak vs. lightning
Angel Ring	Defense +5, Mag.Def +10, Weight 1	Protects vs. Zombie and aging
Wall Ring	Weight 1	Wearer has Reflect during battles
Genji Glove	Defense +12, Mag. Def +1, Weight 6	
DimndArmBand	Defense +4, Mag.Def +5, Weight 3	
Hex Ring	Defense +25, Mag.Def +5, Weight 1	Death-cursed ring
Protect Ring	Stamina +5, Defense +10, Mag.Def +10, Weight 1	Regeneration for person wearing it
KaisrKnuckle	Vigor +5, Defense +8, Weight 1	Raises "Hit" attacks

Items

Name	Use	Function
Tonic	Any time	Restores up to 50 HP
Potion	Any time	Restores up to 500 HP
Tent	Outdoors & Save Points	Restores some HP and MP
Cottage	Outdoors & Save Points	Fully restores HP and MP
Ether	Any time	Restores up to 40 MP
Phoenix Down	Any time	Cures KO Status
Elixir	Any time	Restores full HP/MP
Antidote	Any time	Cures Poison
Soft	Any time	Cures Petrify
Eye Drop	Any time	Cures Dark
Maiden's Kiss	Any time	Cures Frog
Cornucopia	Any time	Cures Mini
Holy Water	Any time	Cures Zombie
Turtle Shell	!Mix item (battle)	Cures Alchemy
Power Drink	!Drink item (battle)	Raises Attack
Speed Drink	!Drink item (battle)	Same effect as Haste
Giant Drink	!Drink item (battle)	2X Max HP
Hero Drink	!Drink item (battle)	Raises Strength
Hard Body	!Drink item (battle)	Raises Defense
Dragon Fang	!Mix item (battle)	Cures Alchemy
Dark Matter	!Mix item (battle)	Cures Alchemy
Omega Badge	None	"Your wisdom/strength have beaten the ancient culture"
Magic Lamp	Battle	Randomly summons Summoner 'Beasts' in battle
Dragon Seal	None	"Replenish lost nutrition from slaying dragons"

Magic

White Magic

Name	Description	Cost	Level #
Cure	Restores small amount of HP	4 MP	1
Scan	View enemy's stats	1 MP	1
Antdot	Removes poison effects	2 MP	1
Mute	Prevents enemy from casting spells	2 MP	2
Protes	Raises defense	3 MP	2
Mini	Shrinks enemies	5 MP	2
Cure2	Restores more HP	9 MP	3
Raise	Recovers fallen allies; adds small amount of HP	29 MP	3
Muddle	Confuses enemy	4 MP	3
Blink	Creates an illusion to prevent attacks	6 MP	4
Shell	Raises Magic defense	5 MP	4
Esna	Cures most abnormal status effects	10 MP	4
Cure3	Fully restores HP	27 MP	5
Rflect	Barrier forms to reflect magic	15 MP	5
Bersrk	Forces a target to go berserk and lose control to automatically initiate physical attacks each turn against one enemy	8 MP	5
Arise	Recovers fallen allies; fully restores HP	50 MP	6
Holy	A sacred attack	20 MP	6
Dispel	Removes magic effects	12 MP	6

Black Magic

Name	Description	Cost	Level #
Fire	Lowest level Flame attack	4 MP	1
Ice	Lowest level Freeze attack	4 MP	1
Bolt	Lowest level Bolt attack	4 MP	1
Poison	Poisons target and gradually lowers HP	2 MP	2
Sleep	Causes target to fall asleep	3 MP	2
Toad	Turns target into a frog	8 MP	2
Fire2	Mid level Flame attack	10 MP	3
Ice2	Mid level Freeze attack	10 MP	3
Bolt2	Mid level Bolt attack	10 MP	3
Drain	Steals HP from enemy	13 MP	4
Break	Petrifies enemy	15 MP	4
Bio	Poisons target and rapidly lowers HP	16 MP	4
Fire3	Highest level Flame attack	25 MP	5
Ice3	Highest level Ice attack	25 MP	5
Bolt3	Highest level Bolt attack	25 MP	5
Flare	Large heat and lightning attack	39 MP	6
Doom	Casts death on some targets	29 MP	6
Asper	Absorbs enemy MP	1 MP	6

Time Magic

Name	Description	Cost	Level #
Speed	Slows down battle speed	1 MP	1
Slow	Slows down enemies	3 MP	1
Regen	Gradually recovers HP	3 MP	1
Mute	Prevents casting of songs & spells	3 MP	2
Haste	Speeds up one ally	5 MP	2
Float	Defends against ground damage	10 MP	2
Demi	Reduces your target's HP by one half	9 MP	3
Stop	Stops enemies	8 MP	3
Telepo	Escape from dungeons and battles	15 MP	3
Comet	Sends down a blast of meteorites	7 MP	4
Slow2	Slows all enemies	9 MP	4
Return	Returns to start of battle	1 MP	4
Demi2	Reduces your target's HP to one quarter	18 MP	5
Haste2	Speeds up entire party	15 MP	5
Old	Ages enemies, causing them to decrease their abilities	4 MP	5
Meteo	Casts an even larger group of meteorites	42 MP	6
Quick	Enables caster to perform twice	77 MP	6
X-zone	Causes enemies to disappear	20 MP	6

Summon Magic

Name	Description	Cost	Level #
Chocobo	Chocobo kick against one enemy, or FatChoc against all enemies	4 MP	1
Sylph	Summons wind attack, plus everyone recovers some HP	8 MP	1
Remora	Sucks an enemy's HP, then stops their movement	2 MP	1
Shiva	Ice-based attack against all all enemies	10 MP	2
Ramuh	Bolt attack against all enemies	12 MP	2
Ifrit	Fire attack against all enemies	11 MP	2
Titan	Earth-based attack against all enemies	25 MP	3
Golem	Guards against physical attacks	18 MP	3
Shoat	Turns one enemy into stone	33 MP	3
Carbuncl	Casts Reflect on entire party	45 MP	4
Hydra	Thunder attack against all enemies	32 MP	4
Odin	Spear attack against one enemy, or attacks with Vengeance Sword against all enemies	48 MP	4
Phoenix	Drains HP of one enemy, and restores HP of K.Oed party member	99 MP	5
Leviathan	Water-based attack against all enemies	39 MP	5
Bahamut	Megaflare attack against all enemies	66 MP	5

Sword Magic

Name	Description	Cost	Level #
Fire	Adds lowest level Fire damage with sword hits	2 MP	1
Ice	Adds lowest level Ice damage with sword hits	2 MP	1
Bolt	Adds lowest level Bolt damage with sword hits	2 MP	1
Poison	Poisons target with sword hits	1 MP	2
Mute	Mutes target with sword hits	1 MP	2
Sleep	Puts target to sleep with sword hits	2 MP	2
Fire2	Adds mid level Fire damage	5 MP	3
Ice2	Adds mid level Ice damage	5 MP	3

Name	Description	Cost	Level #
Bolt2	Adds mid level Bolt damage	5 MP	3
Drain	Transfers enemy HP to your HP	6 MP	4
Break	Turns enemy to stone	8 MP	4
Bio	Casts a Bio germ to target and lowers HP	3 MP	4
Fire3	Highest level Fire damage	15 MP	5
Ice3	Highest level Ice damage	15 MP	5
Bolt3	Highest level Bolt damage	15 MP	5
Holy	Casts a powerful, sacred energy attack	10 MP	6
Flare	Powerful nuclear energy attack	30 MP	6
Asper	Transfers enemy MP to your MP	1 MP	6

Blue Magic

Name	Description	Cost
Condemnd	30 second countdown to Doom	10 MP
Roulette	Random target hit with Doom	1 MP
AquaRake	Water-based attack against all enemies	38 MP
L5 Doom	Casts Death on all enemies with levels divisible by 5	22 MP
L4 Qrtr	Casts Demi2 on all enemies with levels divisible by 4	9 MP
L2 Old	Casts Old against enemies with levels divisible by 2	11 MP
L3 Flare	Casts Flare against enemies with levels divisible by 3	18 MP
ToadSong	Turns one enemy into a Toad	5 MP
LitlSong	Casts Mini against one enemy	5 MP
Flash	Causes most enemies to become blind	7 MP
TimeSlip	Casts Old and Sleep on one enemy	9 MP
MoonFlut	Berserks entire party	3 MP
DoomClaw	Reduces target's HP to single digits	21 MP
Aero	Casts the lowest level Aero attack on any target	4 MP
Aero 2	Casts a mid level Aero attack on any target	10 MP
Aero 3	Casts the highest level Aero attack on any target	24 MP
Burn Ray	Fire attack against one enemy	5 MP
GobPunch	Attack against one enemy	0 MP
BlakShok	Halves level of target	27 MP
GuardOff	Reduces enemy's Defense	19 MP
Pep Up	Restores ally's HP and MP at expense of caster	13 MP
MindBlst	Momentarily stuns and damages one enemy	6 MP
RedFeast	Drains HP from one enemy and gives to caster	2 MP
MagHammr	Halves MP of one enemy	3 MP
Guardian	Casts Safe, Float, and Shell, on entire party	72 MP
Exploder	Causes damage at expense of caster	1 MP
????	Damage equals max HP minus current HP	3 MP
BlowFish	Causes 1000 points of damage to enemy with a needle attack	25 MP
WhitWind	Restores HP equal to caster's current HP to entire party	28 MP
Missile	Cuts any target's HP down to 1/4	7 MP

Earth Magic

Name	Description

Elemental Attacks while in Fields

Gust	Wind attack against one enemy
Earthquake	Earth attack against all enemies
Wind Slash	Wind attack against all enemies
Twister	Reduces target to single digit HP

Elemental Attacks while on Mountains

Gust	Wind attack against one enemy
Earthquake	Earth attack against all enemies
Twister	Reduces target to single digit HP
Stalagmite	Randomly drops four rocks on all enemies

Elemental Attacks while in Forests

Branch Arrow	Attack against one enemy
Rage	Wind attack against all enemies and casts Dark simultaneously
Branch Spear	More powerful attack than Branch Arrow
Vine Hell	Slows all enemies

Elemental Attacks while in Deserts

Dust	Earth/Wind damage to all enemies and casts Dark simultaneously
Desert Storm	Powerful Earth/Wind damage to all enemies
Quicksand	Drags a single enemy into the sand. Same as Time Magic X-zone
Heat Sand	Earth/Fire damage to all enemies

Elemental Attacks while on Water/Waterfall

Whirlpool	Randomly eliminates an enemy in a single shot
Tsunami	Water attack against multiple enemies
Big Wave	Stronger water attack against multiple enemies
Phantom	Normal damage to a single enemy
Waterfall	Water damage to a single enemy

Elemental Attacks while on Marsh lands

Will O' Wisp	Damages and Muddles enemies
Peat Bog	Drags all enemies into marsh
Poison Mist	Causes a single enemy to be near death. HP will drop to 1

Elemental Attacks while in Caves

Wind Slash	Effective windslash attack for multiple, non-Boss enemies
Will O' Wisp	Fire damage to a single enemy. May cast Confuse
Stalagmite	Randomly drops four rocks on all enemies
Stalactite	Drops one giant rock on a single enemy

Elemental Attacks while in Buildings

Wind Slash	Effective windslash attack for multiple, non-Boss enemies
Gust	Wind attack on a single enemy
Twister	Reduces target to single digit HP
Will O' Wisp	Fire damage to a single enemy. May cast Confuse
Sonic Boom	Wind attack on a single enemy

Songs

Name	Description
PowerSong	Increases party's attack power
SpeedSong	Casts Haste on an ally
Str. Song	Regenerates entire party's HP
MP Song	Increase party's Magic ability
LVL Song	Increases party's level
Requiem	Casts Sleep on all undead enemies
Love Song	Stops enemies from attacking for a few turns
TemptSong	Casts Muddle on all enemies

Dance

Name	Description
Wonder Waltz	Drains MP from the enemy
Tempt Tango	Confuses one enemy
Jitterbug	Drains HP from the enemy
Sword Dance	Quadruple damage on your next attack

Critter

Name	Description	Level
Squirrel	Attacks one enemy	1
Mindia Rabbit	Nothing happens	1
Bee Swarm	Attacks all enemies	6
Nightingale	Heals all party members	11
Tree Squirrel	Distracts enemies	16
Falcon	Attacks one enemy and reduces enemy's HP to 1/3	21
Skunk	Casts Dark and Poison to all enemies	31
Wild Boar	Attacks one enemy	41
Unicorn	Restores party members' HP and MP	51

Name	Tonic	Ether	Antidote	Maiden'sKiss	Potion	Turtle Shell	Dark Matter	Dragon Fang	Eye Drop	Elixir	Phoenix Down	Holy Water
Tonic	Tonic+	X-Potion	Neutralize	Maiden'sKiss+	Lifewater	Tincture	Dark Potion	Dragon Power	Eye Drop+	Elixir	Ressurection	Tonic+
Ether	X-Potion	Tincture	ResistPoison	Lilith Kiss	Half-Elixer	X-Potion	Dark Tincture	Dragon Sheid	Resist Fire	Elixir	Reincarnate	Tincture
Antidote	Neutralize	ResistPoison	Antidote	Float	Neutralize	Turtle Shell (1)	Poison	Poison Breath	Tonic2	Elixir	Resist Ice	Samson Might
Maiden'sKiss	Maiden'sKiss+	Lilith Kiss	Float	Maiden'sKiss+	Maiden'sKiss+	Drain Kiss	Toad Kiss	Dragon's Kiss	Lamia's Kiss	Lilith Kiss	Life Kiss	Blessed Kiss
Potion	Lifewater	Half-Elixer	Neutralize	Maiden'sKiss+	Potion+	Dry Tincture	Dark Potion	Dragon Power	Eye Drop+	Elixir	Ressurection	Potion+
Turtle Shell	Tincture	X-Potion	Turtle Shell (1)	Drain Kiss	Dry Tincture	Preventive	Explosive	Dud Potion	Haste Water	Dud Potion	Remedy	Bacchus Wine
Dark Matter	Dark Potion	Dark Tincture	Poison	Toad Kiss	Dark Potion	Explosive	Shadowflare	Dark Breath	Gloom Gas	Dark Elixir	Doom Potion	Dud Potion
Dragon Fang	Dragon Power	Dragon Shield	Poison Breath	Dragon's Kiss	Dragon Power	Dud Potion	Dark Breath	Dragon Breath	Gloom Sigh	Elixir	Dragon Armor	Hoary Water
Eye Drop	Eye Drop+	Resist Fire	Tonic2	Lamia's Kiss	Eye Drop+	Haste Water	Gloom Gas	Gloom Sigh		Elixir	Resist Bolt	ElementMight
Elixir	Elixir	Elixir	Elixir	Lilith Kiss	Elixir	Dud Potion	Dark Elixir	Elixir	Elixir		Reincarnate	Elixir
Phoenix Down	Ressurection	Reincarnate	Resist Ice	Life Kiss	Ressurection	Remedy	Doom Potion	Dragon Armor	Resist Bolt	Reincarnate	Phoenix Down	Life Shield
Holy Water	Tonic+	Tincture	Samson Might	Blessed Kiss	Potion+	Bacchus Wine	Dud Potion	Hoary Water	ElementMight	Elixir	Life Shield	Holy Water+

Tonic2 is called Tonic, but has visual effect like Esna (White Magic)

Name	Description
Tonic+	Restores 90 HP
Potion+	Restores 900 HP
Tincture	Restores 80 MP
Maiden'sKiss+	Cures Frog status and restores HP
Dud Potion	Casts TimeSlip and Muddle
Lifewater	Casts Regen
X-Potion	Recovers all HP
Resurrection	Restores ally from KO'ed status
Neutralize	Cures Poison and recovers HP
Eyedrop+	Cures Blindness and recovers HP
Dragon Power	Raises level by 20
Dark Potion	Causes 666 points of damage
Half-Elixer	Cures HP to maximum
Dry Tincture	Triples the power of normal Ether
Reincarnate	Revives ally and restores HP to maximum
Lilith Kiss	Drains MP from enemy
ResistPoison	Resistant to Poison
Resist Fire	Resistant to Fire attacks
Dragon Shield	Resistant to Ice, Fire, and Thunder attacks
Dark Tincture	Drains MP to 1/4
Giant Drink	Doubles maximum HP
Dark Elixir	Reduces HP and MP to single digits
Life Kiss	Brings KO'ed ally back to life, and recovers 1/2 HP, and full MP

Name	Description
Lifeshield	Resistant to sudden-death attacks
Remedy	Heals all status ailments
Resist Ice	Resistant to Ice attacks
Resist Bolt	Resistant to Thunder attacks
Dragon Armor	Increases Defense and Magic Defense
Doom Potion	Casts Doom
Blessed Kiss	Casts Bersrk, Haste, and Image
Drain Kiss	Drains HP from target
Float	Casts Float on target
Lamia Kiss	Confuses target
Toad Kiss	Transforms victim into a frog
Bacchus Wine	Beserks target
Samson Power	Raises level by 10
ElementMight	Increases magic damage by 50%
Hoary Breath	Casts powerful, holy wind attack
Dud Potion	Poisons target
Preventative	Casts Safe on target
Turtle Shell (1)	Decreases defense by 1/2
Haste Water	Speeds up target
Explosive	Massive Fire damage at cost of user's life
Tonic	Cures status for duration of battle only
Poison Breath	Poisons many targets
Poison	Poisons target

Name	Description
Gloom Sigh	Blinds and Confuses target
Gloom Gas	Blinds target
Dragon Breath	Fire, Thunder, and Ice breath damage
Dark Breath	Casts an unholy fire over targets
Shadowflare	Darkness inflicts massive damage on enemies
Holy Water	Cures Zombie and restores

FINAL FANTASY ANTHOLOGY™
FINAL FANTASY® VI

Characters

Terra Branford

"A mysterious young woman, controlled by the Empire, and born with the gift of magic...."

Terra is one of two characters at the beginning of the game who can use magic. Her knowledge of magic is limited at first but is still very useful. As Terra's skill level grows, she'll slowly learn new spells. Her skill will eventually be supplemented or rather enhanced with the use of Espers, but she can still learn spells until the very end of the game, including the powerful Ultima spell.

Terra's Skill: Morph

Terra has the power to MORPH, which changes her physical appearance to that of an Esper. Doing so doubles the power of her magic. This skill isn't available to her at the beginning of the game.

Morphing puts quite a strain on Terra, so she can't morph as often as you might want. When morphing, a green bar that represents Terra's stamina replaces Terra's ATB bar. When the green bar is depleted, Terra automatically reverts to her normal human form. If this occurs, it may take several battles before Terra is rested enough to use her Morph ability again. Also, the rate at which the stamina bar is depleted is determined by how long since Terra last morphed. It's essential not to overuse her Morph skill, or she'll only be able to hold Esper form in Boss battles for a single turn or less.

`TERRA    4725 ▭▬`

Locke Cole

"Treasure Hunter and trail-worn traveler, searching the world over for relics of the past...."

Locke is a Treasure Hunter (a.k.a. a thief). He possesses greater dexterity and speed than other characters but never really learns to pack much of a punch. However, his skills as a Treasure Hunter make him a valuable asset throughout the game.

Locke's Skill: Steal

As a master Treasure Hunter, Locke has learned to use the Steal skill. Using the Steal command in a battle makes Locke attempt to steal an item from an enemy. At first, Locke's success rate will be pretty low even against weak creatures. Eventually, you can get the Sneak Ring Relic that increases his chances of successfully stealing items. You can also find the Thief Glove Relic, which changes the Steal command into the Capture command.

Capture is different from Steal in that Locke also attacks the enemy while attempting to steal an item. The same "Capture" action can randomly be performed by equipping Locke with a Thief Knife and attacking normally.

Stealing items from enemies is an easy way to increase your inventory of common items. Rarer items like weapons and armor can also be stolen and then sold or equipped. Check the bestiary for specific information on what can be stolen from each monster.

Edgar Roni Figaro

"The young king of Figaro Castle, ally to the Empire, and a master designer of machinery...."

Edgar and his brother, Sabin, are the heirs to Figaro Castle. He is a fair ruler and loved dearly by his subjects. Due to his prowess with machines, Edgar finds useful Tools that can be used in battle, and he has given Figaro Castle the amazing ability to travel underground. As the King of Figaro Castle, Edgar is allowed a 50% discount at the Castle's shops.

Edgar's Skill: Tools

As the game begins, Edgar has a limited number of Tools that he can use in battle. The effects of these Tools vary greatly, but all of them are useful. Some Tools found in the early stages of the game may become obsolete as time passes, but you can count on finding new Tools to take their place. Some Tools must be found, but most others can eventually be purchased at Figaro Castle, so be sure to check back there often.

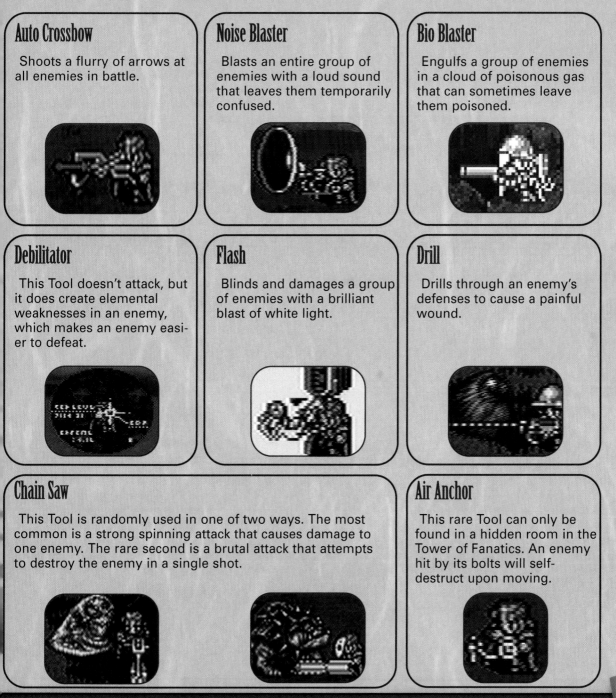

Auto Crossbow

Shoots a flurry of arrows at all enemies in battle.

Noise Blaster

Blasts an entire group of enemies with a loud sound that leaves them temporarily confused.

Bio Blaster

Engulfs a group of enemies in a cloud of poisonous gas that can sometimes leave them poisoned.

Debilitator

This Tool doesn't attack, but it does create elemental weaknesses in an enemy, which makes an enemy easier to defeat.

Flash

Blinds and damages a group of enemies with a brilliant blast of white light.

Drill

Drills through an enemy's defenses to cause a painful wound.

Chain Saw

This Tool is randomly used in one of two ways. The most common is a strong spinning attack that causes damage to one enemy. The rare second is a brutal attack that attempts to destroy the enemy in a single shot.

Air Anchor

This rare Tool can only be found in a hidden room in the Tower of Fanatics. An enemy hit by its bolts will self-destruct upon moving.

125

Sabin Rene Figaro

"Edgar's twin brother, who traded the throne for his own freedom...."

Sabin and his twin brother, Edgar, are the rightful heirs to Figaro Castle. Unlike his brother, who remained behind to rule, Sabin set out to find his own path and to avenge his parents' deaths. He met up with a master of martial arts named Duncan, who taught him the secret of the Blitz techniques.

Sabin's Skill: Blitz

Early in the game, Sabin is the strongest fighter. His Blitz techniques give him a wide variety of special attacks that enable him to rely more on his bare fists than on weapons.

Blitz techniques are slowly learned throughout the game as Sabin gains experience. He begins the game with three: Pummel, Aura Bolt, and Suplex. To use a Blitz technique, select the Blitz command in battle, enter the proper command using the directional pad and buttons on your controller, and then confirm the move with the ⊗ button. If done properly, Sabin will perform the Blitz you've chosen. If you misenter the command, however, Sabin will fumble the move and will miss his opportunity to attack.

> ## Note
> If you've been playing fighting games for years, using Sabin's Blitz techniques will be straight-forward. Unlike a fighting game, it doesn't matter which way Sabin is facing. The commands are always entered the same no matter which side of the screen Sabin is on.

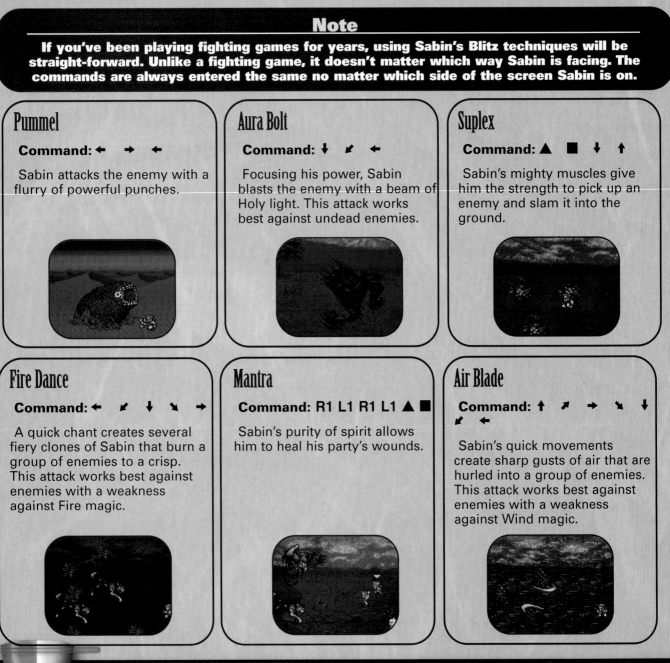

Pummel

Command: ← → ←

Sabin attacks the enemy with a flurry of powerful punches.

Aura Bolt

Command: ↓ ↙ ←

Focusing his power, Sabin blasts the enemy with a beam of Holy light. This attack works best against undead enemies.

Suplex

Command: ▲ ■ ↓ ↑

Sabin's mighty muscles give him the strength to pick up an enemy and slam it into the ground.

Fire Dance

Command: ← ↙ ↓ ↘ →

A quick chant creates several fiery clones of Sabin that burn a group of enemies to a crisp. This attack works best against enemies with a weakness against Fire magic.

Mantra

Command: R1 L1 R1 L1 ▲ ■

Sabin's purity of spirit allows him to heal his party's wounds.

Air Blade

Command: ↑ ↗ → ↘ ↓ ↙ ←

Sabin's quick movements create sharp gusts of air that are hurled into a group of enemies. This attack works best against enemies with a weakness against Wind magic.

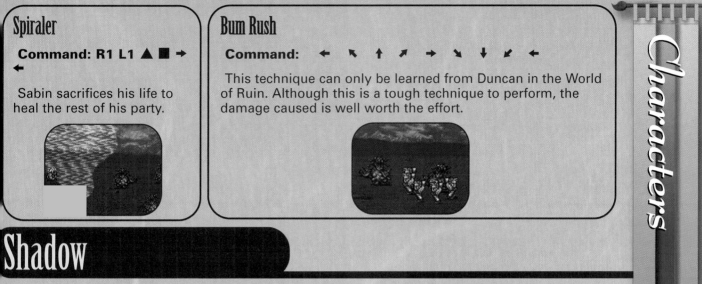

Spiraler

**Command: R1 L1 ▲ ■ →
←**

Sabin sacrifices his life to
heal the rest of his party.

Bum Rush

Command: ← ↖ ↑ ↗ → ↘ ↓ ↙ ←

This technique can only be learned from Duncan in the World
of Ruin. Although this is a tough technique to perform, the
damage caused is well worth the effort.

Shadow

"He owes allegiance to no one, and will do anything for money. He comes and goes like the wind...."

While he may not be the friendliest guy, Shadow is valuable to have around. His ninja skills and
faithful companion, Interceptor, make him a well-balanced character. Unlike most characters, you
don't have much control over Shadow. He comes and goes at his own will and won't join your party
again until he's compelled by money or revenge.

Shadow's Skill: Throw

Like any good ninja master, Shadow has mastered the art of throwing weapons.
He can toss weapons and special magical scrolls at enemies. His most common
throwing weapon is a Shuriken, which can be purchased at a reasonable price
from the various shops scattered throughout the world.

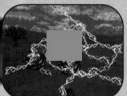

Shadow can also throw weapons from your inventory at enemies, but any
weapon thrown is lost for good. That's why it's usually best to throw the easily
replaced Shuriken.

For an extra kick, Shadow can throw magic scrolls at enemies. They're a bit
more expensive than a Shuriken, but they're also more powerful.

Shadow's Dog: Interceptor

Although you don't have the ability to summon Interceptor into battle,
there's a random chance Shadow's dog may show up on its own. Anytime
Shadow blocks an enemy attack, there's a small random chance that
Interceptor may charge into battle and counterattack the offending enemy.
The dog's attacks are very powerful and a great help at any time.

Celes Chere

"Product of genetic engineering, battle-hardened MagiTek Knight, with a spirit as pure as snow...."

Celes is the second person to join your party with the ability to use magic without the aid of Espers. She
begins the game with a limited number of spells at her disposal, but with time and experience, she'll slowly
learn new spells. Eventually, the use of Espers makes this ability somewhat obsolete.

Celes' Skill: Runic

By equipping certain swords, Celes is able to use the Runic skill.
When selected, she will absorb the next spell cast during battle
whether friend or foe casts it. By absorbing the spell, its effect is
neutralized and Celes gains the amount of MP used to cast the spell.
This is a great way to gain a little extra MP early on in the game. It also
comes in extremely handy in battles against enemies that attack solely with magic.

Cyan Garamonde

"Faithful retainer to his family's liege, with the courage and strength of a hundred men...."

As the master swordsman of Doma Castle, it's no surprise that Cyan is a force to be reckoned with. His power is equal to that of Sabin, but his attacks take time to prepare and can sometimes delay the actions of his allies. Yet even with this shortcoming, Cyan proves to be one of the best characters available to you.

Cyan's Skill: SwordTech

When equipped with the proper weapon, Cyan can use his SwordTech ability in battle. He begins the game with three of the eight SwordTech skills: Dispatch, Retort, and Slash. Over time, he gains additional skills as he gathers experience in battle.

When the SwordTech command is selected, a gauge will appear at the bottom of the screen. You must wait as the gauge slowly fills to the number of the SwordTech skill you wish for Cyan to use, and then press the ⊗ button. If the gauge fills completely, it resets and you must wait again for it to fill to the level you desire.

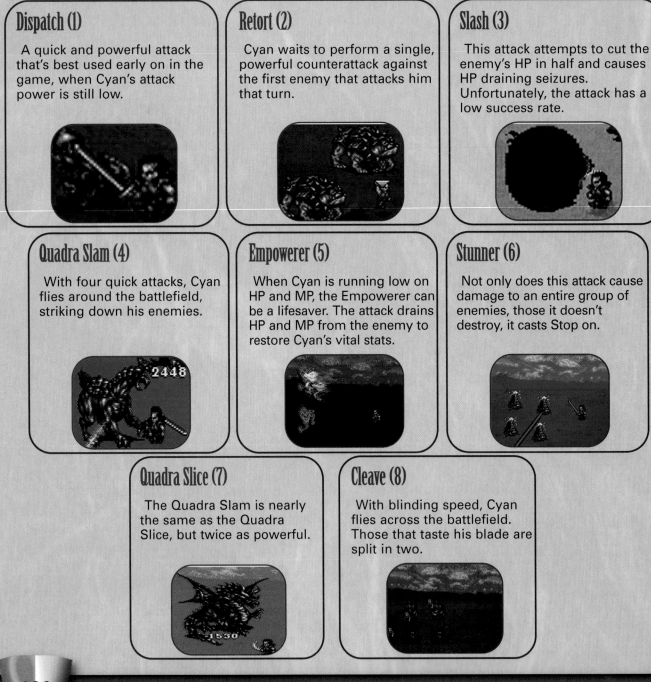

Dispatch (1)

A quick and powerful attack that's best used early on in the game, when Cyan's attack power is still low.

Retort (2)

Cyan waits to perform a single, powerful counterattack against the first enemy that attacks him that turn.

Slash (3)

This attack attempts to cut the enemy's HP in half and causes HP draining seizures. Unfortunately, the attack has a low success rate.

Quadra Slam (4)

With four quick attacks, Cyan flies around the battlefield, striking down his enemies.

Empowerer (5)

When Cyan is running low on HP and MP, the Empowerer can be a lifesaver. The attack drains HP and MP from the enemy to restore Cyan's vital stats.

Stunner (6)

Not only does this attack cause damage to an entire group of enemies, those it doesn't destroy, it casts Stop on.

Quadra Slice (7)

The Quadra Slam is nearly the same as the Quadra Slice, but twice as powerful.

Cleave (8)

With blinding speed, Cyan flies across the battlefield. Those that taste his blade are split in two.

Gau

"Draped in monster hides, eyes shining with intelligence. A youth surviving against all odds...."

Gau is the wild child of the Veldt. After being kicked out into the wild by his father, he learned to live with the animals and began taking on their actions. This gave way to his Rage skill, which imitates creatures that Gau has followed on the Veldt. Although his attacks are powerful, his uncontrollable behavior while using the Rage ability can make him a detriment in some battles.

Gau's Skill: Leap/Rage

Gau's Rage ability allows him to take on the abilities, strengths, and weaknesses of enemies that he's had the chance to run with in the Veldt. This gives him a wide variety of attacks but also limits his usefulness in battle. When a Rage skill is selected, Gau goes into a berserk mode where he randomly uses the selected enemy's attacks against whatever enemy he chooses. Once he enters Rage mode, you cannot change his attacks unless he is K.O.ed and revived.

Gau can learn the abilities of nearly any enemy in the game. However, he must first encounter the enemy on the Veldt and use the Leap command, which only appears there. When you select the Leap command in a battle, Gau will jump into the enemy pack, and the battle will end automatically. Continue to roam the area with your party, and Gau will eventually return to your party after a battle. In the time he was gone, he will have learned how to mimic the creatures he went away with and the creatures he returns with.

As mentioned earlier, Gau can learn to mimic nearly any creature in the game. However, you'll only encounter creatures in the Veldt that you've already encountered elsewhere. To maximize Gau's abilities. you must return to the Veldt often.

Setzer Gabbiani

"A blackjack-playing, world-traveling, casino-dwelling free spirit...."

Setzer's main contribution to your party is his Airship. With it, you'll be able to explore the world freely, visiting new locations and checking back in at old ones. His love of gambling shows up in all aspects of his life, from the décor of his ship, to his choice in weapons. Although he can be a powerful ally, putting him in your party is a gamble in itself.

Setzer's Skill: Slot/GP Rain

Setzer's Slot skill acts just like a normal slot machine, but there's no GP to be earned. Rather, the Slot's outcome determines what type of attack Setzer will use that turn. If you're good, you can almost always get decent results. However, for most people it's just a little too risky to use in most battles.

Once you find the Coin Toss Relic, you can transform Setzer's Slot command into the GP Rain command. With this attack, Setzer actually tosses *your* GP at enemies. It can cause a lot of damage, but it can also drain your party dry of GP.

Slot Combinations

Lagomorph

This is the result of any spin that isn't one of the following. A curious little creature appears and restores a very small amount of HP for the entire party.

Flash

Attacks enemies with a flash of rainbow colored light.

Chocobop

The enemy is trampled by a wild herd of Chocobos.

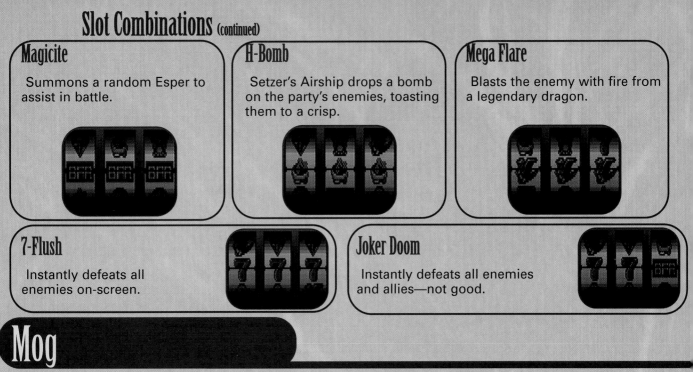

Magicite

Summons a random Esper to assist in battle.

H-Bomb

Setzer's Airship drops a bomb on the party's enemies, toasting them to a crisp.

Mega Flare

Blasts the enemy with fire from a legendary dragon.

7-Flush

Instantly defeats all enemies on-screen.

Joker Doom

Instantly defeats all enemies and allies—not good.

Mog

"Human-loving, fast-talking, street-smart, SLAM-dancing…Moogle…."

Although he isn't the king of the Moogles, he should be. Not only can he speak to humans, but he's also a great dancer, and not bad in a fight. He lives with his Moogle buddies deep inside the Narshe Mines and rarely ventures outside. Still, he's pretty worldy for a fluffy, little, pink-nosed teddy bear.

Mog's Skill: Dance

By traveling around the world and fighting in new areas, Mog learns magical Dances that hurt his enemies and aid his allies. Although Mog starts the game without knowing any Dances, he's a quick learner. One or two fights in the right area are all he needs to pick up some new steps.

To use the Dance command, select it in battle and then select the Dance you want Mog to perform. He'll immediately start showing off some of his fancy moves. Mog then continues to Dance until the battle ends, he's K.O.ed, or he stumbles. Although he's a great Dancer, even the best can sometimes crack under pressure. If Mog stumbles, he'll lose his chance to attack that turn. But he can try to pick up where he left off the next turn if you wish.

Mog's Dances

Wind Song

Learned in grass fields anywhere on the World Map.

Steps	Effect
Wind Slash	Blasts enemies with a gust of wind.
Sun Bath	Restores HP for the entire party.
Plasma	A powerful attack against a single enemy.
Cockatrice	Attack an enemy with a wild Cockatrice.

Forest Suite

Mog learns this Dance when fighting in forests on the World Map.

Steps	Effect
Rage	A ragging wind blasts enemies with dirt and leaves.
Harvester	Cures abnormal status effects.
Elf Fire	A powerful blast of mystical fire magic engulfs an enemy.
Wombat	Attacks an enemy with a wild Wombat.

Desert Aria

The sands of a desert inspire Mog to learn these steps.

Steps	Effect
Sand Storm	Mog's enemies are caught in a violent sand storm.
Wind Slash	Blasts enemies with a gust of wind.
Antlion	The enemy is swallowed up by quicksand.
Kitty	Casts Haste on Mog and his allies.

Love Sonata

Mog learns this Dance when fighting in a town.

Steps	Effect
Elf Fire	A powerful blast of mystical fire magic engulfs an enemy.
Snare	Mog sets a trap for an enemy that eliminates it from battle.
Specter	Casts Confuse on a single enemy.
Tapir	Cures any abnormal status effects.

Earth Blues

Fighting his way up a mountain inspires Mog to create this Dance.

Steps	Effect
Land Slide	Drops a load of rocks on an enemy's head.
Sun Bath	Restores HP for the entire party.
Sonic Boom	Attacks the enemy with a sonic boomerang.
Whump	Attacks an enemy with a herd of wild rock animals.

Water Rondo

Mog can only learn these moves while underwater in the Serpent Trench.

Steps	Effect
El Nino	Pulls an enemy into the undertow.
Specter	Casts Confuse on a single enemy.
Plasma	A powerful attack against a single enemy.
Harvester	Cures any abnormal status effects.

Dusk Requiem

Inspiration sometimes hits Mog while slinking around in dark caves.

Steps	Effect
Cave In	Drops huge boulders on an enemy's head.
Elf Fire	A powerful blast of mystical fire magic engulfs an enemy.
Snare	Mog sets a trap for a single enemy that removes it from battle.
Pois. Frog	A poisonous frog appears and attacks an enemy with Poison.

Snowman Jazz

Mog picks up these steps close to home on the snowy fields above the town of Narshe.

Steps	Effect
Snowball	Cuts an enemy's HP in half.
Snare	Mog sets a trap for a single enemy that removes it from battle.
Surge	A group of enemies is caught in a powerful avalanche.
Ice Rabbit	A cute little bunny heals the party's wounds.

Strago Magus

"An elderly gentleman, pure of heart, and learned in the ways of monsters...."

Strago possesses the rare ability to learn Blue Magic. Unlike normal magic, Blue Magic is the magic used by monsters. Don't confuse this with Gau's Rage ability. Blue Magic is a bit more sophisticated and is used like normal magic. Strago is also quite adept at the use of Rods, which are magical staves with magical powers.

Strago's Skill: Lore

The Lore ability allows Strago to learn Blue Magic from the enemies he fights. If a monster uses a type of Blue Magic that Strago can learn, he'll gain the use of the spell once the battle is finished, but only if Strago is hurt by the spell during battle. Blue Magic tends to use a lot of MP, but it's also very powerful.

Lore Magic

Lore	MP Used	Users	Effect	Element
Aqua Rake	22 MP	Vectagoyle, Rhyos, Chimera	Engulfs the enemies in a seething foam	Water, Wind
Aero	41 MP	Doom Gaze, Tyranosaur, Sprinter	Attacks enemies with a powerful whirlwind	Wind
Blow Fish	50 MP	Brainpan, Phase, Cactrot, Presenter, Mover	Blasts the enemy with a thousand needles, each one causing a point of damage	None
Big Guard	80 MP	Dark Force, Mover, Earth Guard	Protects the entire party with both Shell and Safe	None
Clean Sweep	30 MP	Blue Dragon, Enuo, Dark Force	Summons a tsunami that washes enemies away with Water	None
Condemned	20 MP	Veteran, Critic, Still Life	When the countdown reaches zero, the target is eliminated.	None
Dischord	68 MP	Pipsqueak, Figaliz, Iron Hitman	Reduces the target's level by half	None
Exploder	1 MP	Bomb, Grenade, Balloon, Junk	Caster sacrifices itself to deal an amount of damage equal to the caster's current HP to a single enemy.	None
Force Field	24 MP	Doom	Randomly nullify attacks of certain elemental types. The effectiveness increases with each use.	None
Grand Train	64 MP	Hidon	Blasts a group of enemies with energy that ignores the enemies' defenses	None

Lore	MP Used	Users	Effect	Element
L.? Pearl	50 MP	Dullahan, Critic, Dark Force	Casts Pearl on any enemies whose levels are a multiple of the singles digit of your current GP	None
L.3 Muddle	28 MP	Apokryphos, Goblin, Dark Force	Casts Muddle on any enemies whose levels are a multiple of three	None
L.4 Flare	42 MP	Apokryphos, Goblin, Dueller	Casts Flare on any enemies whose levels are a multiple of four	None
L.5 Doom	22 MP	Sky Base, Didalos, Dark Force, Trapper	Casts Doom on any enemies whose levels are a multiple of five	None
Pearl Wind	45 MP	Sprinter, Peepers, Dark Force, Vectaur	Cures the entire party for an amount equal to the caster's current HP	None
Pep Up	1 MP	Junk, Flan, Muus	Caster sacrifices itself to give an ally full HP/MP and to remove any abnormal status effects	None
Quasar	50 MP	Goddess, Dark Force	Attack a group of enemies with cosmic powers	None
Reflect???	??MP	Dark Force	Casts Dark, Mute, and Slow on any enemies protected by Reflect magic	None
Revenge	31 MP	Dragon, Pan Dora, Dark Force	Deals damage to an enemy equal to the casters maximum HP minus its current HP	None
Rippler	66 MP	Reach Frog, Dark Force	Swaps all status changes between the target and the caster	None
Roulette	10 MP	Dark Force, Veteran, Critic	Randomly selects and eliminates someone in battle	None
Sour Mouth	32 MP	Evil Oscar, Mad Oscar	Casts Mute, Imp, Poison, Dark, Sleep, and Muddle on a single target	None
Step Mine	?? MP	Pug, Mesosaur, Grease Monk	Causes damage to a single enemy equal to 1/32 of the total steps you've taken. MP cost is equal to your elapsed playtime multiplied by two.	None
Stone	22 MP	Iron Fist, Brawler	Caster hurls a stone at an enemy that causes damage and casts Muddle. If caster and target are of the same level the stone causes eight times as much damage.	None

Relm Arrowny

"In her pictures she captures everything: forests, water, light...the very essence of life...."

Relm is the granddaughter of Strago and a talented artist. She's a little rambunctious and sometimes obnoxious, but she'll quickly prove herself in battle.

Relm's Skill: Sketch/Control

Have you ever heard of a good painting gone bad? Relm is such an incredible artist that her paintings not only seem life-like, they *are* alive. By using her Sketch command in battle, Relm quickly paints a replica of one of her enemies. The painting will then use one of the enemy's abilities as if the painting were alive itself.

Once you've found the Fake Mustache Relic, Relm can equip it and change her Sketch command to Control. When Relm takes Control of an enemy, she actually gets to pick and choose what attacks the enemy uses and whom it targets.

Umaro

"Admirer of bone-carvings, as strong as a gigas, a yeti pal with muscle!"

There's a hidden cave in cliffs above the town of Narshe where this giant yeti lives. Umaro may not be the smartest of creatures, but he sure does pack a punch. Just make sure you have Mog with you when you meet him. He's the only one the big guy will listen too. Unlike most characters, Umaro can't equip weapons, armor, or Espers.

Umaro's Skill: None

Umaro doesn't really have any skills. He's just a loose cannon with way too much power. There are two special Relics that only Umaro can use: Rage Ring and Blizzard Orb. The Rage Ring increases his attack options and power. The Blizzard Orb allows him to attack using his blizzard breath.

Gogo

"Shrouded in odd clothing...is this a man...?...a woman...?...or should we ask?"

What do you expect from a person living inside a Zone Eater's belly? Gogo is one strange character. As a mime, Gogo doesn't actually have any actions of its own. Rather, it looks for people that it feels are worthy of its art and mimics that person's actions. It may not sound like much, but it makes Gogo an incredibly versatile character.

Gogo's Skill: Mimic

When you choose Gogo's Mimic ability, it will mimic the actions of the ally that acted just before it takes its turn. Gogo can't mimic most effects granted by Relics. On the other hand, it doesn't cost MP for Gogo to Mimic spells, and it can Mimic other people's skills without having to charge or perform an action.

Another useful thing that's easily overlooked is the fact that you can customize Gogo's command menu. Go to Gogo's status screen and select an empty space in Gogo's command menu. You'll be given a list of commands associated with all of the characters you have at your disposal. You can equip Gogo with three additional commands, so you can give it Sabin's Blitz, Cyan's SwordTech, and even Edgar's Tools at the same time.

If you choose magic as a command for Gogo, you should know that Gogo will have access to any spells the other characters in the current party have learned. Gogo can't equip Espers, so this is the only way it can use magic.

FINAL FANTASY ANTHOLOGY™
FINAL FANTASY® VI

Enemies

Lobo
Guard
Vomammoth
Were-Rat
Repo Man
Vaporite
Whelk (Boss)
Marshal (Boss)

Items

1. Elixir
2. Phoenix Down
3. Sleeping Bag
4. Tonic
5. Sleeping Bag
6. Tincture
   (Later Items)
7. Rune Edge
8. Wall Ring
9. Sneak Ring
10. Hyper Wrist
11. Thief Knife
12. Earrings
13. 5000 GP
14. Elixir
15. Ragnarok (W.o.R.)
16. Cursed Shield (W.o.R.)
17. Moogle Charm (W.o.R.)

Checklist

- [ ] Pilot the MagiTek Armor through town and into the mineshaft at the back
- [ ] Defeat the Whelk inside the mineshaft
- [ ] Approach the frozen Esper, Tritoch
- [ ] Flee into the mine to escape the Narshe guard patrol
- [ ] Meet Locke and the Moogles
- [ ] Battle the Marshal and then flee from Narshe
- [ ] Head south to Figaro Castle

(Optional)

- [ ] Visit Narshe's Training Center

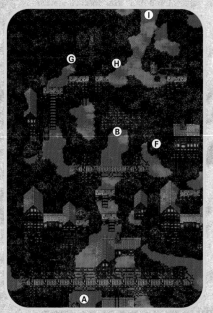

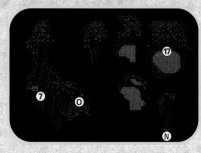

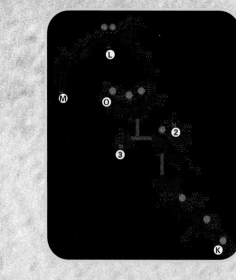

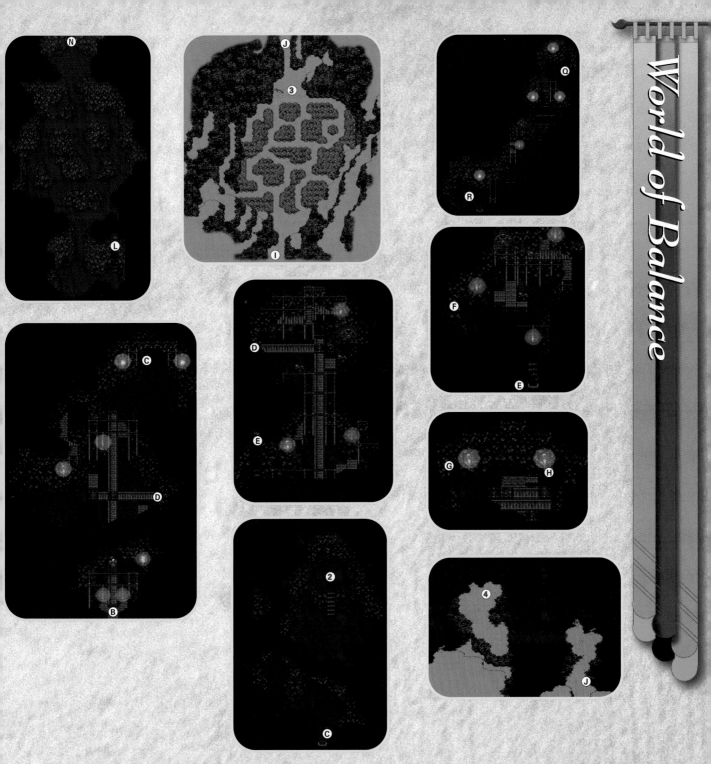

The Grand Entrance

At the beginning of the game, you control two soldiers, Wedge and Biggs, and an unnamed girl. Each character is strapped into what is known as **MagiTek Armor**. Although the three characters are weak on their own, the MagiTek Armor gives them more than enough power to defeat their enemies in Narshe.

Due to the danger of the situation, none of the characters can exit their MagiTek Armor. Therefore, exploring is limited to the main strip right through the center of town. This makes it very easy to navigate Narshe.

Using MagiTek Armor

MagiTek Armor comes with several built-in attacks. The basic armor has three elemental attacks and a healing option for repairing itself and any other allied forces. Later, more advanced models have eight attacks. This includes the three elemental attacks and healing option, plus four more equally powerful attacks. You should be able to eliminate your enemies with any attack, however, the **Bio Blast** is particularly effective against large groups of enemies (except Were-Rats).

Also, make sure you use the healing option often to keep you and your allies in top physical condition. There's no limit as to how many times you can use any of the attacks, so have fun and experiment with them all while you can.

Saving Your Progress

Upon entering the mineshaft, you'll see a shiny, blue-white spot on the ground. This signifies a **Save Point**, where you can save your game to a memory card. Get to know these, as you'll be using them a lot throughout your adventure.

You can only save your game outside on the World Map, or at a Save Point in a town or dungeon. Usually, Save Points are placed right before critical events and challenging battles, so you should always use them. **WARNING!** Failing to save often has been found to be the leading cause of controller breakage.

Whelk

At the end of the mineshaft, you'll face the first Boss in FINAL FANTASY VI, the Whelk. This creature isn't tough if you're careful. There are two parts to the Whelk: the head and the shell. The Whelk's shell can absorb damage and redirect it back at your party. The Whelk's head is its weak spot, so you'll only want to attack its head. When it dies, the rest of the monster goes with it.

Take things nice and slow in this battle, and attack the head with one character at a time. Eventually, the Whelk will pull in its head into its shell without warning. When this occurs, any attacks directed at its head instead target its shell. Accidentally hitting the shell once isn't a big deal, because you can quickly heal your party using the MagiTek Armor's **Heal Force** ability. However, if you've already committed your entire party to attacking the head when the Whelk retreats into its shell, you'll be lucky to survive the flurry of three Mega Volt counterattacks. You can avoid this by attacking the Whelk with one character at a time. Also, don't enter any new commands until the last character's attack is finished.

Locke and the Moogles

Terra is knocked out and hordes of Narshe guards are one step away from capturing her. It's up to Locke and the Moogles to save her. During this event, you gain control of Locke and 11 Moogles split up to form three teams. Your goal is to stop the guards' advance by defeating them in battle. After defeating the roaming guards, you must then defeat the Marshal waiting on the other side.

Have one group block the hall in front of Terra, and use the other two groups to hunt down the guards. You can switch between the three parties by pressing the ⬤ button. You should balance the amount of fighting you do between the groups so that you don't completely drain a group's HP.

The first group contains Locke, but there's a Moogle in the second group named Mog that you should pay attention to. Mog will learn a Dance called **Dusk Requim**, which is a skill unique among the Moogles. This Dance is extremely powerful and can help a great deal during the battles. You may even want to use Mog's group to challenge the Marshal.

Beginner's Training Center

After escaping Narshe, you won't be able to return to the town until things calm down. On the edge of town, you'll find a man in front of a large house. This is the Training Center. Go inside and speak with everyone to learn about the basics of FINAL FANTASY VI. You can also find a few good items. Also, don't forget that you can restore Locke's and Terra's HP and MP by using the recovery water next to the desk.

Enemies
Leafer
Dark Wind
Sand Ray
Areneod
M-Tek Armor

Items
❶ Phoenix Down
❷ Soft
❸ Tonic
❹ Antidote

FIGARO CASTLE

Checklist

☐ **Enter Figaro Castle and speak with King Edgar**

☐ **Find the Matron in the west wing and speak with her**

☐ **Return to the throne room and speak with Edgar**

☐ **Have Edgar speak with Kefka and his guards**

☐ **Speak with Locke and then have Terra follow him**

☐ **Talk to Kefka and then speak with the soldier waiting above**

☐ **Head southeast to a cave leading to South Figaro**

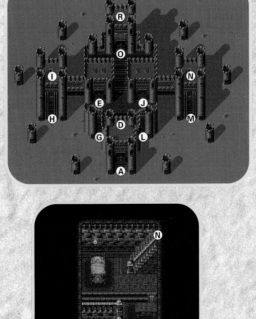

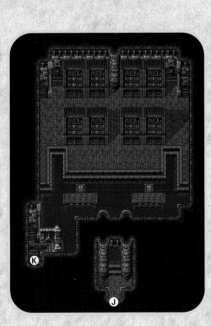

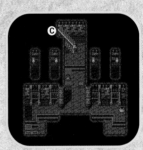

Item Shop #1

Item	Cost
AutoCrossbow	250
NoiseBlaster	500
Bio Blaster	750

Item Shop #2

Item	Cost
Tincture	1500
Antidote	50
Soft	200
Phoenix Down	500
Tent	1200
Potion	300
Revivify	300
Eyedrop	50

Explore Figaro Castle

Take a few moments to explore Figaro Castle. You can find several useful items and two shops. Make sure you purchase a couple of **Phoenix Downs** if you have the GP. Also, make sure you purchase the first set of Edgar's tools. They'll really come in handy later on. Don't miss out on the free room and board if Terra and Locke are in need of a little rest after their long journey.

The Escape

As you flee from Figaro Castle, you're forced into a fight against two of Kefka's guards in MagiTek Armor. However, this battle isn't tough. Have Edgar use his AutoCrossbow and have Terra cast Fire on the enemies.

Casting on Multiple Targets:

To cast a spell on multiple allies or enemies, simply move the targeting cursor over a person (or enemy) in the group you wish to target and press the R1 button. Note that this doesn't work with all spells.

Casting Fire will cause the battle to pause for a while, as Edgar and Locke marvel at Terra's magical gift. If you don't use magic during this battle, you'll see this event the first time you use magic in a battle.

Enemies
Hornet
Crawly
Bleary

Items
1 Tincture
2 Tincture
3 Phoenix Down
4 Recovery Spring

FIGARO AREA CAVE

Checklist
☐ **Use the recovery spring to heal your party**

☐ **Exit the cave and head southeast to South Figaro**

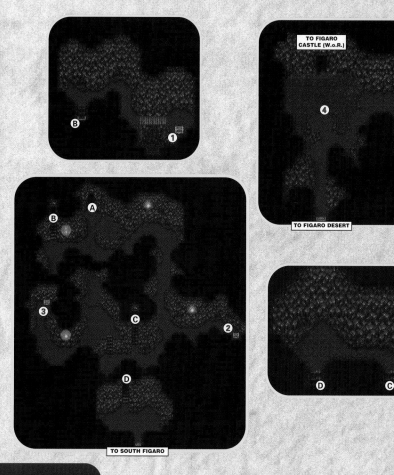

TO FIGARO CASTLE (W.o.R.)

TO FIGARO DESERT

TO SOUTH FIGARO

Recovery Spring

There's a **recovery spring** just inside the cave. If you visited the Beginner's Hall in Narshe, then you already know about these. Stop in the middle of the spring, and your entire party will be healed, plus their MP will be restored. There's no limit to how many times you can use the recovery spring.

Recovery spring

Stock Up on Healing Items

Thanks to Edgar's **NoiseBlaster**, it's easy to stock up on healing items while venturing through the cave. Use the NoiseBlaster to confuse your enemies, and then have Locke steal from them. If an enemy recovers, you can eliminate them or use the NoiseBlaster again.

Also, take note that Edgar's **AutoCrossbow** is great for eliminating the large groups of enemies that often appear inside the cave.

Treasure Trick

The chests inside the cave contain some very basic items that can come in handy. If, however, you're willing to hold off on opening the chest until later in the game (we'll tell you when later), you can receive even better items, such as a **Thunder Rod** and an **X-Potion**.

Enemies
Rhodox
Rhintaur
Grease Monkey

Items
1. Tonic
2. Soft
3. Antidote
4. Eyedrop
5. Green Cherry
6. Tonic
7. Tonic
8. Warp Stone
9. Phoenix Down
10. Hyper Wrist
11. Running Shoes
12. 500 GP
13. 1000 GP
14. 1500 GP
15. Tincture
16. Elixir

(Later Items)
17. Elixir
18. Iron Armor
19. Heavy Shield
20. Regal Cutlass
21. X-Potion
22. Ribbon
23. Ether
24. Earrings

SOUTH FIGARO

Checklist

☐ *Meet the mysterious ninja, Shadow, at the Pub*

☐ *Go to Duncan's house and speak to his wife to learn about Mt. Kolts*

☐ *Head northeast to Mt. Kolts*

(Optional)

☐ *Sneak into Owzer's secret basement and take everything you can find*

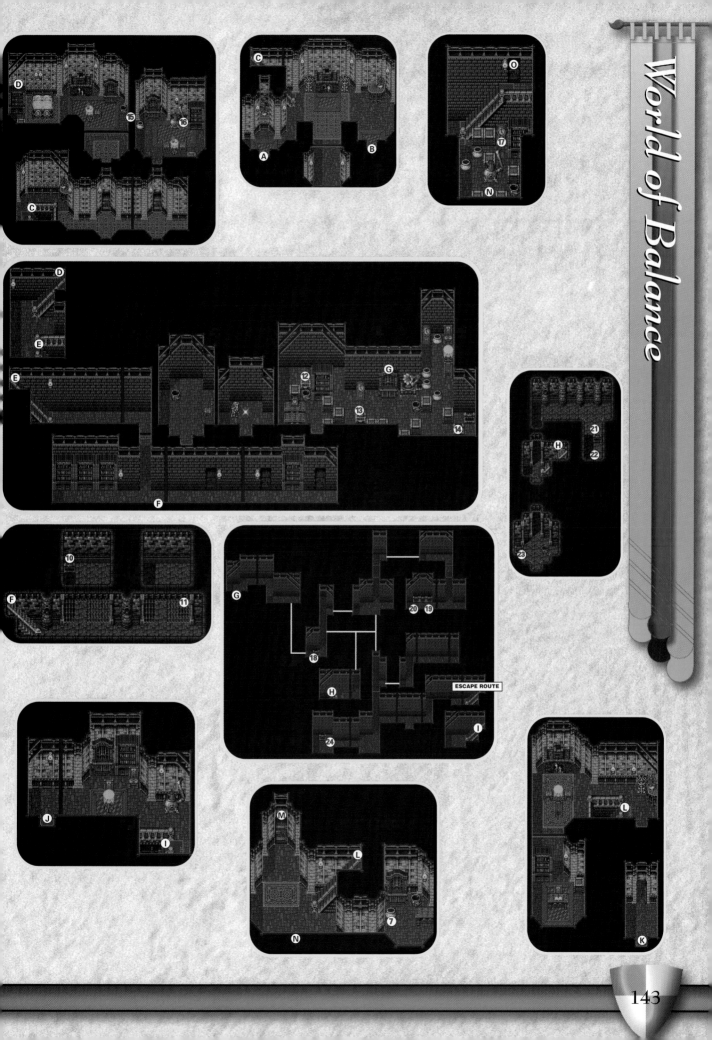

Chocobo Stable	
Item	Cost
Chocobo Rental	80

Inn	
Item	Cost
Room	80

Relic Shop	
Item	Cost
Sprint Shoes	1500
Goggles	500
Star Pendant	500
Jewel Ring	1000
True Knight	1000

Weapon Shop	
Item	Cost
Dirk	150
Mythril Knife	300
Mythril Blade	450
Regal Cutlass	800
NoiseBlaster	500
Bio Blaster	750

Armor Shop	
Item	Cost
Buckler	200
Heavy Shield	400
Hair Band	150
Plumed Hat	250
Cotton Robe	200
Kung Fu Suit	250

Item Shop	
Item	Cost
Tonic	50
Antidote	50
Soft	200
Eyedrop	50
Echo Screen	120
Phoenix Down	500
Sleeping Bag	500
Tent	1200

The Old Man and the Cider

Don't drive yourself nuts trying to figure out how to get some Cider for the old man. You can't do this quite yet, but you'll get your chance eventually.

Upgrading Weapons and Armor

This is your first chance to upgrade each party member's weapons and armor. Don't miss out on the great deals South Figaro's shops have to offer. You'll need the added attack and defense power in the battles to come.

Precious Relics

Relics are a very important part of the game. There are several Relics you can purchase or find in South Figaro. You should get two for each character, but don't forget to equip them.

In particular, you'll want the **Running Shoes** and **Hyper Wrist** from Owzer's basement. You may also want to purchase **Sprint Shoes** so you can walk faster in towns and dungeons.

Millionaire's Basement

Owzer is the town's richest citizen, but not the smartest. Check behind the bookcase in Owzer's room to find a hidden passage that leads to a basement full of treasure. Robbing Owzer blind will give you the extra GP you need to upgrade each party member's weapons and armor before heading to Mt. Kolts.

Enemies

Brawler
Trilium
Tusker
Cipius
Ipooh
Vargas (Boss)

Items

❶ Tonic (Sabin's Hut)
❷ Guardian
❸ Atlas Armlet
❹ Tent
❺ Tent

MT. KOLTS

Checklist

- ☐ **Head northeast to Mt. Kolts**
- ☐ **Follow the shadowed figure across the mountain**
- ☐ **Battle Vargas and the Ipoohs**
- ☐ **Meet Sabin and equip him once he joins the party**
- ☐ **Continue over Mt. Kolts and head north to the Returners' Hideout**

(Optional)

- ☐ **Visit Sabin's hut (north of South Figaro) to rest for free**

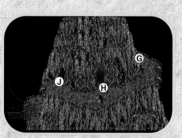

TO RETURNERS' HIDEOUT

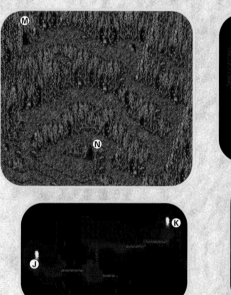

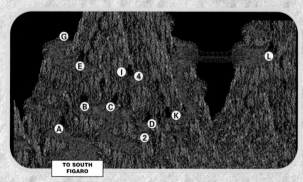

TO SOUTH FIGARO

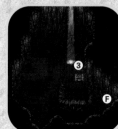

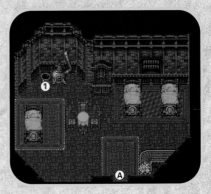

Sabin's Hut

There's a lone hut to the north of South Figaro. As you explore the inside, Edgar will recognize various items as some of Sabin's favorite things.

You can rest here for free at any time by getting into any of the three beds. Also, don't miss out on the hidden **Tonic** in the bucket next to the stove. As you leave the hut, speak with the old man outside and he'll tell you that Sabin headed to Mt. Kolts.

Brawler Bandanas

There are Brawlers all over Mt. Kolts. These tough fighters carry **Bandanas**, which Locke can steal from them. Try to get a few of them, because they're slightly better armor than the Plumed Hats you can purchase in South Figaro. Also, keep in mind that you can sell any extra Bandanas for additional GP.

Be Sure to Save

There's a Save Point near the end of Mt. Kolts. Make sure you use it to save your game. You may also want to use a Tent to heal your characters before moving on.

Vargas & Ipoohs

Vargas is well protected by the Ipoohs. Use Edgar's **Bio Blaster** and Terra's **Fire** magic to quickly eliminate them so that you can begin attacking Vargas. You must be prepared to cast **Cure** at all times, because Vargas' attacks are very strong. Continue using the Bio Blaster on Vargas and, in a few short turns, Sabin will jump into battle. To finish the fight, select Sabin's **Blitz** command and quickly enter the **Pummel** command ← , → , ← and then press the ⬤ button). If you have difficulty entering the Blitz command, access the Main Menu and select "Config." While in the Config sub-menu, set the battle speed to 6. This will give you a bit more time to enter Sabin's Blitz commands.

Sabin Joins

Sabin becomes a member of your party after the battle with Vargas. Quickly check his equipment and relics, because you may have useful items for him. Also, examine Sabin's skills in the main menu and check out his Blitz commands. Sabin starts with three: **Pummel**, **AuraBolt**, and **Suplex**. Start practicing them now.

Enemies

Rhintaur
Grease Monkey
Rhodox

Items

- Phoenix Down
- Antidote
- Tincture
- True Knight
- Phoenix Down
- Air Lancet
- White Cape
- Green Cherry
- Potion

RETURNERS' HIDEOUT

Checklist

☐ **Enter the Returners' Hideout and speak with Banon**

☐ **Talk to everyone inside the Hideout and collect all items**

☐ **Return to the Hideout's entrance and answer Banon's request**

☐ **Hurry to the raft and hop onboard**

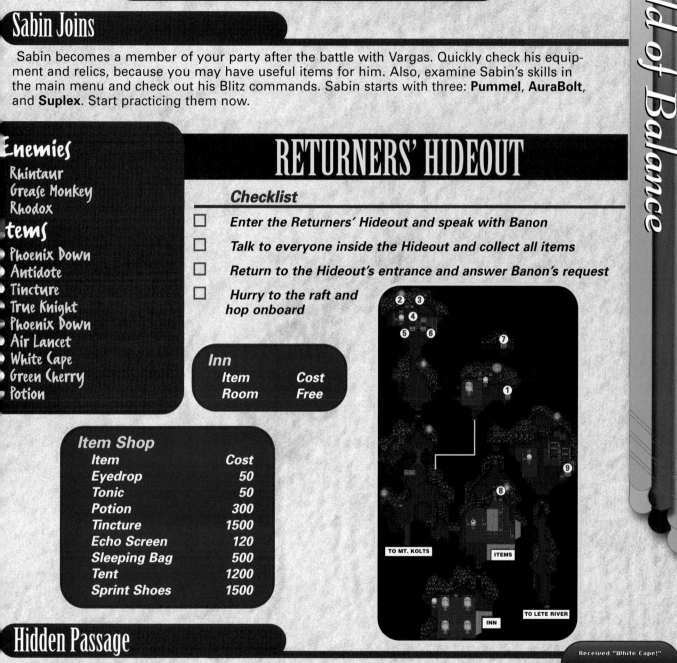

Inn

Item	Cost
Room	Free

Item Shop

Item	Cost
Eyedrop	50
Tonic	50
Potion	300
Tincture	1500
Echo Screen	120
Sleeping Bag	500
Tent	1200
Sprint Shoes	1500

Hidden Passage

There's a hidden passage in the right wall of the "treasure room." Work your way through the invisible path to find a new relic, the **White Cape**.

Received "White Cape!"

Banon's Request

Received "Genji Glove!"

Banon asks Terra to assist the Returners, and awaits her answer near the Hideout's entrance. If you agree to help, you'll later be given a **Gauntlet**, but you can get a better item if you hold out. Say no to Banon three times, and you'll receive a **Genji Glove** instead of the Gauntlet, which in my opinion is a much better relic because it enables you to equip two weapons on a party member and attack an enemy with both.

147

Enemies

Nautloid
Exocite
Pterodon
Ultros (Boss)

Checklist

☐ **Direct the raft down the river**

☐ **Keep Banon from being K.O.ed during battles**

☐ **Defeat Ultros the octopus**

☐ **Choose which character's adventure to follow**

TO RETURNERS' HIDEOUT

ULTROS

Raging River

The Lete River is a twisting mess of channels. Your goal is to figure out the path to the end. Each time the raft stops, choose one of the listed directions. If you choose poorly, you get returned to a point you've previously passed, which forces you into additional encounters. Also note that there are two Save Points along the way.

Big Boost

You can easily boost your characters' levels near the beginning of the river. At the first Save Point, go into the sub-menu. Go to "Cmd. Set", select "short" and press the ⓧ button. You can now place Banon's Health spell in place of the Fight command. This means that he will cast his health spell every turn. Back on the river, select to go up the river at the first intersection and then tape down the ⓧ button and tape the D-pad in the up position. The raft will then circle the area and your characters will fight and heal automatically. Leave the game running in this fashion over night, and the next day you'll find that your character's level has increased significantly.

Protect Banon

If Banon gets K.O.ed at any time during your trip down the river, you'll be forced to start over from the Returner's Hideout or wherever you last saved on the river. To prevent this from occurring, make good use of Banon's **Health** skill, which heals the entire party without using MP. Also, conserve Terra's MP to heal Banon if his HP gets too low.

Edgar's NoiseBlaster comes in handy by turning away enemy attacks from Banon and the rest of the party. Make sure you stick Banon in the back row. This will offer him a bit more protection, which is worth it although it cuts down on the power of his attack.

Ultros

Ultros is a very tough Boss due to its strong attacks. In fact, protecting Banon during this battle isn't always possible, because a single Tentacle attack can knock him out.

Have Sabin use **Pummel** (◄, ►, ◄, and ⊗) and have Terra use **Fire** magic. Both attacks will cause 300+ points of damage each time. If you have the **Genji Glove**, make sure it's equipped on Edgar. With two swords, even the king of Figaro Castle can cause about 300 points of damage each turn. Leave most of the healing up to Banon's **Health** skill, but be prepared to use Terra's **Cure** magic if you encounter trouble.

Separate Quests

After the battle with Ultros, you must choose which character(s) you'll control next. You'll eventually take all three groups through their adventures, so pick your favorite character and enjoy.

You Choose...	Go to...
Edgar, Terra, & Banon	Page 149
Locke	Page 150
Sabin	Page 154

Enemies

1st Class
Wild Rat
Dark Side
Repo Man
Vaporite
Spectre
Rinn

Items

Rune Edge (Chest in Moogle's Lair)
*Maps on page 136

EDGAR, TERRA, & BANON'S QUEST (NARSHE)

Checklist

☐ *Continue down the Lete River until the raft reaches the coast*

☐ *Head northwest to Narshe*

☐ *Use the secret door from earlier to get into the mines*

☐ *Follow the star through the security checkpoint room*

☐ *Find Arvis' house and speak with him*

Getting Into Narshe

EDGAR: Knowing him, there's probably some secret switch in this rock wall...

Because of Terra's bad reputation in Narshe, you won't be able to stroll through the front gate. Instead, you must use Locke's secret door next to the Training Center to get into the Narshe Mines. Before you go, you may want to use the recovery water inside the Training Center to restore your party's HP and MP.

Security Checkpoint

Since the battle with the Marshal's troops, the people of Narshe have installed a security system to stop unwanted visitors. As you enter the room, you'll see a white star that resembles a Save Point. Watch the path the star takes through the room, which is the only safe route. Follow the star's path exactly to reach the opposite side; if not, you're forced to fight, plus you must start over from the beginning.

NOTE

If they go the wrong way, a chain of light surrounds your party. When caught, you can avoid going into battle if you "tag", press ⬤ the button, the gold link in the light-chain that surrounds the party. If you manage to touch the gold light, the chain is broken and your party can move on without fighting or starting over.

What's Next?

This quest is complete once you speak to Arvis. You'll either get the chance to choose from any remaining quests, or the story will pick back up with all the characters congregating in Narshe.

You Choose...	Go To...
Locke	Page 150
Sabin	Page 154
All Complete	Page 155

Enemies

Merchant
Officer
Heavy Armor
Vector Pup
Commander

Items

Elixir ((lock in secret passage)
❶ Iron Armor
❷ Heavy Shield
❸ Regal Cutlass
❹ X-Potion
❺ Ribbon
❻ Ether
❼ Earrings
*Additional maps on pages 142-143

LOCKE'S QUEST (SOUTH FIGARO)

Checklist

- ☐ Equip Locke with armor, weapons, and relics
- ☐ Steal the clothes from the merchant in the Item Shop
- ☐ Use the merchant's clothes to pass through the old man's house
- ☐ Steal the clothes from the Officer on the upper level
- ☐ Speak with the soldier in town and go to the Pub
- ☐ Steal the clothes and cider from the merchant below the Pub
- ☐ Deliver the cider to the old man
- ☐ Talk to the old man's grandson and choose the password "Courage"

- ☐ Enter the secret passage to Owzer's house
- ☐ Go to Owzer's room and enter the secret passage behind the bookcase
- ☐ Find Celes in the first room
- ☐ Free Celes and steal the guard's Clock Key
- ☐ Equip Celes with armor, weapons, and relics
- ☐ Use the Clock Key to wind the stopped clock in the basement
- ☐ Find your way through the secret section of the basement and escape from South Figaro
- ☐ Head for the cave northwest of Narshe

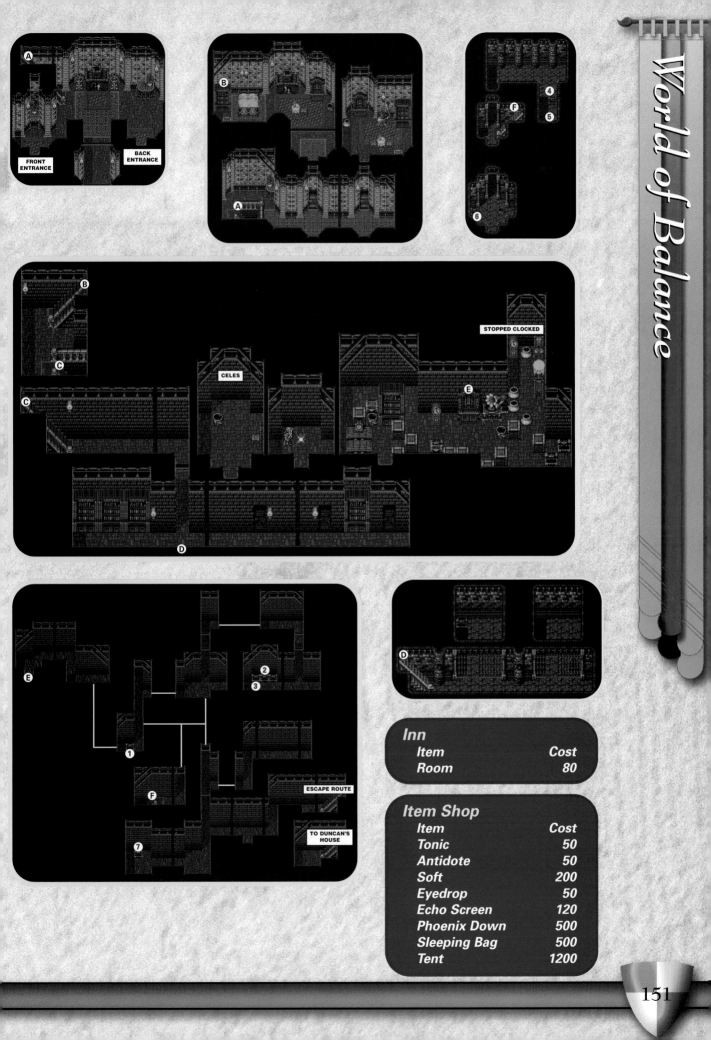

FRONT ENTRANCE

BACK ENTRANCE

STOPPED CLOCKED

CELES

ESCAPE ROUTE

TO DUNCAN'S HOUSE

Inn

Item	Cost
Room	80

Item Shop

Item	Cost
Tonic	50
Antidote	50
Soft	200
Eyedrop	50
Echo Screen	120
Phoenix Down	500
Sleeping Bag	500
Tent	1200

Armor Shop		Weapon Shop		Relic Shop	
Item	Cost	Item	Cost	Item	Cost
Buckler	200	Dirk	150	Sprint Shoes	1500
Heavy Shield	400	Mythril Knife	300	Goggles	500
Hair Band	150	Mythril Blade	450	Star Pendant	500
Plumed Hat	250	Regal Cutlass	800	Jewel Ring	1000
Cotton Robe	200	NoiseBlaster	500	True Knight	1000
Kung Fu Suit	250	Bio Blaster	750		

Occupied South Figaro

Getting around in South Figaro isn't easy now that the town is under Empire control. Most of the townspeople are more than happy to share information with you, however, the Empire's soldiers block your path at almost every major intersection. You should avoid contact with soldiers in MagiTek armor, because they're just itching for a fight. If Locke gets K.O.ed in battle, he'll get dropped off back at the point where he originally entered town and you may have to start all over again.

The only way to make your way around town is to steal the clothes from either a Merchant or an Officer. While dressed as a Merchant, the townsfolk are happy to provide you with safe passage and information, but soldiers will still be very rude. However, if you dress as an Officer, the soldiers will gladly give you information and passage, but the townsfolk will be very cold toward you.

Merchants look like this.

Officers look like this.

Changing Clothes

To change clothes, you must use Locke's **Steal** skill in battle against either a Merchant or an Officer. There are three Merchants and two Officers in town.

You can find the Merchants in the Item Shop, Inn, and Pub. You only need to steal the clothes from the Merchants in the Item Shop and the Pub, but that doesn't mean that you can't rob the one in the Inn just for the extra item.

You can find the Officers on the wall above the city and roaming around near the Café. In this case, you only need the clothes from the Officer on the wall, so you can get the soldier blocking your path to the Pub to move.

Getting the Cider

In the large house on the right side of the city, you'll find an old man who wants Cider before he'll talk to you. To get the Cider, you must go into the Pub's basement and steal the Merchant's clothes and Cider. Take the Cider back to the old man, and he'll almost tell you his grandson's password. No matter; you don't need it! Go downstairs and talk to the grandson after you've taken the old man his Cider, and he'll ask you for the password. Choose **"Courage"** from the list of passwords, and the grandson will open a secret passage that leads to Owzer's house.

Saving Celes

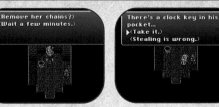

To find Owzer's hidden basement, check behind the book-case in Owzer's room. You may have already been here earlier during your first visit. Inspect the first basement door to find Celes, who's being held captive. Free her and then inspect the sleeping guard to steal the **Clock Key**. Make sure you equip Celes before moving on.

As you proceed further into the basement, use the Clock Key on the stopped clock to open a secret passage. The secret passage is full of dangerous enemies, plus it's very difficult to navigate. There are a lot of good items, so check the map and don't miss a single one. Also, don't forget to visit the basement's lower level. When you're done, head for the exit and escape from town.

Enemies

Primorde
Gold Bear

Items

None
*Maps on page 141

LOCKE'S QUEST CONTINUED (FIGARO AREA CAVE)

Checklist

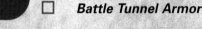

☐ *Enter the cave and head for the recovery spring*

☐ *Battle Tunnel Armor*

Time to Collect

Did you leave the treasure chests unopened the first time you came through this area? If so, it's time to collect. Most of the chests will now contain much better items than they did earlier. Proof that good things come to those that wait!

Tunnel Armor

Before this fight, make sure you use the mines' recovery spring to heal Locke and Celes. As you exit the mine, Tunnel Armor attacks.

This is an easy battle if you follow Celes' advice. Each turn, have her use her **Runic Blade**, which will absorb Tunnel Armor's powerful magic attacks. Locke can then steal

from the Boss, and slowly pick away at its defenses. If the party needs to heal, have Locke use **Tonics** or **Potions**, but don't stop using Celes' Runic Blade.

What's Next?

After defeating Tunnel Armor, Locke and Celes will exit the mine on their own. At this point, you're prompted to choose your next adventure.

You Choose...	Go to...
Terra, Edgar, & Banon	Page 149
Sabin	Page 154
All Complete	Page 164

Enemies
None

Items
None

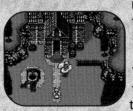

SABIN'S QUEST (HOUSE ON THE VELDT)

Checklist

- [ ] **Go to the house near Sabin's starting point**
- [ ] **Speak with Shadow and have him join your party**
- [ ] **Talk to the Aged Man inside the house**
- [ ] **Head south-southeast to the Imperial Camp**

Item Shop

Item	Cost
Tonic	50
Phoenix Down	500
Tent	1200
Plumed Hat	250
Shuriken	30
Inviz Edge	200
Shadow Edge	400
Sprint Shoes	1500

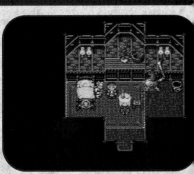

Traveling Merchant

Upon first entering the yard around the house, a Chocobo-riding Merchant will run in from the side. Quickly speak with the Merchant if you want to make purchases or the Merchant will quickly leave.

You can make the Merchant reappear by going back to the World Map and then returning to the yard. Don't miss out on the useful **Skeen** and **Shuriken** items for Shadow. He can throw these at enemies during battle.

Inside the House

The man inside the house may seem a bit confused, but pay attention to his ramblings. They'll come in handy sooner or later. You can rest in his bed for free if you like.

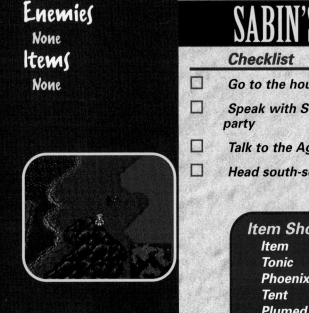

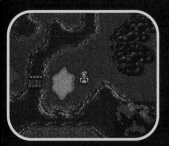

IMPERIAL CAMP

Enemies

Soldier
Leader
Doberma
Templar
Grunt
Cadet
M-Tek Armor
Kefka
Telstar

Items

1. Star Pendant
2. Mythril Glove
3. Green Beret

Checklist

- [ ] Hide behind the wall and listen to the soldiers
  (As Cyan)
- [ ] Challenge the Commander of the Imperial Forces to a battle
  (As Shadow & Sabin)
- [ ] Sneak through the camp and listen to General Leo's conversation
- [ ] Battle Kefka and chase him through the camp
  (As Cyan)
- [ ] Find the King of Doma Castle
- [ ] Search the room to the right of the throne room
  (As Shadow & Sabin)
- [ ] Assist Cyan with defeating the Imperial forces
- [ ] Use the MagiTek Armor to escape the camp
- [ ] Head for the forest to the south

TO DOMA CASTLE

Saving Doma Castle

Cyan is too strong for the enemy. If you want, you can pick off the enemy soldiers attacking the castle just for the fun of it, but you'll end up using a lot of Tonics or Potions for very little gain.

When attacking the Leader, simply charge Cyan's **SwordTech** to Level 2, the **Retort** attack. When the Leader attacks, Cyan will counterattack and defeat the Leader with a single blow.

Getting the Goods

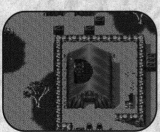

There are treasures in the Imperial Camp. To get those in the Imperial Camp, you must grab them from the chests inside the tents during your chase with Kefka.

Enemies
Ghost
Poplium

Items
None

Checklist

- ☐ **Enter Phantom forest east of Doma Castle**
- ☐ **Find your way through the forest to the Train Station**
- ☐ **Board the Phantom Train**

Navigating the Forest

This side perspective may seem odd at first, but it isn't tough to follow. Just head to the right and look for passages in the background and foreground. It is possible to get turned around if you take the one wrong path, which drops you off near the entrance. Don't worry, though, because there's a recovery spring here, so you can afford to explore.

recovery spring

From the entrance of the Phantom Forest, follow the path right to the end. Go up into the next screen to find the Recovery Spring. Go right to the end and go down into the next screen. Go right and then up into the next screen. Walk right and take the first path up to reach the station.

TO WORLD MAP

Ⓐ

RECOVERY
SPRING

Ⓐ   Ⓑ

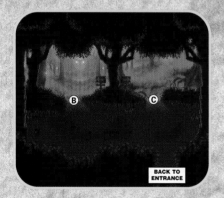

Ⓑ   Ⓒ

BACK TO
ENTRANCE

TO TRAIN
PLATFORM

Ⓒ

Enemies

- Whisper
- Hazer
- Bomb
- Still Going
- Over-Mind
- Specter
- Phantom Train (Boss)

Items

1. Earrings
2. Monster-in-a-Box
3. Hyper Wrist
4. Phoenix Down
5. Sniper Sight
6. Phoenix Down

SABIN'S QUEST (PHANTOM TRAIN)

Checklist

- ☐ Try to exit the train the way you entered
- ☐ Go to the caboose and save your game
- ☐ Enter the fourth car and then fight your way out
- ☐ Climb the fourth car and jump to the fifth car
- ☐ Enter the sixth car and detach the other cars by flipping the yellow switch
- ☐ Flip the yellow switch again to enter the sixth car
- ☐ Take a break in the dining car
- ☐ Throw the two switches inside the engine's cabin and then the one on the smokestack
- ☐ Battle the Phantom Train
- ☐ Try to speak to Cyan and then leave the forest
- ☐ Continue through the mountains to Barren Falls

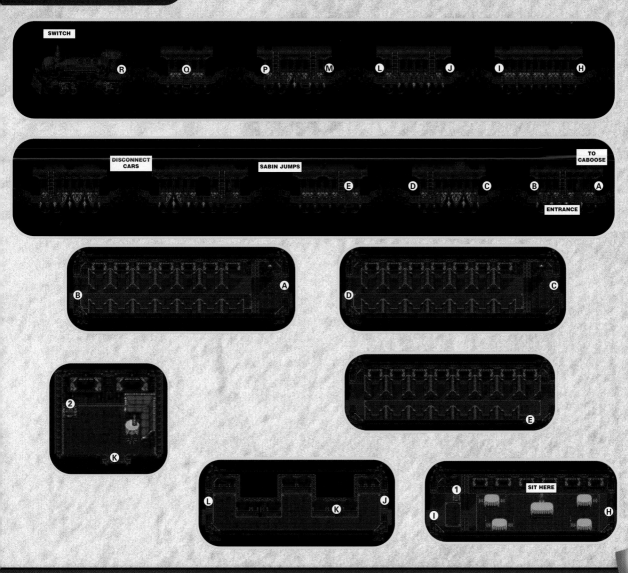

157

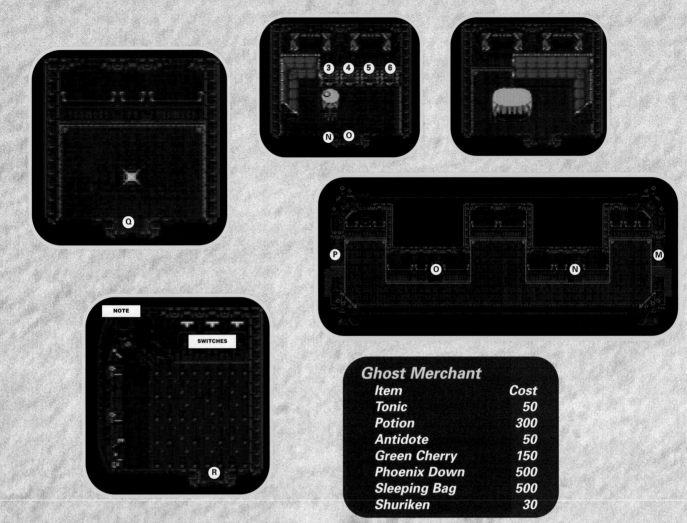

Ghost Merchant	
Item	**Cost**
Tonic	50
Potion	300
Antidote	50
Green Cherry	150
Phoenix Down	500
Sleeping Bag	500
Shuriken	30

Friendly Ghosts

Not all spirits are evil. Some may even want to join you, which makes your trek through the train much easier. The first of such spirits are in the caboose. You can also find the spirit of a Merchant if you talk to the right spook.

There are two things you should know about Ghosts. First, their **Possess** attack will completely eliminate an enemy. Unfortunately, it also eliminates the Ghost, so don't use it unless you don't mind losing your friend. Second, Ghosts take damage from healing items, so healing a Ghost during battle is impossible. However, healing items work normally on Ghosts outside of battles.

Trapped

A spirit will lock you in the fourth car. Defeat the spook and you'll be placed outside, but your situation won't improve. Climb the ladder on the side of the car and make a daring leap to the fifth… er… sixth car. To leave the evil spirits behind, enter the sixth car and throw the yellow switch on the wall. This detaches the other cars from the train. Flipping the yellow switch again will enable you to enter the sixth car.

The Dining Car

If you stop at the middle table of the dining car, you'll get treated to a free meal, which restores your party's HP and MP. This may be just the boost your party needs to reach the engine room alive. By the way, switch the leader of your party and have everyone eat. Check out each party member's reaction.

Ziegfried

If you try to open the treasure chest in the first passenger car, you'll run into a fighter named Ziegfried. Ziegfried talks a lot of smack, but can't live up to the hype. You can win this battle easily, however, Ziegfried gets the last laugh by running off with the treasure.

MAN: I am Ziegfried, the world's greatest swordsman! That treasure chest is mine.

Stopping the Train

To stop the train, shut the first and third pressure valves, and operate the switch outside, near the

When you reach the engine, inspect the top-left corner of the room to find instructions on how to stop the train. The note tells you to shut off the *first* and *third* switches on the wall, and then it says to throw a switch near the engine's smokestack outside. Doing so throws you into battle against the Phantom Train.

Phantom Train

GhostTrain	SHADOW	131
	SABIN	194
	CYAN	212

⬥Fight	SABIN	105
SwdTech	CYAN	81
Item		

This Boss isn't tough, but it has some powerful attacks. **Acid Rain** is the worst of them all, because it causes about 150 points of damage to each party member and it causes them to have HP-draining seizures. Have Sabin use either the **Aura Bolt** or **Pummel Blitz**, have Shadow toss **Shurikens**, and make Cyan use the Level 1 **SwordTech**. Using these three attacks, the Phantom Train won't last long.

ONE-HIT KILL:

Because the Phantom Train is an undead enemy, you can use a Phoenix Down against it and destroy it with one shot.

SABIN'S QUEST CONTINUED (BARREN FALLS)

Enemies

Piranha
Rizopas (Boss)

Items

None

Checklist

☐ *Walk to the edge of Barren Falls and bid farewell to Shadow*

☐ *Walk to the edge again and jump off*

☐ *Battle the Piranhas until Rizopas appears*

☐ *Defeat Rizopas to reach the Veldt*

☐ *Head east-southeast across the Veldt to Mobliz*

159

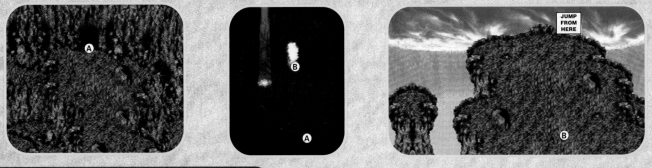

Shadow Departs

When you reach Barren Falls, Shadow will leave your party. There's a chance he may even leave before that point after a battle. Either way, there's nothing you can do to get him back for now.

Rizopas

After jumping off of Barren Falls, you're forced to fight 10 to 12 Piranhas in succession. After eliminating them, an even more powerful creature, Rizopas, will appear.

This creature lacks a lot of HP, however, it does have an extremely powerful attack called **El Nino** that causes about 250-300 points of damage to Sabin and Cyan. Use **Blitz** attacks and the Level 1 **SwordTech** when possible, but keep both characters' HP high by using **Potions** or **Tonics**.

Gau

You first meet Gau when you arrive at the Veldt, but he quickly disappears. As you make your way to Mobliz, you're bound to run into Gau a few times. He'll beg for food, but you don't have anything to offer him. Attack him and he'll run away.

SABIN'S QUEST (MOBLIZ)

Enemies
All regular enemies in the game

Items
❶ Elixir

Inn
Item	Cost
Room	100

Checklist

☐ **Talk to the townsfolk to learn about Gau and the Diving Helmet**

☐ **Purchase Dried Meat from the Item Shop**

☐ **Explore the Veldt and find Gau**

☐ **Give Gau the Dried Meat to get him to join your party**

☐ **Take Gau to Mt. Crescent Cave and the Serpent Trench, located to the southwest of Mobliz**

(Optional)

☐ **Mail the letter for the wounded soldier in Mobliz**

RELICS

ITEMS

WEAPONS ARMOR

INN

Weapon Shop

Item	Cost
Mythril Knife	300
Mythril Blade	450
Mythril Claw	800
Kotetsu	800

Armor Shop

Item	Cost
Buckler	200
Heavy Shield	400
Plumed Hat	250
Magus Hat	600
Bandana	800
Iron Helmet	1000
Kung Fu Suit	250
Iron Armor	700

Item Shop

Item	Cost
Dried Meat	150
Tonic	50
Potion	300
Eyedrop	50
Green Cherry	150
Phoenix Down	500
Sleeping Bag	500
Tent	1200

Relic Shop

Item	Cost
Sprint Shoes	1500
White Cape	5000

Talk to Everyone

After speaking with everyone in the town, you'll learn two things. First, the wild child, Gau, likes Dried Meat. One villager mentions throwing Dried Meat into a pack of animals once, which caused Gau to appear. Second, you'll hear of the **Serpent Trench**, which can take you to a town known as Nikeah. Unfortunately, you need an underwater breathing device that was recently stolen from Mobliz.

Get Gau

Purchase some **Dried Meat** from the Item Shop in Mobliz, and then return to the Veldt. After a battle, you'll eventually meet up with Gau. Select the Dried Meat from your item inventory and use it on Gau. The hungry wild child will gobble down the food and join your party in appreciation of the kind act.

Gau has a skill that enables him to learn the attacks of creatures found in the Veldt. This is the only area in the world where Gau can learn these attacks, and once he learns them, they can be used at any time during battle anywhere in the world.

Teaching Gau a new attack is simple, but time consuming. Wander the Veldt until you get into a battle. Have Gau "Leap" into an enemy(ies) you want him to learn from. The battle will end, and Gau will no longer be in your party. Continue fighting on the Veldt, and Gau will eventually reappear with a new **"Rage"** skill.

Gau learns skills from the enemies he disappears with, and from any enemies in the battle in which he reappears. You can use a skill by selecting Gau's Rage skill in battle, and then choose one of the monsters listed. Once Gau goes into Rage mode, you lose complete control of him. He'll continue to use the selected beast's attacks until the battle ends.

Avoid the Inn

The Inn at Mobliz isn't cheap. Instead of wasting 100 GP to rest there, go to the Relic Shop at the back of the town. There's a bed in the back that you can sleep in for free.

The Wounded Soldier

In one of the houses at Mobliz, you'll find a wounded soldier who speaks of his true love back at his hometown. You can help him out by taking the letter from the desk, and paying to have it mailed at the house with the carrier pigeons.

SABIN'S QUEST
(MT. CRESCENT CAVE & SERPENT TRENCH)

Enemies
Actaneon
Anguiform
Aspik

Items
① Elixir
② Diving Helmet
③ X-Potion
④ Green Beret

Checklist

☐ *With Gau, head southwest from Mobliz to find Mt. Crescent Cave*

☐ *Explore the area to find the Diving Helmet*

☐ *Hop into the Serpent Trench and steer your way through the murky waters*

☐ *Arrive at the town of Nikeah*

Searching for Treasure

As you walk around the cave, Gau will automatically react whenever you get near a treasure or event. You must be careful though. If you go to the top-left corner of the cave, Gau will pull a practical joke that causes Sabin to lose 500 GP. Check the map and screenshots for assistance in locating items.

Navigating the Serpent Trench

The Serpent Trench is full of monsters, so be prepared to fight. Watch out for Anguiforms. Their **Aqua Rake** attack can easily knock out injured characters. Make sure you heal your party members in any cave you find.

As you travel, always take the right path when given a choice. There are a couple of caves to the right that have some useful items. Caves also provide the only opportunity for you to heal your characters in-between battles.

Anguiform	CYAN	311
Actaneon	SABIN	220
ik	GAU	350

SABIN'S QUEST (NIKEAH)

Checklist

- [ ] **Visit Nikeah's shops**
- [ ] **Talk to the boat's captain and travel to South Figaro**

Enemies

None

Items

1. Elixir

Relic Shop

Item	Cost
Goggles	500
Star Pendant	500
White Cape	5000
Fairy Ring	1500

Weapon Shop

Item	Cost
Mythril Claw	800
Kotetsu	800
Mythril Pike	800

Chocobo Stable

Item	Cost
Ride	80

Item Shop

Item	Cost
Tonic	50
Potion	300
Echo Screen	120
Smoke Bomb	300
Green Cherry	150
Phoenix Down	500
Sleeping Bag	500
Tent	1200

Armor Shop

Item	Cost
Heavy Shield	400
Plumed Hat	250
Magus Hat	600
Bandana	800
Iron Helmet	1000
Kung Fu Suit	250
Silk Robe	600
Iron Armor	700

Inn

Item	Cost
Rest	150

CHOCOBO STABLE · INN · 1 · ITEMS · WEAPONS · ARMOR · CAFE · RELICS · A

Exploring Nikeah

DANCER: Yoo hoo!
You handsome thing.
How 'bout joining me?
Tee hee!

There isn't much to do in this town except shop. You should definitely purchase armor, because there are a lot of new items to find. Don't neglect to buy for people who aren't in your party yet. They'll need new equipment soon.

Also, stop by the local Pub. There's a funny scene inside between Cyan and a dancing girl.

When finished shopping, speak to the captain of the boat docked at Nikeah. He'll give you a ride to South Figaro.

What's Next?

After you set sail, Sabin's quest is essentially finished. After a short conversation, you're prompted to choose your next adventure.

You Choose...	Go to...
Terra, Edgar, & Banon	Page 149
Locke	Page 150
All Complete	Page 164

Enemies

Trooper
B_____y Man
Heavy Armor
Fidor
Rider

Items

Elixir (Clock in Elder's House)
Wall Ring (Chest in Old Man's house)
Sneak Ring (Chest in Old Man's house)
Hyper Wrist (Chest in Old Man's house)
Thief Knife (Chest in Old Man's house)
_____ngs (Chest in Old Man's house)
5000 GP (Chest in Old Man's house)
Sleeping Bag (Training Center)
Tincture (Training Center)
Tonic (Training Center)
*Maps on Page ??

NARSHE (KEFKA'S ASSAULT)

Checklist

- [ ] **Update everyone's equipment and choose your battle parties**
- [ ] **Fight your way through Kefka's troops while protecting Banon**
- [ ] **Challenge Kefka to a battle**
- [ ] **Meet the frozen Esper**
- [ ] **Explore Narshe and then head to Figaro Castle**

Armor Shop

Item	Cost
Mythril Shield	1200
Magus Hat	600
Bandana	800
Iron Helmet	1000
Silk Robe	600
Iron Armor	700

Weapon Shop

Item	Cost
Regal Cutlass	800
Mythril Claw	800
Kotetsu	800
Mythril Pike	800
Air Lancet	950
Flail	2000
Full Moon	2500

Inn

Item	Cost
Rest	200

Relic Shop

Item	Cost
Sprint Shoes	1500
Jewel Ring	1000
Fairy Ring	1500
Barrier Ring	500
Mythril Glove	700
True Knight	1000

Item Shop

Item	Cost
Tonic	50
Potion	300
Tincture	1500
Soft	200
Phoenix Down	500
Smoke Bomb	300
Sleeping Bag	500
Tent	1200

Kefka's Charge

You can split up your party in one of two ways: balance or power. With a balanced party, you have a main group of three characters and two guard groups with two characters apiece. A power group focuses on a main group of four, and two guard groups with the remaining characters.

Either way, place your guard groups at the end of the trails so that the enemy can't get past without fighting. Send the main group out to plow through the onslaught and onto Kefka.

You don't need to defeat all of Kefka's army, so a power group can easily blast through by fighting a minimal number of battles. Also, keep in mind that you can heal between battles. Don't send a weak party against Kefka or the last of Kefka's guards.

Kefka

Kefka isn't very tough, but he does use some powerful magic. Ideally, you'll have Celes in your party for this battle. Her Runic blade can absorb Kefka's magic, which makes him much less threatening. Use powerful attacks like magic, SwordTechs, Blitz attacks, and Tools to really hurt Kefka. It helps a lot to have Cyan at Level 15. His Level 4 SwordTech, **QuadraSlam**, causes close to 1000 points of damage.

Exploring Narshe

Once again, you'll find a lot of new items in the shops around town. Make sure you buy only what you can afford. The Inn is very expensive, however, you can cheat the Innkeeper out of his money by sleeping in the back room at the Weapon Shop. Also, there's always the recovery water in the training hall (Classroom). Don't miss out on all the free items. There's one locked chest you can't yet open, so don't worry about it right now.

FIGARO CASTLE

Enemies
Leafer
Dark Wind
Sand Ray
Areneid
M-Tek Armor

Items
None

Checklist

☐ **Enter the castle and head down to the engine room**

☐ **Ask the old man to take the castle to Kohlingen**

☐ **Leave the castle and head north to find Kohlingen (Optional)**

☐ **Explore the castle with Edgar and Sabin to learn more about their past**

Item Shop #1

Item	Cost	Sale
Potion	300	150
Tincture	1500	750
Phoenix Down	500	250
Revivify	300	150
Antidote	50	25
Eyedrop	50	25
Soft	200	100
Tent	1200	600

Item Shop #2

Item	Cost	Sale
AutoCrossbow	250	125
NoiseBlaster	500	250
Bio Blaster	750	375
Flash	1000	500
Drill	3000	1500

Leaving So Soon?

Upon reaching Figaro Castle, speak with the man in the engine room and he'll take the castle to Kohlingen. But wait! There's more to do if you have Sabin and Edgar in your party.

Explore the castle and take a nap in the castle's chambers. Also, have Edgar go shopping. If he is leading the party at a shop, you'll receive a 50% discount on anything you purchase. You may want to stock up a bit before heading for Kohlingen.

EDGAR: SABIN, let's settle this with a toss of a coin.

MERCHANT: I can't take money from the King!

KOHLINGEN

Checklist

☐ **Go to Rachel's house and listen to Locke's story**

☐ **Visit the basement of the house in the northeast corner of town**

☐ **Learn about the flying creature's visit and head south to Jidoor**
(Optional)

☐ **Head north from Kohlingen to find a lone house**

Enemies

Fossil Fang
Vulture
Iron Fist
Red Fang
Mind Candy
Over Gunk

Items

Elixir
Green Beret
Hero Ring (Pot in house north of Kohlingen)

Inn

Item	Cost
Rest	200

Weapon Shop

Item	Cost
Air Lancet	950
Flail	2000
Full Moon	2500
Shuriken	30
Fire Skean	500
Water Edge	500
Bolt Edge	500
Inviz Edge	200

Item Shop

Item	Cost
Potion	300
Tincture	1500
Revivify	300
Antidote	50
Green Cherry	150
Phoenix Down	500
Sleeping Bag	500
Tent	1200

Armor Shop

Item	Cost
Mythril Shield	1200
Magus Hat	600
Bandana	800
Head Band	1600
Iron Helmet	1000
Silk Robe	600
Iron Armor	700

RACHEL'S ①
②
WEAPONS
ARMOR
ITEMS
INN
CAFE

Visiting Kohlingen

That? Oh, that's LOCKE's... Dear, me! Almost spilled the beans! Kwa, ha!

Everyone was scared when the glowing creature stopped here. It left to the south, toward Jidoor.

Your main purpose in this town is to find out if anyone witnessed the flying creature. Sure enough, you'll find that there are several signs of the creature's visit. One witness will point you south toward the town of Jidoor.

Also, you'll learn more about Locke if you visit two of the houses. Locke's old flame, Rachel, lived in this town and visiting her home sparks some painful memories for Locke.

Hidden Chest

Received "Green Beret!"

There's a hidden chest in the home on the northeast corner of town. To get it, you must enter through the back door and then search behind the suit of armor. You'll find a **Green Beret** inside.

Dreamer's House

Several people in town mention a house to the north. If you head that way, you'll discover a man who dreams of one day owning a coliseum. You can also find a Relic, the **Hero Ring**, hidden in a pot.

JIDOOR

Checklist

☐ **Enter Jidoor and talk to everyone**

☐ **Head north to Zozo**

(Optional)

☐ **Go south to the Opera House**

Enemies

None

Items

❶ Tincture

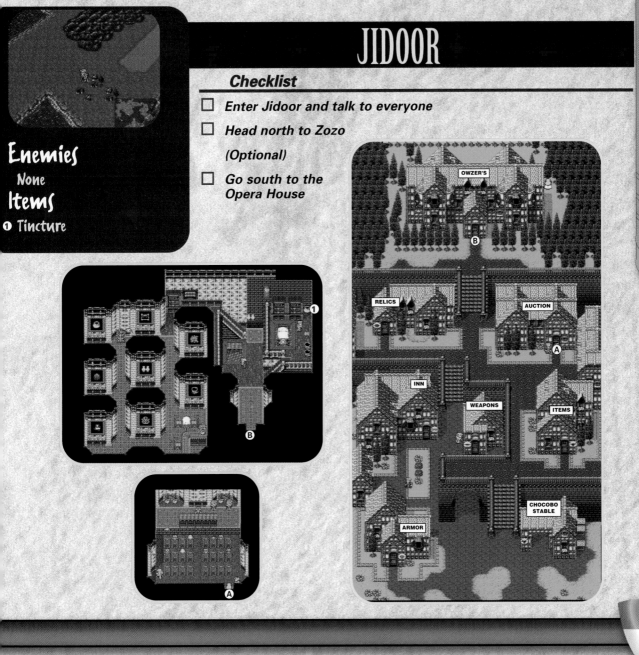

Chocobo Stable

Item	Cost
Ride	250

Inn

Item	Cost
Rest	250

Armor Shop

Item	Cost
Mythril Shield	1200
Head Band	1600
Mythril Vest	1200
Ninja Gear	1100
White Dress	2200

Weapon Shop

Item	Cost
Forged	1200
Kaiser	1000
Kodachi	1200
Full Moon	2500
Fire Skean	500
Water Edge	500
Bolt Edge	500
Shadow Edge	400

Relic Shop

Item	Cost
Peace Ring	3000
Barrier Ring	500
Mythril Glove	700
Earrings	5000
True Knight	1000
Sniper Sight	3000

Item Shop

Cost	Item
Potion	300
Tincture	1500
Antidote	50
Soft	200
Revivify	300
Phoenix Down	500
Echo Screen	120
Tent	1200

The Search Continues

There's some good shopping in Jidoor, but that seems to be about it at the moment. The **Auction House** may seem intriguing, but there's nothing going on there at this point in the game. You'll also hear talk of an **Opera House** to the south, but for the moment you don't need to go there unless you can't wait to check it out.

By talking to Jidoor's citizens, you learn that the creature was seen flying north toward the town of Zozo. Although you don't learn much about Zozo, you may get the feeling it isn't a very friendly place. Stock up on weapons, armor, and healing items because you'll need them in Zozo. You may want to consider renting a Chocobo for the long journey north to conserve your party's energy.

Enemies

Hades Gigas
Slam Dancer
Harvester
Gabledegak
Dadaluma (Boss)

Items

1. Tonic
2. Thief Glove
3. Tincture
4. Potion
5. Fire Knuckle
6. Tincture
7. Chain Saw
8. X-Potion
9. Running Shoes

Magicite

10. Ramuh
11. Stray
12. Siren
13. Kirin

ZOZO

Checklist

- [ ] Go to the Inn and inspect the clock
- [ ] Talk to everyone in town to get the correct time
- [ ] Set the Inn's clock to the proper time
- [ ] Get Edgar's Chainsaw
- [ ] Climb the center tower
- [ ] Battle Dadaluma
- [ ] Find Terra at the top of the tower
- [ ] Rejoin your comrades and split into two parties.

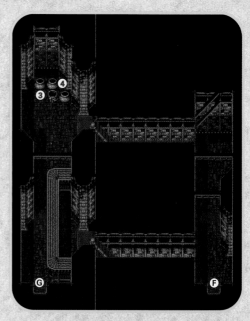

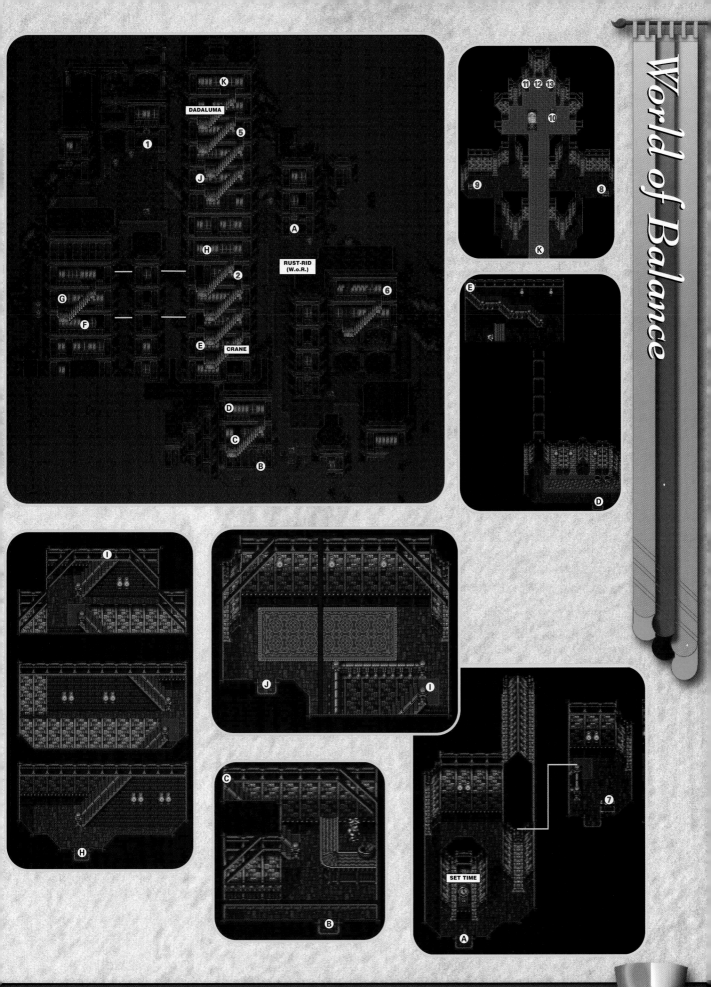

Unwelcome Visitors

Zozo is anything but a friendly town, but what do you expect with the constant downpour and dark streets? Lying seems to be the only acceptable form of communication, and thugs fill the streets.

Expect to get attacked regularly while walking around town. Make sure you've saved your game before entering the town, and consider Zozo to be *extremely* hostile.

> **Hades Gigas: Use Edgar's NoiseBlaster to confuse this enemy. This gives Locke an opportunity to steal an Atlas Armlet Relic from the enemy. It also causes the Hades Gigas to waste its MP by casting Magnitude 8 on itself, which saves your party a lot of damage.**
> **As a general rule you can steal a lot of good items from the enemies in Zozo, but they may also try to steal from your party as well.**

The Broken Clock

There's a stopped clock on the wall inside the Inn. After inspecting it, you're asked to set the correct time. However, to get the correct time, you must decipher the vague clues given to you by the locals, which are all lies, of course.

First, visit the "Weapon Shop" and talk to the person there. Since you know he's lying, the clock is pointing at 10 minutes after. Next, go to the middle tower on the south side of town. The line of liars will help you decipher that the hour isn't 2, 12, 10, 4, or 8. Continue talking to some of the townsfolk to learn that the seconds is neither 30 nor 20. You'll also learn that the seconds *cannot* be divided by 20.

So what's the answer? It's currently 6:10:50 in Zozo. Set the time on the "Inn's" clock to open a secret passage that leads to a chest containing a **Chain Saw**. This is a powerful new tool for Edgar that's sure to come in handy.

Finding Terra

It should quickly become apparent that you'll need to climb the large tower in the center of town to find Terra. Climbing the tower isn't easy, because you'll encounter a lot of enemies and dead ends before reaching the top.

When you reach a spot where you can't seem to go any farther, look around for an open window on the side of the building. You can leap out an open window to an adjacent tower, which you must do more than once. To get out of the tower, you must use the crane found on the main tower's stairs.

Dadaluma

At the top of the tower, you'll face the powerful warrior, Dadaluma. This Boss has powerful physical attacks and uses a variety of support magic. Use your most powerful attacks, especially Sabin's **Blitz** skills, Edgar's **Chain Saw**, Cyan's **SwordTech**, and Celes' **Magic** if they're in your party.

As you deplete Dadaluma's HP, it will begin to heal itself with Potions and two Iron Fists will join the battle. If you defeat the Iron Fists, they are quickly replaced, so you should continue to focus your attacks on Dadaluma.

You can make the Iron Fists fight *for* you instead of *against* you by using Edgar's **NoiseBlaster** to confuse them. The Iron Fists are automatically defeated after you defeat Dadaluma.

What's Magicite?

You're about to receive your first four **Magicite crystals**. Magicite is the remains of a defeated Esper. Each character can equip one Magicite crystal in the Skills menu. By equipping Magicite, a character can assume the lost Esper's powers. Over time, the character will learn new spells from the Esper's Magicite, and will no longer need to have the Magicite equipped to use the spells. This is accomplished with Magic Points won in battle. Also, while a character has an Esper equipped, he/she can summon the Esper into battle. This is very handy, because each Esper has a different attack and some are more powerful than others.

As your characters learn from Espers, they can trade Magicite crystals so that everyone can have the same list of spells as everyone else. Note, however, that this takes a lot of time and effort. Also, some Espers have bonuses connected to them that characters receive when leveling up. For example, whenever a character equipped with Ramuh levels up, that character's Stamina increases by one point. Use these bonuses to help round out your characters' vital statistics.

Enemies

Sewer Rat
Vermin
Ultros (Boss)

Items

None

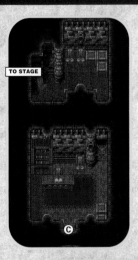

THE OPERA HOUSE

Checklist

- [ ] Go to Jidoor and speak with the Impresario at Owzer's house
- [ ] Pick up and read the letter left by the Impresario
- [ ] Head south from Jidoor to the Opera House and find the Impresario
- [ ] Go to the dressing room and speak with Celes
- [ ] Read the score and memorize Celes' lines
- [ ] Go onto the stage and perform
- [ ] Return to the dressing room and read Ultros' letter
- [ ] Find the Impresario and warn him of Ultros' plan
- [ ] Rush to the right side of the balcony and throw the right switch
- [ ] Rush back to the left side of the balcony and enter the door leading to the rafters
- [ ] Cross the rafters quickly to stop Ultros

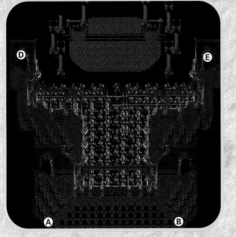

Setzer's Item Shop

Cost	Item
Potion	300
Tincture	1500
Revivify	300
Phoenix Down	500
Remedy	1000
Smoke Bomb	300
Warp Stone	700
Tent	1200

The Big Performance

Oh my hero, so far away now!
Will I ever see your smile?
Love goes away, like night
into day. It's just a fading

Before going onstage as Celes, you should study her part by reading the book on the table. You must memorize her lines, because you'll periodically be asked to recite a line at the proper moment. If you mess up, the opera will be ruined and you'll be forced to start over again. The following are the lines you must remember:

- Oh my hero...

- I'm the darkness...

- Must I...

After the last line, Draco will appear and request that Celes dance with him. Follow his lead. You don't have to mimic his movements, but you must quickly get in front of him each time he stops and speak to him.

After completing the dance, quickly grab the bouquet and walk up the stairs to the balcony where the rest of the opera will play itself out. Remember that if you mess up the dance, or you don't get up the stairs fast enough, the opera will stop and you'll be forced to start over from the beginning.

Stop Ultros

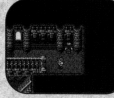

After Locke reads Ultros' letter, run back to the Impresario and tell him what's going on. Run to the right side of the balcony and speak with the man there. He'll tell you to throw the switch on the right side of the wall. After doing so, race back to the left side of the balcony and head through the door to the rafters.

To cross the rafters, you must get past a bunch of rats. You can dodge the rats if you cross the beams at the right time, but running into a rat initiates a battle. Quickly eliminate any Vermin, and then destroy any remaining Sewer Rats during a battle. If you destroy the Sewer Rats first, the Vermin will call in reinforcements. Remember that you only have five minutes, so you may want to run from battle or use Smoke Bombs to escape if time is short.

Ultros

The royal octopus, Ultros, has improved a lot since your last meeting. It now has magic attacks that can be difficult to overcome. Make sure you have a supply of **Green Cherries** and **Remedies** before the fight begins. You may also want to equip your characters with Relics that prevent **Imp** and **Confused** statuses. This will put a dent in Ultros' battle plan.

Ultros will cast two negative status effects on your party, Imp and Confuse. While "imped," your characters can still attack, so this effect isn't a major deal. However, when confused, your characters can turn on each other in the worst of ways. Quickly strike a confused character to snap him/her out of it. Also, make sure you use your new magic abilities and summon your Espers into battle. The Espers will make this battle a lot quicker.

Setzer's Airship

After gaining control of Setzer's Airship, you'll automatically head for your next destination. Once there, you should jump back onboard the ship and take advantage of its features.

There are other men onboard the Airship. One will heal your party, another will sell you items, and the last will enable you to un-equip characters that aren't in your current party so that you can redistribute equipment.

ALBROOK

Enemies

Giga Toad
Chitonid
Peepers
Gilmantis
Mesosaur
Black Dragon
Earth Guard
Osprey
Lunaris

Items

❶ Tincture
❷ Elixir
❸ Potion
❹ Warp Stone

Checklist

☐ **Prepare for the journey to Vector**

☐ **Leave the town and head east to Vector**

(Optional)

☐ **Visit the town of Tzen (far to the north) or Maranda (far to the west)**

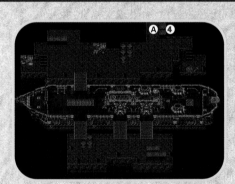

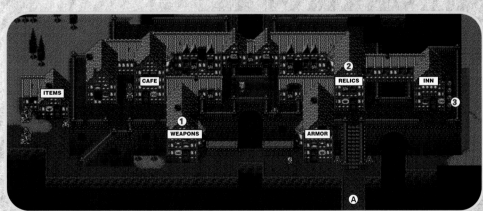

Inn

Item	Cost
Rest	300

Item Shop

Item	Cost
Potion	300
Tincture	1500
Eyedrop	50
Remedy	1000
Revivify	300
Phoenix Down	500
Tent	1200
Warp Stone	700

Weapon Shop

Item	Cost
Forged	1200
Poison Claw	2500
Epee	3000
Blossom	3200
Shuriken	30
Fire Skean	500
Water Edge	500
Bolt Edge	500

Armor Shop

Item	Cost
Head Band	1600
Bard's Hat	3000
Mythril Vest	1200
Ninja Gear	1100
White Dress	2200

Relic Shop

Item	Cost
Goggles	500
Peace Ring	3000
Earrings	5000
Sniper Sight	3000
Wall Ring	6000
Amulet	5000

Shop Around

There's not much to do here except shop, which is fine. Take a moment to stock up and get your party ready for the battles to come. When you're finished, you may want to find the far-off towns of Tzen and Maranda before heading for Vector.

Enemies

None

Items

❶ Magicite Sraphim (Purchase for 3,000 GP in W.o.B. or 30 GP in W.o.R.)

TZEN

Inn

Item	Cost
Rest	350

Chocobo Stable

Item	Cost
Ride	100

Item Shop

Item	Cost
Potion	300
Tincture	1500
Eyedrop	50
Green Cherry	150
Echo Screen	120
Revivify	300
Phoenix Down	500
Tent	1200

Weapon Shop

Item	Cost
Air Lancet	950
Full Moon	2500
Epee	3000
Boomerang	4500

Armor Shop

Item	Cost
Bard's Hat	3000
Mythril Helm	2000
Mythril Vest	1200
Ninja Gear	1100
White Dress	2200

Relic Shop

Item	Cost
Earrings	5000
Running Shoes	7000
Black Belt	5000
Amulet	5000

Looking Around

At this point, all you really want to do in Tzen is purchase some new items. There are plenty of shops to visit. Also, there's a hidden **Chocobo Stable** in the woods to the east of town. You should rent one if you plan to go to Maranda before heading to Vector.

Chocobo ride, 100 GP!
How about it?
▶ Yes

Enemies

None

Items
1. Revivify
2. Remedy

MARANDA

Checklist

☐ *Visit Laura's house*

Inn

Item	Cost
Rest	200

Chocobo Stable

Item	Cost
Ride	100

Armor Shop

Item	Cost
Bard's Hat	3000
Green Beret	3000
Mythril Helm	2000
Mythril Vest	1200
Mythril Mail	3500

Weapon Shop

Item	Cost
Mythril Pike	800
Trident	1700
Poison Claw	2500
Epee	3000
Boomerang	4500

Soldier's Lost Love

Remember the wounded soldier in Mobliz? His lost love is here in Maranda. Make sure you pay her a visit!

Hidden Chocobo Stable

There's a hidden Chocobo Stable outside of town. Search in the southern part of the woods to the east of Maranda.

Enemies

Guard
Garm
Commando
Proto Armor
Pipsqueak
Guardian

Items

None

VECTOR

Checklist

- ☐ **Find the Returner Sympathizer**
- ☐ **Sneak past the guards and into the Magitek Factory**

Inn

Item	Cost
Rest	Free (Sort of)

Weapon Shop

Item	Cost
Forged	1200
Poison Claw	2500
Epee	3000
Blossom	3200

Armor Shop

Item	Cost
Head Band	1600
Bard's Hat	3000
Mythril Vest	1200
Ninja Gear	1100
White Dress	2200

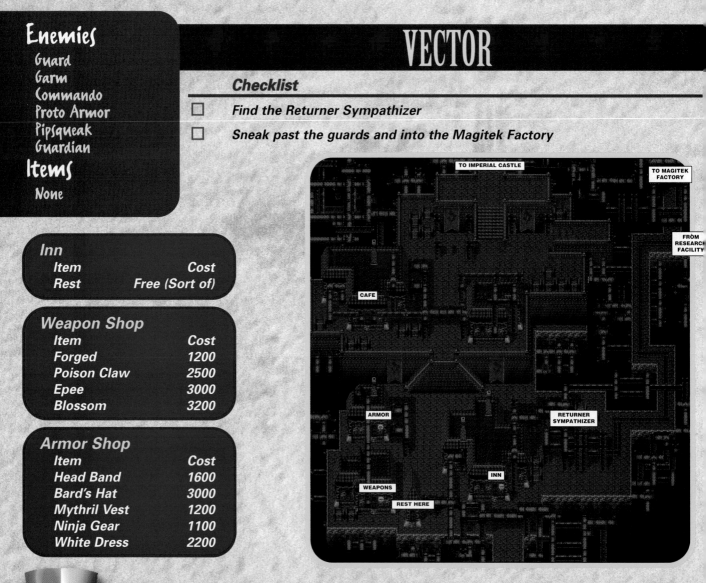

Unfriendly Inn

Upon arrival in Vector, you may be in serious need of rest. The Inn offers a "free" stay, but there's a hidden cost. In the middle of the night, a thief will steal 1000 GP from your party. Fortunately, you can avoid this.

Check out the smallest house in town. When asked about your allegiance, respond that you aren't loyal to the Empire, which prompts a fight with two Guards. After defeating them, the house's owner will gladly restore your party's HP and MP for free.

The Imperial Palace

The entrance to the Imperial Palace is heavily guarded. If a soldier spots your party, you'll be forced into battle. Even if you do get past the soldiers, you'll find the **Guardian**, a large, seemingly invincible machine protecting the entrance. Still, this is a great place to build levels and earn GP if your characters need a boost.

Returner Sympathizer

The **Returner Sympathizer** is hiding behind some crates near the entrance to the Magitek Factory. Speak with him, and then follow his orders. Climb onto the box and then sneak past the guards.

Enemies
Garm
Commando
Pipsqueak
Proto Armor
Trapper
General
Ifrit (Boss)
Shiva (Boss)

Items
Flame Sabre
X-Potion
Tincture
Thunder Blade
Remedy
Dragoon Boots
Gold Shield
Tent
Gold Armor
Gold Helmet
Blizzard
Zephyr Cape

Magicite
Ifrit
Shiva

MAGITEK FACTORY

Checklist

☐ **Find Kefka and follow the Espers**

☐ **Save your game and battle Ifrit and Shiva**

☐ **Go to the Magitek Research Facility**

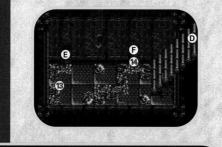

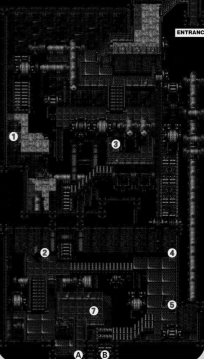

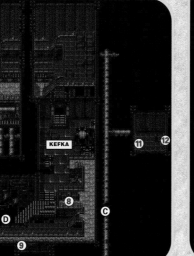

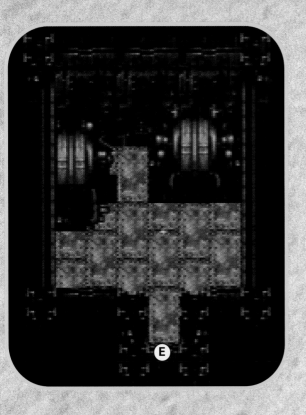

TO
RESEARCH
FACILITY

E

F

Navigating the Factory

This area can be a bit confusing at first. To get to some areas, you must crawl through pipes, ride lifts, and hop onto conveyor belts. Use the maps to help guide you, and try and get all of the chests.

Your ultimate goal is to find Kefka. You'll find his location marked on the maps. You must ride a conveyer belt in the second area to find him. Once he leaves, follow the Espers to continue your quest.

Ifrit and Shiva

When you find the two Espers, don't immediately inspect them. Instead, enter the left door and save your game. You may want to use a Tent if you've been in a lot of fights.

When you're ready for battle, inspect Ifrit and the battle will begin. Use **Ice** magic on Ifrit and **Fire** magic on Shiva. Most physical attacks won't cause much damage, unless you've equipped your characters with the **Flame Sabre** and **Blizzard** found in the factory. Avoid using the Flame Sabre against Ifrit, or the Blizzard against Shiva or you'll heal them.

As the fight goes on, the two Espers will sense Ramuh's presence and will turn themselves into Magicite. Continue by going through the door Shiva was blocking.

Enemies

Rhinox
Gobbler
Trapper
Chaser
Mag Roader
024 (Boss)
Number 128 (Boss)
Crane (Boss)

Items

Break Blade

Magicite

Unicorn
Maduin
Shoat
Phantom
Carbunkl
Bismark

MAGITEK RESEARCH FACILITY

Checklist

- ☐ *Find and defeat 024*
- ☐ *Throw the switch in the Esper containment chamber*
- ☐ *Follow Cid out of the M.R.F.*
- ☐ *Save your game and then talk to Cid*
- ☐ *Fight your way out of the M.R.F.*
- ☐ *Run into town until you meet Setzer*
- ☐ *Destroy Kefka's Cranes to release the Airship*

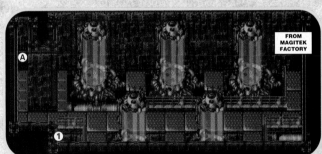

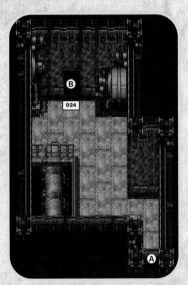

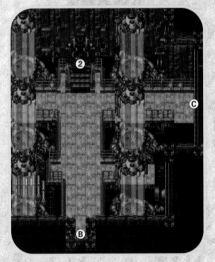

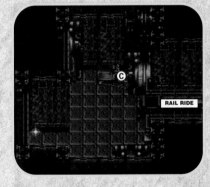

024

This Boss has a lot of powerful magic attacks and a shifting weakness. At the start of the battle, use everything you've got against 024. Several turns later, 024 will use **Wall Change** to shift its strengths and weaknesses. Use special attacks like Cyan's **Dispatch**, Sabin's **Pummel**, and Edgar's **Chain Saw**.

You can use **Scan** magic to take a peak at 024's new weakness, and take advantage of it if you have the right kind of magic. If you keep your HP up, this shouldn't be a tough fight.

Escape by Rail

Your only way out of the Magitek Research Facility is by rail. As you travel, Mag Roaders will periodically attack. Eliminate them quickly, and make sure you keep your party's HP up because you won't get a chance to heal between battles. As you near the end, Number 128 will challenge you.

Number 128

This battle can be challenging after fighting so many Mag Roaders. If any party member's HP is low, immediately use **Cure** magic or **Potions** for a boost.

Number 128 is comprised of three parts. The center body is the main target, and it's the hardest part to eliminate. You can destroy Number 128's arms, but they'll quickly regenerate. Still, it's worthwhile to destroy its arms because it reduces the amount of damage the Boss can cause to your party each turn.

Use special attacks that target all parts of the Boss, such as Sabin's **Fire Dance**. Powerful magic, for example **Bolt**, works especially well. If Cyan is in your party, use his **Retort SwordTech** to inflict extra damage.

Cranes

Kefka's Cranes are deceptively tough. Whatever you do, avoid casting a **Bolt** spell on the left crane or a **Fire** spell on the right crane. Doing so only powers them up. When a Crane powers up to level three, it casts a powerful spell on your entire party. The Cranes also use other types of powerful magic, and will occasionally power up each other.

Have one or two characters act as medics by casting **Cure** or **Cure 2** on the party. Fortunately, you now have Setzer's aid. Use his **Slot** command to attack the enemy. His most common combination, **Three Diamonds**, attacks the enemies with the **Flash** attack. This attack causes around 400 points of damage to each Crane. You can also cast **Fire** on the left crane and **Bolt** on the right crane. The Level 2 Bolt and Fire spells can cause as much as 1000 points of damage.

Enemies
None
Items
None

ESPER WORLD

Checklist

☐ *Return to Zozo with the Espers (automatic)*

☐ *As Maduin, find Madonna and take her back to the Elder's home*

☐ *Speak with Madonna*

☐ *Head past the point where Maduin found Madonna, and find Madonna again*

☐ *Speak with the Elder*

☐ *Attempt to leave the Elder's home and speak with the Espers*

☐ *Follow Madonna toward the gate and speak with her*

☐ *Fly the Airship northeast to Narshe*

Switching Up

Now that everyone is back together, you can change your party around if you like. To change your party, simply speak with any one of your characters inside the ship. Remember to take the time to equip Setzer and Terra properly.

Before Heading to Narshe

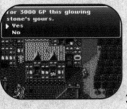

There are a few things that you can do now that you have an airship at your disposal. First, you should revisit the town of Tzen. In the northeast corner of town, there's a thief hiding in the woods. Talk to him, and you can purchase a Magicite crystal, **Sraphim**, that he stole from the Magitek Research Facility after your assault. The price is a little steep (3000 GP), but well worth it. If you want, you can hold off until later in the game and get the same piece of Magicite for 30 GP, but that opportunity is a long way off.

You can return to Mobliz and assist the wounded soldier a second time by sending a letter to his love in Maranda.

The auction house in Jidoor is open for business. Stop by and check out some of the auctions. You can actually win a couple of Espers at the auction[md]if you're willing to pay the price. Come back here regularly.

Figaro Castle now has a new Tool for sale, the **Drill**. It isn't cheap, but you should definitely pick one up. Just make sure that Edgar is leading your party so you can get the Drill for half price.

Enemies
None
Items
None

*Maps on page 136

NARSHE

Checklist

☐ *Enter Narshe and follow the guard to the Elder's house*

☐ *Board the airship and head for the Imperial Base on the southern continent*

(Optional)

☐ *Go to the treasure house and find Lone Wolf*

☐ *Chase Lone Wolf through the mines*

☐ *Choose to save either Mog or obtain the Gold Hairpin*

Inn

Item	Cost
Rest	200

Weapon Shop

Item	Cost
Poison Rod	1500
Trident	1700
Boomerang	4500
Morning Star	5000
Hawk Eye	6000
Blossom	3200

Armor Shop

Item	Cost
Gold Shield	2500
Bard's Hat	3000
Green Beret	3000
Mythril Helm	2000
Tiara	3000
Gold Helmet	4000
Mythril Mail	3500
Power Sash	5000

Relic Shop			Item Shop		
Item	**Cost**		**Item**	**Cost**	
Earrings	5000		Potion	300	
Sniper Sight	3000		Tincture	1500	
Running Shoes	7000		Phoenix Down	500	
Wall Ring	6000		Green Cherry	150	
Black Belt	5000		Tent	1200	
			Fire Skean	500	
			Water Edge	500	
			Bolt Edge	500	

Lone Wolf, the Pickpocket

Remember that chest you couldn't open earlier? Return to the treasure house and check on it. Upon doing so, you'll find Lone Wolf, the guy who was locked up in Figaro Castle's prison, busy tinkering with the locked chest. He'll run away with the treasure, but all is not lost.

Chase the thief through Narshe toward the mines. Inside the mines, take the first right and follow the path until you catch up with Lone Wolf. Now you must make a choice. You can either save the treasure, a **Gold Hairpin**, or you can save Mog. Gold Hairpins are *very, very* rare, but Mog will join your party if you save him. The choice is yours, but who could stomach letting a little fuzzy guy like Mog fall off a cliff?

If you choose Mog, you can find another Gold Hairpin later in the game. If you take the item, you'll find Mog later in the game as well. However, you'll benefit more from having Mog now than you will the Gold Hairpin.

Restocked

Due to the impending war, most of Narshe's shops have received some powerful new items. Check out every store, and take along lots of GP!

Enemies
- Lich
- Apparite
- Zombone
- Ing
- Ninja
- Kefka

Items
1. Assassin
2. Tempest
3. Coin Toss
4. X-Potion
5. Ether
6. Genji Glove
7. Tent
8. Ether
9. Elixir
10. Magicite
11. Ether
12. Atma Weapon
13. Magicite
14. Magicite

CAVE TO THE SEALED GATE

Checklist

☐ **Land outside the Imperial Base**

☐ **Walk through the Imperial Base and continue on to the cave beyond it**

☐ **Make your way through the cave to the sealed Esper Gate**

☐ **Use the "emergency exit" to leave the cave, and return to the airship**

☐ **Walk to the town of Vector**

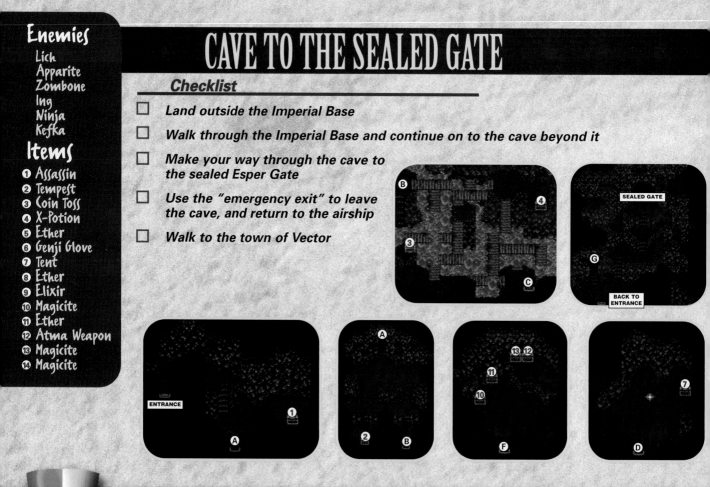

Map labels (top map):

OPENS "D"   NINJA DROP
D
CREATES STAIRS
E
SWITCH 1
6 1
C
5

Map labels (bottom map):

14
E
MOVES ISLAND
MOVES ISLAND
STAIRS
CREATES STAIRS
G
9
F
OPENS "F"
8

Basement 2

This area has a wooden path that constantly switches between two patterns. Before going anywhere, sit for a moment and compare the two paths. You must cross one path and be prepared to hop to the next when the paths switch. If you're not ready to hop onto the next path, your party will fall into the lava below, which causes some damage and throws them back to the left shore. This sounds and looks more complicated than it actually is.

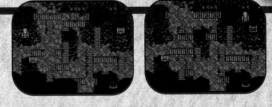

Basement 3

Now you must deal with a bunch of switches and alternating landscape. There's a lot of treasure in this area; however, the problem is figuring out how to get to it all. Check the map for help in deciphering which switch leads to each treasure.

You must be careful, though, because the monsters in this area are powerful. There's also a hidden **Save Point** just in case you need to save and rest.

Stranded

As the party flies off, several Espers cause the Airship to crash. Your next stop should be Vector, but it's a long walk from the crash site. Search the woods northwest of the crash site to find a **Chocobo Stable** if you don't feel like fighting your way to Vector.

Enemies

Commando
Mega Armor
Special Forces

Items

① Gale Hairpin
② Revivify
③ Tincture
④ Back Guard
⑤ Potion

⑤ Soldiers

IMPERIAL PALACE

Checklist

☐ Head for the Imperial Palace and speak with the Emperor's guard

☐ Follow the guard to Gestahl's throne room

☐ Search the Palace and talk to as many Imperial Soldiers as possible in four minutes

☐ Join Gestahl and Cid for the banquet

☐ Answer Gestahl's questions

☐ Battle the Special Forces, and then continue to the banquet

☐ Get information on your reward from Gestahl's trooper

☐ Go to the Albrook's port and speak with General Leo

☐ Spend the night at the Inn

☐ Return to the dock and set sail with General Leo

(Optional)

☐ Return to the Imperial Base and collect your reward

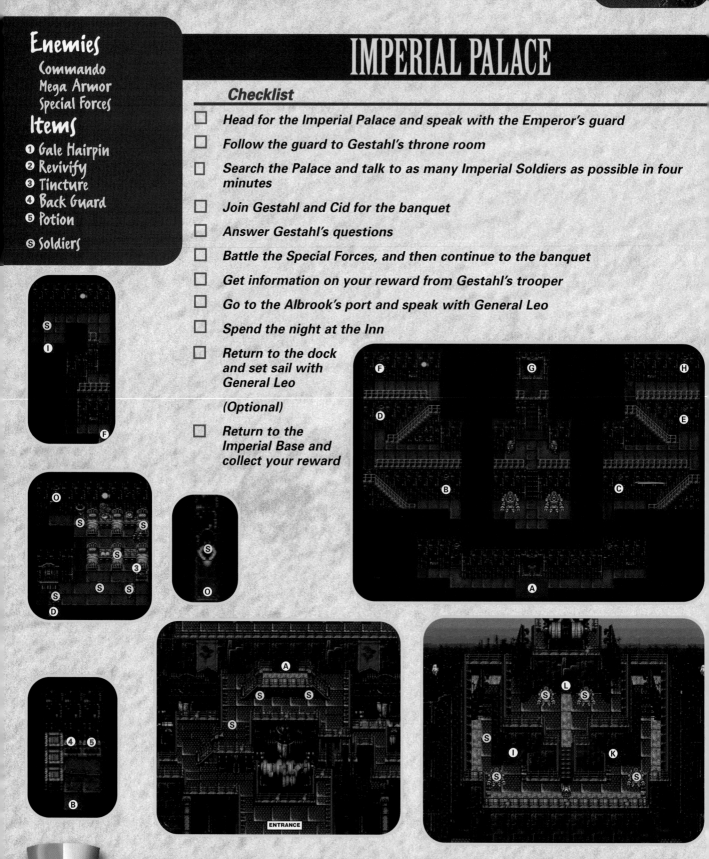

Vector in Flames

What's this? The town is full of Returners, nearly everything is on fire, and there are no Imperials anywhere. Although the town is in chaos, you can still shop and the woman who healed you before is still willing to lend you a helping hand. When you're finished, head for the Imperial Palace.

The Banquet

Please, before we dine, talk to as many soldiers as you can! Make them understand!

Gestahl asks you to join him for a banquet, and to help him make his soldiers understand. You have four minutes to talk to every soldier you can find. Some soldiers are easily swayed, while others will challenge you to battles.

Avoid visiting the jail cell, because you'll run into Kefka and lose approximately twenty seconds. It's best to keep moving, and end every battle as quickly as possible. The total number of soldiers you sway will be added to your score at the end of the banquet.

GESTAHL: I truly apologize about the poisoning of Doma. No one dreamed Kefka would use poison.

At the end of four minutes, you'll get taken to the banquet room and the feast will begin. During the banquet, Gestahl will ask you many questions. Follow the answers listed below to receive the highest score possible. Also note that when you take a break, you should talk to Gestahl's soldiers, who challenge you to a battle. Once the battle ends, return to the banquet room to continue the discussion.

The Toast

Answer	Score
To the Empire.	2 Points
To the Returners.	1 Point
To our hometowns.	5 Points

Kefka's Fate

Answer	Score
Leave him in jail.	5 Points
Pardon him.	1 Point
Execute him.	3 Points

Apology for Doma

Answer	Score
What's done is done.	1 Point
That was inexcusable.	5 Points
Apologize again!!	3 Points

General Celes

Answer	Score
Was she an Imperial spy?	1 Point
Celes is one of us!	5 Points
We trust Celes!	3 Points

Further Questions

Answer	Score
Ask a question once.	2 Points Each
Repeat any question.	- 10 Points Each

The Espers

Answer	Score
Yes, the Espers have gone too far.	5 Points
But you unleashed their power!!	2 Points

Your First Question

Answer	Score
Answer Correctly.	5 Points
Answer Wrong.	0 Points

Care for Rest?

Answer	Score
Take a rest.	5 Points
Keep talking.	0 Points

What to say?

Answer	Score
That all you really want is peace.	3 Points
That your war's truly over.	5 Points
That you're sorry...	1 Point

Will you accompany Gestahl?

Answer	Score
Yes	3 Points
No	0 Points

Gestahl's Generosity

When the banquet ends, you'll get stopped by Gestahl's trooper and the party will be rewarded. What you receive depends upon your final score:

Imperial troops have withdrawn from South Figaro.

Total Score	Gestahl's Actions
0-39 Points	South Figaro is liberated
40-49 Points	South Figaro and Doma are liberated
50-59 Points	South Figaro and Doma are liberated, and the Imperial Base's stock room is unlocked
60-69 Points	South Figaro and Doma are liberated, the Imperial Base's stock room is unlocked, and the party receives a Tintinabar
70+ Points	South Figaro and Doma are liberated, the Imperial Base's stock room is unlocked, and the party receives a Tintinabar and a Charm Bangle

Before Heading to Albrook

If Gestahl opens the Imperial Base's supply room for you, go there before you go to Albrook. There are a lot of rare items and GP waiting for you.

Also, don't forget about South Figaro and Doma Castle. You can't go there right now, but later you can get items from both places that you might have earlier missed.

Enemies
Balloon
Flame Eater (Boss)

Items
1. Eyedrop
2. Phoenix Down
3. Green Cherry
4. Soft
5. Echo Screen
6. Fire Rod
7. Ice Rod

Item Shop
Item	Cost
Tonic	50
Potion	300
Tincture	1500
Remedy	1000
Warp Stone	700
Revivify	300
Phoenix Down	500
Tent	1200

Relic Shop
Item	Cost
Earrings	5000
Sniper Sight	3000
Running Shoes	7000
Wall Ring	6000
Black Belt	5000
Dragoon Boots	9000
Sprint Shoes	1500

Inn
Item	Cost
Rest	1500/1

Weapon Shop
Item	Cost
Mythril Rod	500
Fire Rod	3000
Ice Rod	3000
Thunder Rod	3000
Morning Star	5000
Hawk Eye	6000
Stout Spear	10,000
Darts	10,000

THAMASA

Checklist

- ☐ Equip your party and travel northeast to Thamasa
- ☐ Explore the town and observe Thamasa's citizens
- ☐ Meet Strago and Relm
- ☐ Spend the night at the Inn
- ☐ Go to the house in flames and speak with Strago
- ☐ Fight your way through the fire to the Boss, Flame Eater
- ☐ Defeat Flame Eater and save Relm
- ☐ Head for the Espers' Gathering Place set in a cave in the mountains west of Thamasa

Armor Shop
Item	Cost
Gold Shield	2500
Tiger Mask	2500
Tiara	3000
Gold Helmet	4000
Mystery Veil	5500
Power Sash	5000
Gaia Gear	6000
Gold Armor	10,000

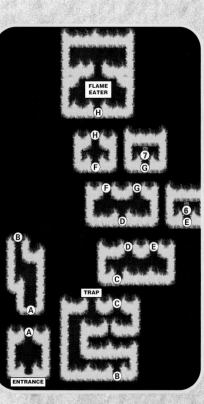

187

What's Going On?

After exploring the town, you'll quickly discover the citizens have a secret. A secret they're not about to divulge to outsiders like Terra, Locke, and Shadow. When you've finished exploring, find Strago to learn a bit more about this mysterious town. Then go to the Inn, where you'll find that the innkeeper has lowered his price from 1500 GP to a measly 1 GP. I guess at 1500 a night for visitors, this guy can afford such a ridiculously low price once in a while!

Fire!

In the middle of the night, you'll awake to the sounds of a panicked Strago. As you follow him into the town, you'll discover that the little boy who likes to play with fire may have had a bit too much success with his spell. The party must rush inside to rescue Relm.

You'll see lots of small flames dancing on the floors inside the building. If you get too close to a flame, you'll fight Balloons. If this occurs, make sure you equip Ice weapons (if you have them), such as the **Ice Rod**, which Strago wields well. You should also equip **Shiva**, the Ice Esper, and be prepared to use lots of Ice magic. Flames are very susceptible to Ice attacks. By the way, don't forget that Strago is new to your party and could use some refitting, such as Relics and an Esper.

Flame Eater

When you reach the back of the house, you'll face Flame Eater. This is a tough Boss because of its strong Fire attacks. Keep up each party member's HP, and unload on the Boss with Ice magic. Summon **Shiva** to battle (if she's equipped), and she'll put the hurt on Flame Eater.

Strago's skill is called **Lore,** a type of magic learned from enemies in battle. He joins you with a Lore spell known as **Aqua Rake**, which just happens to work really well against Flame Eater. Use this attack any time the Boss calls for Balloon reinforcements.

Also, watch for Flame Eater to cast **Reflect** on itself. When this occurs, stop casting magic on the Boss; if not, the magic will get reflected back at your party. You can counter this by casting **Reflect** on your own party, and then bouncing Ice spells off your characters and onto the Boss.

Enemies

Slurm
Admancht
Abolisher
Mandrake
Insecare

Items

❶ Heal Rod
❷ X-Potion
❸ Chocobo Suit
❹ Tabby Suit

ESPERS' GATHERING PLACE

Checklist

☐ **Enter the cave and find your way to the "Statues"**

☐ **Battle Ultros (Boss)**

☐ **Meet the Espers**

☐ **Board the Airship**

Ultros

Once again, you must battle the octopus king. This battle is actually easier than the battle at the Opera House. Use **Fire 2** or **Fire** if that's all you have. This should quickly deplete Ultros' health.

Near the end of the battle, Relm will appear. Use her **Sketch** skill to draw a picture of Ultros, which attacks the angry octopus. When she uses this ability successfully, which may take a while, the battle automatically ends.

The Three Holes

There are three holes in the floor just past the "Statues." The hole closest to the stairs leads to the Espers, while the other two holes lead to valuable treasures. You should get the treasures before going to the Espers.

Before You Head Off to the Floating Continent...

When all is said and done, you'll end up in the Airship with the option to lift off or to find the Floating Continent. Before rushing off, you should collect your rewards from the banquet. There may be treasure at Doma Castle and South Figaro if you missed it earlier. Also, revisit the auction house in Jidoor and attempt to get the **Zone Seek** and **Golem** Espers, if you haven't already.

Enemies

Sky Armor
Spit Fire
Ultros (Boss)
Chupon (Boss)
Air Force (Laser Gun &
Missile Bay & Speck;
Boss)
Dragon
Brainpan
Misfit
Apokryphos
Gigantos (Boss)
Behemoth
Ninja
Wirey Dragon
Atma Weapon (Boss)
Naughty
Nerapa

Items

- Murasame
- Monster-in-a-Box
- Beret
- Elixir

FLOATING CONTINENT

Checklist

☐ **Go to the Airship's deck and choose to "Find the Floating Continent"**

☐ **Battle the Imperial airforce until Ultros arrives**

☐ **Defeat Ultros and Chupon**

☐ **Destroy the Air Force**

☐ **Land on the Floating Continent and save your game**

☐ **Find your way across the landscape to Atma Weapon**

☐ **Defeat Atma Weapon and then confront Kefka and Gestahl**

☐ **Run to the edge of the continent and wait for Shadow**

☐ **If time is under five seconds, proceed without Shadow**

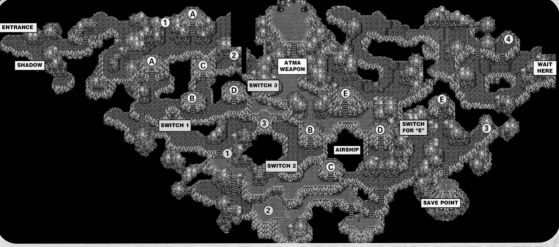

189

Air Assault

As the party heads for the Floating Continent, they are attacked by the entire Imperial Air Force. You must fight a seemingly never-ending assault of Sky Armors and Spit Fires until Ultros shows up. The battles aren't difficult, but you'll want to heal between them to save time in battle.

Also, if you switched around your party before the battles, you'll need to equip everyone who's new after the first battle.

Eventually, one of your characters will notice something strange headed your way. Check the back of the ship to find Ultros. Approach Ultros to initiate a battle.

Ultros & Chupon

Ultros still isn't very tough, but the crafty octopus has brought along a friend, Chupon. After landing a few good hits against Ultros, Chupon will join the battle. Focus your attacks on Chupon or use attacks that hit both enemies. Chupon uses strong magic, so prepare to heal everyone. Throw a couple of powerful Level 2 spells at Chupon as well. The battle ends when Chupon blows your party off the Airship.

Air Force

As your party falls through the sky, they're attacked by Air Force, the ultimate Imperial flying machine. This Boss has three parts: the main body, a Laser Gun, and a Missile Launcher. You can target each part of this Boss, and you can destroy the Laser Gun and Missile Launcher separately from the main body. However, doing so will only cause the Boss to launch a Speck, which can absorb any magic cast during the battle no matter who it's targeted toward. Specks aren't tough enemies, and you can easily eliminate them if Air Force launches one. Just do it quickly, because you must rely upon **Potions** and **Tonics** for healing while the Speck is present.

Cast Level 2 spells at all parts of Air Force. This causes damage to the main body and to its other parts. After eliminating the parts, quickly eliminate any Specks the Boss launches by using physical attacks. You can then finish off the Boss with powerful **Bolt** and **Fire** spells. Don't worry about your MP; you'll have a chance to rest as soon as you reach the Floating Continent.

Arriving at the Floating Continent

When you reach the Floating Continent, you should immediately rest to restore your party from the previous battles. Also, save your game now while you can.

Near the Save Point, you'll spot a man on the ground. After talking to the man, you discover that it's Shadow. He decides to join your group and give you a little extra firepower.

Shifting Landscape

A lot of the paths in this area won't open up until your party is right on top of them. Check the map for help in finding these hidden paths. Also, you need to use "teleporters" to get around. You'll also find these locations on the maps.

Gigantos

In one treasure chest you'll encounter a monster-in-a-box, however, this is no ordinary monster. Gigantos is perhaps the most powerful creature you've fought thus far. It has rapid, powerful attacks that can wipe out a party in just a few turns. What can you do?

This is by far my favorite strategy, but it isn't the only one as it relies on Cyan's presence. Begin the battle by casting **Vanish** on your party members, especially Cyan. While your characters are protected by Vanish, Gigantos can't hurt them because it doesn't use magic. Have Cyan charge his SwordTech to Level 4, **Quadra Slam**. Cyan will attack the giant four times, but the Vanish spell won't be broken. This way, Cyan can stay under cover the entire fight without becoming vulnerable to Gigantos' attacks and can single-handedly eliminate the enemy. If you don't have Cyan, you can use a similar strategy, or have one character attack while another continues to use Vanish on him/her.

Back to the Ship

If things are just too hot for your party, or you're running out of supplies, you can escape this area. Just before Atma Weapon, you'll see the Airship floating below the island. You can choose to leap onto the Airship if you like, but keep in mind that you must return later and start back at the beginning. Still, this isn't a bad idea if this area is just too tough for you at this point.

Atma Weapon

Atma Weapon uses extremely powerful magic to wear down your party, and in this case you can't reflect it back at the Boss. Instead, you must devote a couple of characters to healing your party with **Cure 2**, while the other party members attack. There's a lot of variety to the magic Atma Weapon uses, but you can count on most of its spells causing somewhere between 200-600 points of damage.

On each turn, have your two healers cast Cure 2 on the entire party whether or not they need it. This will quickly drain their MP, so it helps if they have the **Osmose** spell, which takes MP from the Boss and gives it to the spellcaster.

This also drains Atma Weapon's MP, which severely limits its attacks. But with 5000 MP, it takes a long time to completely drain it. Just keep your two powerhouse characters focused on attacking with their special skills each turn, and you'll be surprised at how quickly Atma Weapon falls.

Run for Your Life

There isn't a lot of ground to cover between the statues and the Airship, but you don't have much time. Quickly equip Celes, and run along the path to the Airship. You'll face a lot of enemies along the way, so use physical attacks, especially special skills like Sabin's or Cyan's.

As you go down the stairs near the end, make sure that you go around the long way! At the very edge, you'll have the option of jumping to the Airship or waiting for Shadow. Wait! If you leave Shadow behind, you'll never see him again. Only go on without him if there's less than five seconds and he's still not there, or you can reload your game prior to Atma Weapon and try to get to the Airship faster next time.

Enemies
Peepers
Black Dragon
Earth Guard

Items
None

CASTAWAYS

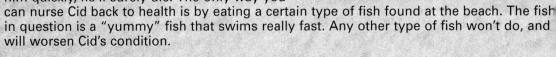

Checklist

- [ ] **Go to the beach and catch fish for Cid**
- [ ] **Get Cid's raft and leave the island**
- [ ] **Once on shore, go west to Albrook**

CATCH FISH

RAFT

Cid's Peril

Cid is in bad shape and if Celes doesn't help him quickly, he'll surely die. The only way you can nurse Cid back to health is by eating a certain type of fish found at the beach. The fish in question is a "yummy" fish that swims really fast. Any other type of fish won't do, and will worsen Cid's condition.

To fish, run Celes to the beach and go as far into the water as possible. When the super fast fish swims by, press the ⊗ button to catch it. Make sure you grab the correct fish by checking your item inventory under "Rare" items. If it doesn't describe the fish as "yummy," you didn't get the right one. You can also keep him alive by feeding him the medium speed fish, but this won't keep him alive for long.

If you go to the beach and there aren't any "yummy" fish, you can go back and speak to Cid. This will reset the fish in the water, however, Cid's condition will worsen a bit each time you do so. Still, this is better than accidentally feeding him a rotten fish.

If you save Cid, he'll tell you about the raft and send you on your way to find your friends. If Cid dies, Celes will eventually find a note from Cid telling her about the raft and instructing her to use it.

ALBROOK

Enemies
Chitonid
Peepers
Gilmantis
Mesosaur
Black Dragon
Earth Guard
Osprey
Lunaris
Giga Toad

Items
None

Checklist

- [ ] **Talk to everyone and learn about the "new" world**
- [ ] **Leave town and head north to Tzen**

Weapon Shop

Item	Cost
Flame Sabre	7000
Blizzard	7000
Thunder Blade	7000

Item Shop

Item	Cost
Potion	300
Tincture	1500
Phoenix Down	500
Revivify	300
Remedy	1000
Sleeping Bag	500
Smoke Bomb	300
Warp Stone	700

Inn

Item	Cost
Rest	300

Armor Shop

Item	Cost
Gold Shield	2500
Bard's Hat	3000
Green Beret	3000
Gold Helmet	4000
Gold Armor	10,000

Relic Shop

Item	Cost
Sprint Shoes	1500
Atlas Armlet	5000
Earrings	5000
Barrier Ring	500
Mythril Glove	700
True Knight	1000
Wall Ring	6000
Jewel Ring	1000

Talk to the Locals

First, you need some information. Talk to everyone in town to learn a lot about the state of the world. Kefka's located in a large tower north of Albrook, and exacts vengeance on anyone who opposes him with something called the "Light of Judgement."

You'll also hear about some legendary monsters that have been unleashed on the world. The most notable comment is about something called "Crusader" and the eight dragons that guard it.

Also, there's a painter who sold a portrait of Emperor Gestahl to a man named Owzer in Jidoor. Lastly, and most importantly, you'll learn that someone like Celes was here recently looking for friends. Who can it be? A woman tells you that he headed north to Tzen, so Tzen is your next destination.

Enemies

Hermit Crab
Pm Stalker
Scorpion

Items

Heal Rod ((Chest in collapsing house)
Pearl Rod ((Chest in collapsing house)
Tincture ((Chest in collapsing house)
Hyper Wrist ((Chest in collapsing house)
Magicite ((Chest in collapsing house)
Drainer ((Chest in collapsing house)

TZEN

Checklist

- ☐ **Upon arriving rush to the back of town and find Sabin**
- ☐ **Enter the collapsing house**
- ☐ **Find the child**
- ☐ **Quickly exit the house**
- ☐ **Equip Sabin and head east to Mobliz**

Inn

Item	Cost
Rest	350

Weapon Shop

Item	Cost
Kaiser	1000
Poison Claw	2500
Flame Sabre	7000
Blizzard	7000
Thunder Blade	7000
Fire Knuckle	10,000

Armor Shop

Item	Cost
Gold Shield	2500
Beret	3500
Tiger Mask	2500
Gold Helmet	4000
Power Sash	5000
Gold Armor	10,000

Item Shop

Item	Cost
Potion	300
Tincture	1500
Green Cherry	150
Phoenix Down	500
Echo Screen	120
Revivify	300
Sleeping Bag	500
Super Ball	10,000

Relic Shop

Item	Cost
Dragoon Boots	9000
Sneak Ring	3000
Black Belt	5000
Back Guard	7000
Sniper Sight	3000
Peace Ring	3000
Jewel Ring	1000
Amulet	5000

Collapsing House

You only have six minutes to get in and out before the house collapses. Before you go, make sure Celes is equipped with a relic that protects against the Stone status. **Ribbon** is the best choice, but a **Jewel Ring** also works. If you don't, Celes might get turned to stone, which would mean game over!

Once inside, collect the treasures, but don't waste any time. During battles, use Level 2 spells or run from battle, because you don't have time to fight every monster. There are two chests full of monsters. Try to avoid opening them. When you find the child, get out fast.

Sraphim Esper

Did you get the **Sraphim Esper** earlier? If not, go to the right side of town and look for any movement in the woods. Talk to the hidden thief, and he'll sell you the Sraphim Esper for 10 GP. That's quite a discount from his earlier asking price of 3000 GP.

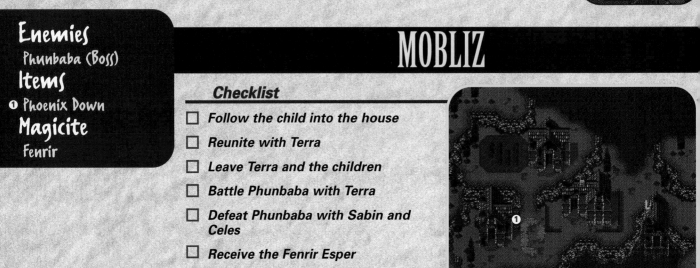

Enemies
Phunbaba (Boss)
Items
❶ Phoenix Down
Magicite
Fenrir

MOBLIZ

Checklist

☐ *Follow the child into the house*

☐ *Reunite with Terra*

☐ *Leave Terra and the children*

☐ *Battle Phunbaba with Terra*

☐ *Defeat Phunbaba with Sabin and Celes*

☐ *Receive the Fenrir Esper*

☐ *Leave Terra behind and follow the Serpent Trench to Nikeah*

Phunbaba

Terra *cannot* defeat Phunbaba on her own. Her defeat is inevitable, so don't think that you're doing something wrong. If you haven't used Sabin and Celes much yet, you might have a tough time with this fight. In fact, you may want to spend some time fighting enemies outside the village to boost Sabin and Celes' levels, and to teach them some basic spells like **Cure 2** and **Life**.

You need to keep the party's HP over 1,000 while Sabin uses **Blitz** techniques to chase Phunbaba away. During the battle, Celes can use her **Runic** skill to absorb Phunbaba's powerful magical attacks. If you do so, Sabin will need the **Cure 2** ability. Otherwise, Celes will need to act as a medic when Phunbaba uses one of its powerful physical attacks.

It's best that both Celes and Sabin have the ability to cast Cure 2.

On Your Way Out

You'll automatically get the Fenrir Esper as you leave Terra. However, Celes and Sabin are bound to need rest after the battle. Go to the Relic Shop at the back of town, and use the bed there.

No Need to Walk

There's a hidden **Chocobo Stable** in the forest south of Mobliz. For 100 GP, you can ride in comfort to the town of Nikeah instead of battling enemies every few feet. Nikeah is at the end of the Serpent Trench, and it's a very long walk. The choice is yours.

NIKEAH

Enemies
Bloompyer
Delta Bug
Lizard
Buffalax
Items
None

Enemies
Bloompyer
Delta Bug
Lizard
Buffalax
Items
None

Checklist

- [ ] **Go to the Pub and speak with the thieves**
- [ ] **Find Gerad near the Armor Shop and talk to him**
- [ ] **Pursue Gerad back to the dock**

Inn

Item	Cost
Rest	150

Chocobo Stable

Item	Cost
Ride	80

Item Shop

Item	Cost
Potion	300
Tincture	1500
Soft	200
Phoenix Down	500
Revivify	300
Remedy	1000
Sleeping Bag	500
Tent	1200

Weapon Shop

Item	Cost
Rune Edge	7500
Flame Sabre	7000
Blizzard	7000
Thunder Blade	7000
Enhancer	10,000

Armor Shop

Item	Cost
Diamond Shield	3500
Bard's Hat	3000
Green Beret	3000
Diamond Helm	8000
Gaia Gear	6000
Power Sash	5000
Diamond Vest	12,000

Relic Shop

Item	Cost
White Cape	5000
Cure Ring	8000
Zephyr Cape	7000
Gale Hairpin	8000
Hyper Wrist	8000
Beads	4000
Amulet	5000
Czarina Ring	3000

Spotting Gerad

Gerad blends in pretty well with the background. You'll find him "hiding" behind the merchandise to the left of the Armor Shop.

Bring Lots of GP

The stores in Nikeah have lots to offer, but they aren't cheap. You should stock up on the latest in protective wear—**Diamond Vests**, however, it will cost you 48,000 GP for four vests! Add on **Diamond Helms** and **Diamond Shields,** and you're looking at a lot of GP. Of course, if you really want to splurge, hold off until you get to South Figaro and go for Diamond Armor instead of Diamond Vests.

you're obligated to buy from me, now!

SOUTH FIGARO

Enemies
Nohrabbit
Sand Horse
Maliga
Latimeria
Items
None

Enemies
Nohrabbit
Sand Horse
Maliga
Latimeria
Items
None

Checklist

- [ ] **Track Gerad to the Inn and talk to him**
- [ ] **Follow Gerad and friends to the cave west of South Figaro**

Inn

Item	Cost
Rest	80

Chocobo Stable

Item	Cost
Ride	80

Relic Shop

Item	Cost
Goggles	500
Star Pendant	500
Fairy Ring	1500
Amulet	5000
Running Shoes	7000
Wall Ring	6000
Cure Ring	8000
Czarina Ring	3000

Weapon Shop

Item	Cost
Trident	1700
Stout Spear	10,000
Enhancer	10,000
Gold Lance	12,000

Armor Shop

Item	Cost
Diamond Shield	3500
Bard's Hat	3000
Green Beret	3000
Diamond Helm	8000
Gaia Gear	6000
Diamond Vest	12,000
Diamond Armor	15,000

Item Shop

Item	Cost
Potion	300
Tincture	1500
Eyedrop	50
Echo Screen	120
Phoenix Down	500
Revivify	300
Remedy	1000
Tent	1200

Duncan Lives

Remember Sabin's teacher, Duncan? Speak with his wife to learn that Duncan is alive and well, meditating north of Narshe. Hmm… Perhaps this information will come in handy later.

> DUNCAN'S WIFE: No, dear! Duncan's still alive and well! He's meditating just north of Narshe.

Enemies

Neck Hunter
Cruller
Humpty
Dante

Items

None

FIGARO AREA CAVE

Checklist

- [ ] Speak with Ziegfried and then move on
- [ ] Find the recovery spring
- [ ] Follow Gerad and his thieves across the water by hopping off of the turtle's shell
- [ ] Enter Figaro Castle

Cave's Dangers

The cave isn't quite the way you remember it. Now it's packed full of undead creatures. Use Sabin's **Flame Dance** Blitz to eliminate entire groups of Humptys and Crullers in a single attack.

Also note that the recovery spring has apparently lost its power to heal the injured. By the way, it's never a good idea to travel behind a bunch of thieves. You'll quickly notice that they will clean out every chest along the way.

Enemies

Neck Hunter
Cruller
Humpty
Dante
Drop
Tentacle (Boss)

Items

1. Crystal Helm
2. Gravity Rod
3. Ether
4. X-Potion
5. Regal Crown
6. Soul Sabre

FIGARO CASTLE

Checklist

- [ ] Follow Gerad into the castle and down to the basement
- [ ] Take the middle passage to the engine room
- [ ] Talk to Gerad and battle the Boss Tentacle
- [ ] Head back upstairs and ask the old man to take the castle to Kohlingen
- [ ] Leave the castle and go west to Kohlingen

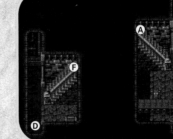

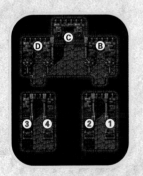

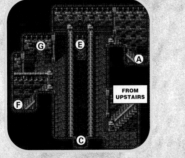

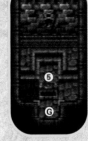

Item Shop #1

Item	Cost	Sale
Potion	300	150
Tincture	1500	750
Antidote	50	25
Eyedrop	50	25
Echo Screen	120	60
Phoenix Down	500	250
Remedy	1000	500
Tent	1200	600

Item Shop #2

Item	Cost	Sale
Auto Crossbow	250	125
Noise Blaster	500	250
Bio Blaster	750	375
Flash	1000	500
Debilitator	5000	2500
Drill	3000	1500

Tentacle

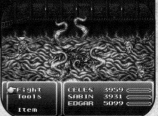

There are four Tentacles, and only three people in your party. This spells trouble. To make matters worse, the Tentacles can grab your party members and hold them captive while draining their HP.

Edgar doesn't have any Espers, so he won't know any magic unless you had him in your party earlier in the game and he's already learned some. Therefore, count on using Sabin and Celes to heal Edgar. Fortunately, he's well equipped, so he can cause lots of damage.

Start the battle by having Sabin use the **Fire Dance**. This will heal one of the Tentacles, but the rest will take damage. Then have Edgar use the **Drill** on one of the three enemies that wasn't healed by the Fire Dance. Finally, have Celes follow Edgar's lead. You can **Scan** each Tentacle and check it's weaknesses if you want, and then blast it with magic. Using this attack pattern takes out the three Tentacles, followed by the one healed by the Fire Dance.

If a Tentacle grabs a party member, have another character attack the Tentacle holding your party member. This should get the enemy to drop whoever it's holding.

Stupid Thieves

Check the treasure room after the thieves leave. Sure enough, they opened every chest, but they failed to check the statue in the middle of the room. Locke would be so proud of you right now!

New Tool

Before you leave the castle, stop in at the Item Shop (#2) and purchase Edgar's new tool, the **Debilitator**. Also, take advantage of Edgar's discount by having him in the lead when you talk to the shop owner.

KOHLINGEN

Enemies
Harpiai
Muus
Bogy
Deep Eye

Items
None

Checklist

☐ **Go to the Pub and find Setzer**

☐ **Leave town and head southwest to Darill's Tomb**

Inn

Item	Cost
Rest	200

Item Shop

Item	Cost
Potion	300
Tincture	1500
Antidote	50
Phoenix Down	500
Revivify	300
Remedy	1000
Sleeping Bag	500
Tent	1200

Armor Shop

Item	Cost
Diamond Shield	3500
Bard's Hat	3000
Green Beret	3000
Diamond Helm	8000
Diamond Vest	12,000
Diamond Armor	15,000

Weapon Shop

Item	Cost
Darts	10,000
Dice	5000
Doom Darts	13,000
Enhancer	10,000
Gold Lance	12,000

Locke's Quest

You may remember this is where Locke's true love sleeps. Visit her and speak with the man watching over her. He'll mention that Locke has gone on a quest to find the ultimate treasure. Hmm… Wonder what that is?

Find the treasure, and you'll find LOCKE!

Enemies

Orog
Osteosaur
Mad Oscar
Exoray
Power Demon
Presenter
Dullahan (Boss)

Items

1. Crystal Mail
2. Czarina Gown
3. Genji Helmet
4. Exp. Egg
5. Man Eater
6. Monster-in-a-Box

DARILL'S TOMB

Checklist

- [ ] Go down to Basement 3 and throw the door switch
- [ ] Inspect the tombstone on the right side of Basement 2
- [ ] Go through the door and throw the switch to flood the tomb
- [ ] Hop on the turtle in Basement 2 and throw the switch where you're dropped off
- [ ] Ride the nearby turtle and then save and rest
- [ ] Inspect the memorial and battle Dullahan
- [ ] Keep talking to Setzer and go get your new Airship

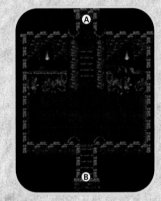

ENTRANCE

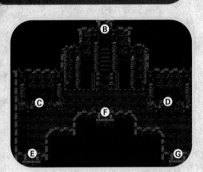

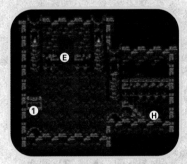

SWITCH

FLOOD SWITCH

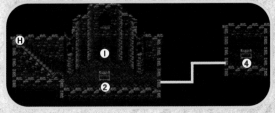

BLANK TOMBSTONE

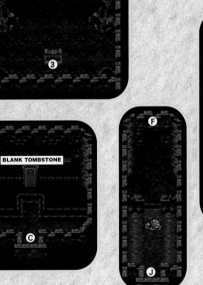

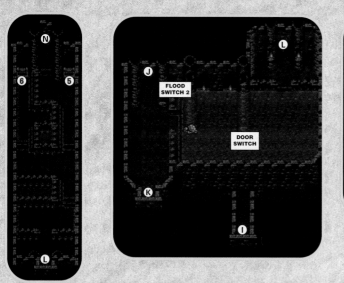

The Blank Tombstone

There's a blank tombstone in the tomb. Upon inspecting it, you're asked if you'd like to write something. Don't do it just yet. First, find a group of four tombstones. Read them all, and then return to the blank one. Write down the messages in the following order:

THEW   ORLD   ISSQ   UARE

You'll then discover how to find the rare **Experience Egg** (Exp. Egg). It's located in Basement 3 through a secret passage. You need this Relic! It doubles the amount of experience a character receives in battle.

Presenter

Just before the end of this area, you'll find a monster-in-a-box named Presenter. This isn't a tough battle. For a one-hit kill, immediately cast **Break** on the enemy and watch with glee. You receive a **Dragon Claw** for winning the fight.

Dullahan

Once again, you're faced with an enemy that uses a nonstop assault of powerful magic. However, Celes' **Runic** skill can absorb just about any spell the Boss throws at you. Of course, that doesn't mean the Boss is powerless just because Celes is in your party.

Aside from using Celes' Runic skill, you must be able to heal your party. Potions won't do the trick, so you must use **Cure 2** instead. However, avoid casting Cure 2 when Celes is waiting to catch a spell with her Rune Blade, or you'll end up transferring MP. If this occurs, have another character follow up with a second Cure 2.

Use Edgar's **Drill**, Sabin's best **Blitz**, and have Setzer do whatever he can to help. You may also want to use the new **Debilitator** you picked up at Figaro Castle so you can give the Boss an elemental weakness and use spells to put it away.

MARANDA

Checklist

☐ *Land the Airship and enter Maranda*

☐ *Go to Lola's house and speak with her*

☐ *Read the letter on Lola's desk*

☐ *Agree to mail a letter for Lola*

☐ *Attach the letter to the carrier pigeon*

☐ *Watch where the carrier pigeon flies*

☐ *Get back in the Airship and head for Zozo*

Enemies

Muus
Bogy
Deep Eye
Harpiai

Items

None

Inn

Item	Cost
Rest	200

Weapon Shop

Item	Cost
Gravity Rod	13,000
Sword Breaker	16,000
Falchion	17,000
Fire Skean	500
Water Edge	500
Bolt Edge	500
Inviz Edge	200
Shadow Edge	400

Armor Shop

Item	Cost
Crystal Shield	7000
Crystal Helm	10,000
Oath Veil	9000
Dark Gear	13,000
Tao Robe	13,000
Crystal Mail	17,000

A Strange Occurrence

LOLA: Look!
My boyfriend in Mobliz sent me
all these flowers!

When you visit Lola, you'll discover that her lover has been sending her lots of flowers and letters. But wait—Mobliz was destroyed and her lover passed away. Check the letters and you'll soon determine who the author is. Agree to Lola's request and take the letter outside and inspect the pigeon on the ground. Carefully watch the map to see where the pigeon goes. This is your next destination.

ZOZO

Checklist

☐ *Enter Zozo and inspect the carrier pigeon*

☐ *Purchase Rust-Rid from the merchant*

☐ *Enter the "Pub" and climb up to the rusted doorway*

☐ *Use the Rust-Rid on the doorway and enter to find Mt. Zozo*

Enemies

Hades Gigas
Gabledegak
Slam Dancer
Harvester

Items

Rust Rid

Rust-Rid

Rust dissolved.

After inspecting the pigeon, it will fly past the Pub. This is a hint as to where you must go. If you remember, there's a rusted door on the top floor. Looks like you need a bottle of **Rust-Rid**.

Go behind the Pub and talk to the Merchant. He'll sell you a bottle of Rust-Rid for a measly 1000 GP. It's no bargain, but you don't have a choice. Climb the stairs to the rusted door and, presto, you're in!

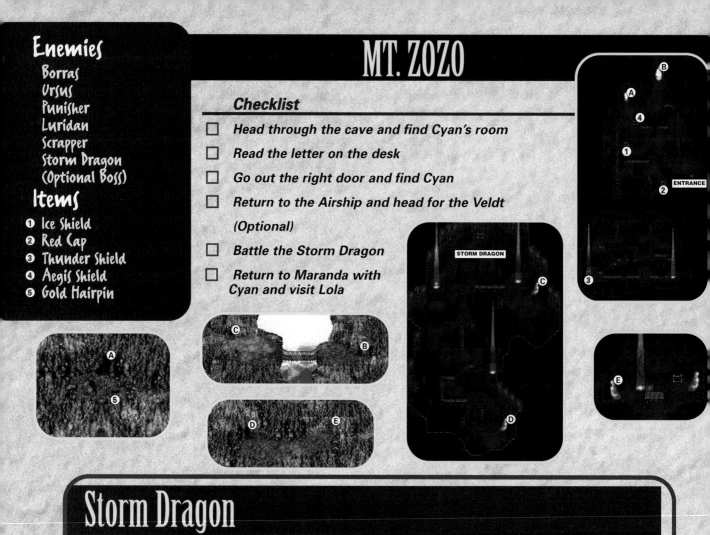

Enemies

Borras
Ursus
Punisher
Luridan
Scrapper
Storm Dragon
(Optional Boss)

Items

❶ Ice Shield
❷ Red Cap
❸ Thunder Shield
❹ Aegis Shield
❺ Gold Hairpin

MT. ZOZO

Checklist

- [ ] **Head through the cave and find Cyan's room**
- [ ] **Read the letter on the desk**
- [ ] **Go out the right door and find Cyan**
- [ ] **Return to the Airship and head for the Veldt (Optional)**
- [ ] **Battle the Storm Dragon**
- [ ] **Return to Maranda with Cyan and visit Lola**

Storm Dragon

There's a switch set in the ground near the Save Point. Stepping on the switch opens the chest above, which contains the **Storm Dragon**. This is one of the eight dragons you've been hearing so much about. You don't have to fight it right now; you can return later when your party is powered up more. Whatever you do, make sure you save your game and use a Tent before challenging Storm Dragon.

There's really only one safe way to fight the Storm Dragon. Have three of your characters act as healers, while the fourth character attacks the Storm Dragon with **Bolt 2**. On each turn, have your healers cast **Cure 2** on the entire party. This should keep their HP high enough that the Storm Dragon can't easily eliminate them. When their MP starts to get low (around 100), have each one take a turn using the **Osmose** magic to draw MP from Storm Dragon.

Make sure at least two characters are still healing the party, but it's even better to have your attacker take a break and become a healer while everyone refills. The Storm Dragon doesn't have an unlimited amount of MP, so when it runs out you must attack it normally. However, this should be manageable because it can no longer attack the entire party with a spell each turn.

The Locked Chest

After Cyan joins your party, return to the cliff where you found him. There you'll see a shiny blue spot on the edge. Inspect the spot to find the **key** to Cyan's treasure chest. Open the chest to find Cyan's **"Machinery Manual"** and **"Book of Secrets."** The two books do not serve a useful purpose in the game. They are only rare items, and aren't used.

Revisiting Lola

You can tie up a loose end by taking Cyan back to see Lola. Speak with her, and then have Cyan inspect the letter on the desk to make his final delivery.

202

THE VELDT

Checklist

- ☐ *Fly to the Veldt and search for Gau*
- ☐ *Head southwest to the Cave in the Veldt*

Finding Gau

Gau has returned to his original lifestyle of running with the creatures on the Veldt. To get him to rejoin your party, simply search the Veldt as you normally would when Gau uses his Leap ability. Also, make sure you only have three people in your party or Gau won't show up. He needs to be able to join your party after a battle.

Enemies

Toe Cutter
Allo Ver
Rhyos
Sr. Behemoth (Boss)

Items

1. Rage Ring
2. Monster-in-a-Box
3. Striker

CAVE IN THE VELDT

Checklist

- ☐ *Enter the cave and spot Interceptor*
- ☐ *Follow Interceptor's path*
- ☐ *Speak with the thieves*
- ☐ *Pull the wall switch to move the stones blocking the path*
- ☐ *Find either Shadow or Relm*
- ☐ *Battle the Sr. Behemoth*
- ☐ *Rush Shadow or Relm to Thamasa*

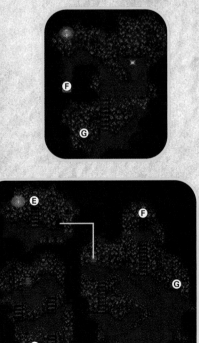

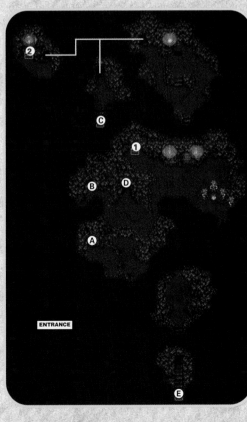

The Thieves

If Gau is already in your party, the Thieves won't have much new information for you. There is one thief who mentions a dragon in a forest to the north. Although this isn't one of the eight dragons you've been hearing about, it's worth knowing. Its name is Bracheosaur, and it lives in a forest shaped like a dinosaur head. It isn't easy to defeat, but if you do, you receive 10 Magic Points and lots of experience. The Bracheosaur will also randomly leave behind the **Economizer Relic**. This valuable relic will let a party member cast any spell at a cost of only one MP.

Shadow or Relm

Your earlier actions on the Floating Continent have a big effect on this part of the game. If you waited for Shadow and he made it off of the Floating Continent with you, then you'll find him collapsed inside the cave.

However, if Shadow didn't make it, he's gone for good. In this scenario, you'll find Relm inside the cave. If you don't find Relm here, you'll still eventually find her.

Sr. Behemoth

Although the Sr. Behemoth is tough, it's nothing compared to some of the enemies you've already fought. Use two healers to keep the party healthy, and attack with your most powerful skills. Celes can use the **Runic** ability to stop the Boss' powerful magic, but this won't cripple the Boss. It still has powerful physical attacks. Avoid using **Ice** magic; the Sr. Behemoth absorbs it, so you'll only end up healing it.

After defeating the Sr. Behemoth, the ghost of the Sr. Behemoth immediately attacks from behind the party. You can finish this battle quickly by using a **Revivify** on the dead spirit.

THAMASA

Enemies
None

Items
None

Checklist

- ☐ **Talk to Shadow**
- ☐ **Explore Thamasa**
- ☐ **Head for Doma Castle**

Inn

Item	Cost
Rest	1

Armor Shop

Item	Cost
Mystery Veil	5500
Circlet	7000
Dark Hood	7500
Light Robe	11,000
Diamond Vest	12,000

Weapon Shop

Item	Cost
DaVinci Brush	7000
Gravity Rod	13,000
Pearl Rod	12,000
Doom Darts	13,000
Gold Lance	12,000
Man Eater	11,000
Shuriken	30
Ninja Star	500

Item Shop

Item	Cost
Potion	300
Tincture	1500
Phoenix Down	500
Revivify	300
Remedy	1000
Smoke Bomb	300
Sleeping Bag	500
Tent	1200

Relic Shop

Item	Cost
Barrier Ring	500
Fairy Ring	1500
Wall Ring	6000
Jewel Ring	1000
Czarina Ring	3000
Guard Ring	5000
Peace Ring	3000
Cure Ring	8000

Shadow Rests

Because of his injuries, Shadow can't go with the team. Leave him behind for now, and explore Thamasa. One man will mention that there's a demon in Doma Castle that came to him while he was sleeping. Perhaps you should check it out.

When I would try to sleep there, demons would come for me... Oh! I don't want to remember that!

DOMA CASTLE

Checklist

- ☐ *Enter Doma Castle and find the "bedroom"*
- ☐ *Take a rest in the bedroom*
- ☐ *Find two of your three missing party members*
- ☐ *Battle the Dream Stooges*
- ☐ *Enter the last door*
- ☐ *Go through the train and solve the puzzles*
- ☐ *Shut down and exit the engine*
- ☐ *Follow Cyan through the mines*
- ☐ *Backtrack to find the bridge*
- ☐ *Go to the throne room to find Wrexsoul and Cyan*
- ☐ *Defeat Wrexsoul*
- ☐ *Get the Alexander Esper from the throne room*

Enemies

Allosaur
Parasite
Critic
Pan Dora
Parasite
Samurai
Rain Man
Barb-e
Suriander
Plute Armor
Sky Cap
Io
Larry (Boss)
Moe (Boss)
Curly (Boss)
Wrexsoul (Boss)
Soul Saver (Boss)

Items

- Remedy
- X-Potion
- Elixir
- Ether
- Phoenix Down
- Beads
- Genji Glove
- 'Lump of Metal'
- Flame Shield
- X-Potion
- Ice Shield

Magicite

Alexander

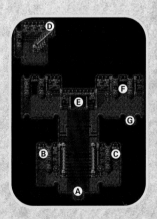

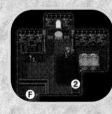

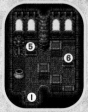

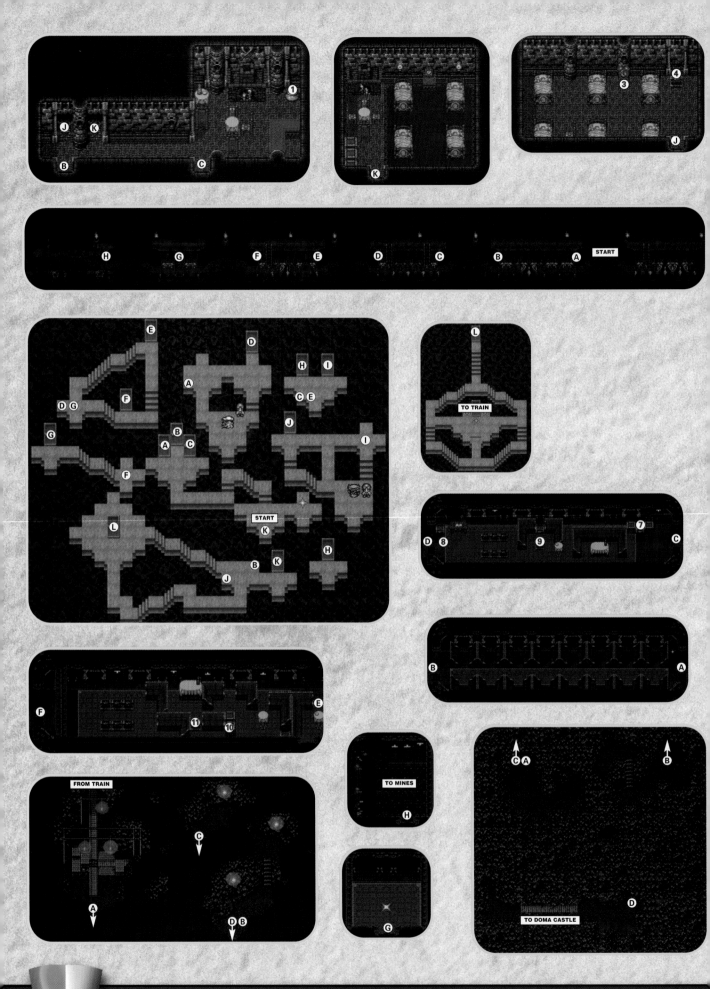

Dream World

We're the 3 Dream Stooges!

Upon first entering the dream world, one of your characters will be alone. However, off to the side you'll see one of your other characters on the ground. Your goal is to reunite three of your characters, and then search for Cyan.

Take the left door to find your first party member. Exit that area, then take the high door, and then the right door to find the next party member. Finally, exit that area and take the door to the left to find the Dream Stooges.

Dream Stooges

This man's soul is ours!

After reuniting three of your party members, you'll fight the Dream Stooges. These creatures support each other during battle, and have a powerful attack that can petrify a member of your party. If this occurs, quickly cast **Remedy** on the petrified party member.

Begin the battle by attacking Curly (the one at the top) with **Ice** magic. You should hit it first, because it has the ability to revive its partners. With Curly out of the way, none of the Dream Stooges can be revived once eliminated.

Then focus your attacks on either Larry or Moe. **Fire** works well against Larry, but avoid **Ice** and **Wind** attacks. Moe absorbs **Bolt** spells, and doesn't have a weakness to any element. However, you can cast Berserk to put an end to its magic. Without its Bolt spells, it's easy to defeat.

Chest Puzzle 1

The first puzzle is easy. Flip the wall switch twice to move the second box next to the chest.

Chest Puzzle 2

To stop the moving chest, go to the end of the car and get the **"Lump of Metal."** Now put the "Lump of Metal" in the moving chest, which weighs it down so that it can't block your path.

Chest Puzzle 3

Flip the wall switch above the six chests. Memorize which chests close, and then go to the next car. When you reach the end, close the three chests that were closed by the switch on the other set of chests, and then throw the wall switch.

Couch Puzzle

Throw the switches in the following order: RIGHT, LEFT, RIGHT, MIDDLE, RIGHT, LEFT. This should open a path on the bottom. Don't miss the two chests!

Stop the Engine

Use the right switch, and then exit the engine. This takes you to the Narshe mines.

MagiTek Puzzle

OK, so you're suited in MagiTek Armor and stuck in what looks like the Narshe Mines. Where do you go? If you continue forward, you'll get stuck in a loop. Backtrack a bit to find Cyan crossing a bridge. The bridge collapses under the weight of the MagiTek Armor, which drops you into Doma Castle.

Doma Castle

In the throne room, you'll encounter Wrexsoul, who has a hold on Cyan. At the start of the fight, Wrexsoul will possess one of your characters, leaving its cronies behind to attack the party. Ignore them. If you destroy either of the Soul Savers, they'll just regenerate.

WREXSOUL: I'm gonna possess your body!

SoulSaver	CELES	1814
	EDGAR	1711
	SABIN	1215

To make Wrexsoul reappear, you must KO the possessed character. The bad thing is, there's no indication as to which party member is possessed. So, one by one, you must KO your own characters and revive them until Wrexsoul is once again visible. After doing so, throw your most powerful **Ice** magic and any other strong attacks. You don't have long to attack, because Wrexsoul will soon possess another character.

There is a simpler way to win. After Wrexsoul has possessed a character, cast the **X-Zone** spell. This may not work at first, but if both Soul Savers are caught by X-Zone, you'll win the battle.

Great Rewards

For completing the Doma Castle event, you receive two rewards. First, Cyan becomes a true master of the sword and can now use all eight of his SwordTech skills. Second, you can pick up the **Alexander Esper** in the Doma Castle throne room.

Enemies

Nightshade
Dahling
Soul Dancer
Crusher
Wild Cat
Vindr
Still Life
Chadarnook (Boss)

Items

① Moogle Suit
② Relic Ring
③ 2000 GP
④ Potion
⑤ Ether
⑥ Remedy

Magicite

⑦ Starlet

JIDOOR

Checklist

☐ *Follow up on the lead about Emperor Gestahl's Painting and head to Jidoor*

☐ *Enter Owzer's House and attempt to enter the gallery*

☐ *Read the diary on the hall table*

☐ *Turn on the lamp at the base of the stairs*

☐ *Inspect the painting of a lady*

☐ *Enter the new door*

☐ *Enter the left moving door*

☐ *Battle the Still Life to reveal a door*

☐ *Talk to Owzer and Relm*

☐ *Defeat Chadarnook*

☐ *Get the Starlet Esper from the bookcase*

LAMP

ENTRANCE

A

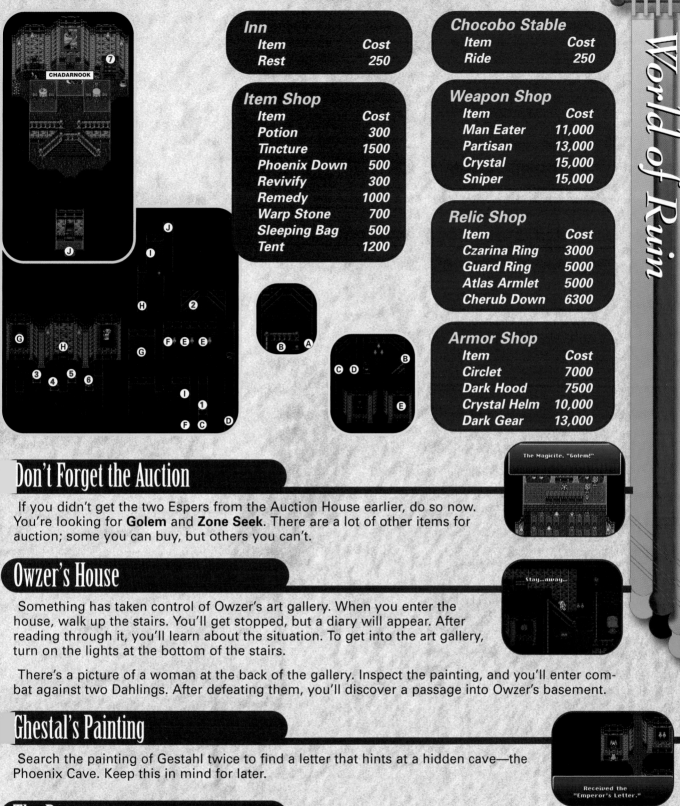

Inn

Item	Cost
Rest	250

Chocobo Stable

Item	Cost
Ride	250

Item Shop

Item	Cost
Potion	300
Tincture	1500
Phoenix Down	500
Revivify	300
Remedy	1000
Warp Stone	700
Sleeping Bag	500
Tent	1200

Weapon Shop

Item	Cost
Man Eater	11,000
Partisan	13,000
Crystal	15,000
Sniper	15,000

Relic Shop

Item	Cost
Czarina Ring	3000
Guard Ring	5000
Atlas Armlet	5000
Cherub Down	6300

Armor Shop

Item	Cost
Circlet	7000
Dark Hood	7500
Crystal Helm	10,000
Dark Gear	13,000

Don't Forget the Auction

If you didn't get the two Espers from the Auction House earlier, do so now. You're looking for **Golem** and **Zone Seek**. There are a lot of other items for auction; some you can buy, but others you can't.

The Magicite, "Golem!"

Owzer's House

Something has taken control of Owzer's art gallery. When you enter the house, walk up the stairs. You'll get stopped, but a diary will appear. After reading through it, you'll learn about the situation. To get into the art gallery, turn on the lights at the bottom of the stairs.

There's a picture of a woman at the back of the gallery. Inspect the painting, and you'll enter combat against two Dahlings. After defeating them, you'll discover a passage into Owzer's basement.

Stay...away...

Ghestal's Painting

Search the painting of Gestahl twice to find a letter that hints at a hidden cave—the Phoenix Cave. Keep this in mind for later.

Received the "Emperor's Letter."

The Basement

Most of the paintings in this area are possessed. You must inspect some of them to fight, but others will attack you automatically. This area loops a bit, but overall you don't have many options. Follow the maps to find Owzer.

The Floating Chests

In one room, there are several chests floating in the air. When you step under them, they'll drop. You must fight enemies, but there's an item to win. When you're done collecting, inspect the painting on the middle of the back wall. Defeat the Still Life to open a door leading to Owzer.

Chadarnook

This Boss has two forms: the demon and the goddess. Your attacks should focus more on the demon than on the goddess, because its HP is lower and it doesn't counterattack with quite as much force.

When the goddess is present, she'll attack with different abnormal status effects. If a party member is under the goddess' control, attack the affected character. When you attack the goddess, there's a good chance that she'll counterattack with an attack that acts like poison. Each time she counterattacks, the effect is added to any previous effects, so a character may lose hundreds of HP each turn.

When the demon appears, attack it full force with **Fire** magic or strong attacks. Wait to heal your party until the goddess reappears.

Starlet Esper

After the battle with Chadarnook, Owzer mentions that there's an Esper in his bookcase. Search the bookcase to the right to find **Starlet**.

Received the Magicite "Starlet."

Enemies

Magic Urn
L.10 Magic
L.20 Magic
Magic
L.40 Magic
L.50 Magic
L.60 Magic
L.70 Magic
L.80 Magic
L.90 Magic
White Dragon (Boss)
Mage Master (Boss)

Items

1. Safety Bit
2. Air Anchor
3. Genji Shield
4. Stunner
5. Force Armor
6. Gem Box

TOWER OF FANATICS

Checklist

☐ **Place Relm in your party and enter the tower**

☐ **Strago will join your party**

Waking Strago

RELM: You!! You old fool!!! You're still standing!?

With Relm in your party, getting Strago to snap out of it is easy. She'll automatically call out to him, and Strago will immediately join you. There's more to do here, but not right now.

210

RETURN TO MOBLIZ

Enemies
Phunbaba (Boss)

Items
Ether

Checklist

☐ Go to Mobliz and check in on Terra

☐ Check the house next door and follow the dog to the hidden staircase

☐ Talk with Terra

☐ Rush out of the house to confront Phunbaba

☐ Defeat Phunbaba and Terra joins

Phunbaba

As the fight begins, you'll discover that Phunbaba isn't quite so tough this time around. Attack the demon with **Bio** and **Poison** magic or any other strong attacks. Then when Phunbaba's HP gets low, it will blow away two of your characters and the battle will come to a screeching halt.

Terra joins the battle in Esper form, prepared to eliminate Phunbaba for good. Have her attack with **Bio** or **Poison** magic. In Esper form, she can cause about 5000 points of damage with each Bio attack. After the battle, Terra will join you.

Enemies
Trixter
Necro Man
Phase
Cha▮▮▮agon
Uroburos
Sea Flower
Parasoul
Aquila
Red Dragon (Boss)

Items
❶ Wing Edge
❷ Warp Stone
❸ Ribbon
❹ Dragon Horn
❺ (Locke's Treasure)
　　X-Potion
　　Phoenix Down
　　X-Ether
　　E▮▮▮▮
　　Flame Shield
　　Valiant Knife

Magicite
❾ Phoenix

PHOENIX CAVE

Checklist

☐ Find the "Mountains that form a star" near Tzen

☐ Land the Airship in the center of the star

☐ Break your party into two teams

☐ Use teamwork to get the teams through the cave

☐ Find Locke and return to Kohlingen

(Optional)

☐ Battle the Red Dragon

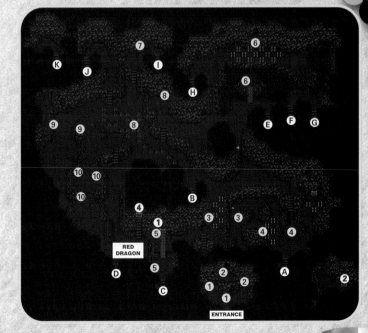

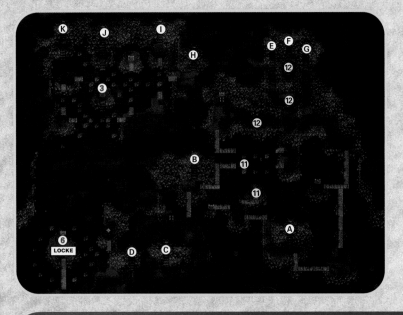

Getting Inside

You'll get a quick lesson in teamwork right at the start of this area. Have one party stand on the switch inside the door, while the other party goes through the opened door. Have the second party perform a hard right, and step on the switch above the first party. This opens the second door, letting them go inside.

Getting around the rest of the area is basically a matter of taking turns. One team flips a switch, which enables the other party to move forward.

Red Dragon

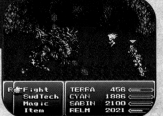

Just before this area ends, there's a side path leading to a dragon protecting a chest. This is one of the eight dragons of legend. You don't have to fight it at this time, however, this is one of the easier ones.

During battle, have the entire party cast **Ice 2** or **Ice 3** on the dragon, which will quickly deplete its energy. If Strago is in your party, use his **Aqua Rake Lore** to cause some heavy damage. Also, Terra should undergo her transformation if she's with you. In Esper form, she can cause around 6000 points of damage with a simple **Ice 2** spell. Resist using Celes' **Runic** skill. This consumes too much magic, and she'll just end up absorbing your spells.

Locke's Treasure

After finding Locke, you'll immediately get rushed back to Kohlingen, where Locke's lost love rests. After a short event, you'll receive the **Phoenix Esper** and several items that Locke found in the Phoenix Cave. Remember all of those empty chests? Locke is a true treasure hunter.

THE COLOSSEUM

Enemies
None

Items
None

Checklist

☐ **Go to the Inn and speak with the people**
☐ **Bet the Striker**
☐ **Defeat Shadow in the arena**
☐ **Shadow joins the party**

Inn	
Item	Cost
Rest	400

One Man's Dream Fulfilled

Remember the man you met earlier who mentioned one day owning a grand colosseum where legendary battles would take place? Well, his dream comes true in the World of Ruin. You'll find this testament to war in the northwest corner of the world, just north of Kohlingen.

Search for Shadow

If you talk to the men in the Inn, you'll discover that a ninja has been hang-ing around looking for an item named **Striker**. This is a weapon you should have picked up while in the Cave in the Veldt. If you don't have it, go get it. If you sold it, well, there's only one in the world, so you're in deep trouble.

If you have the Striker, talk to the man standing in the middle of the lobby. Agree to do battle and bet the Striker. You'll soon see that Shadow will be your adversary. Choose a strong character, and you shouldn't have any trouble defeating him. Shadow then joins your party when you win.

NOTE
Shadow will only join your party if you saved him on the Floating Continent and you've already found him in the Cave in the Veldt.

Fighting at the Colosseum

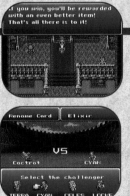

The Colosseum offers a great opportunity to win rare items through one-on-one combat. Don't get too excited, though, because it's not as easy as it sounds.

By betting an item, you have a chance to win an even better item. This isn't always the case, but most of the time it is. (You'll find a list of the items you can bet, who you'll fight, and what you can win on page 277 of this book.)

Battles in the arena are somewhat tricky. No matter how buff your character may be and despite lots of powerful spells, there's no such thing as a sure win. For this reason, it's impor-tant to save before entering the arena. You're betting some very rare items, so second chances are sometimes hard to come by.

To make battles easier, analyze your enemy and prepare for battle. For example, betting an Elixir earns you a battle against a Cactrot. Under normal circumstances, this is a tough battle. Cactrots have a high evade ability, plus they're immune to most magic. However, if you equip a character with a Genji Glove and the Sniper Sight Relic, you won't have any problems. The Sniper Sight ensures that you'll hit the enemy each time, even with its high evade ability. It also caus-es two points of damage each turn; that may not sound like much, but the Cactrot only has three HP!

Enemies

Test Rider
Nastidon
Red Wolf
Wizard
Psychot
Mag Roader
Kiwok
Ceritops
Poppers
Anemone
Tomb Thumb
Pug
Pugs
Ice Dragon (Boss)
Tritoch (Boss)
Umaro (Boss)

Items

Moogle Charm
❶ Monster-in-a-Box
❷ Gauntlet
❸ X-Ether

Magicite

Ragnarok
Tritoch
❹ Terrato

NARSHE

Checklist

- ☐ Check the door to the Weapon Shop with Locke in your party
- ☐ Talk to the Weapon Shop owner
- ☐ Choose to get either the Ragnarok Esper or Ragnarok Sword
- ☐ Go to the Moogle cave and talk to Mog
- ☐ Put Mog into your party
- ☐ Head for the cliff where Tritoch is located
- ☐ Battle Tritoch to get the Tritoch Esper
- ☐ Jump into the pit left behind after the battle
- ☐ Find Umaro's lair and inspect the bone statue
- ☐ Take the Terrato Esper
- ☐ Battle Umaro
- ☐ Talk to Umaro and get him to join your party

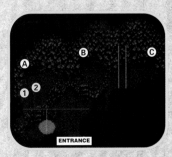

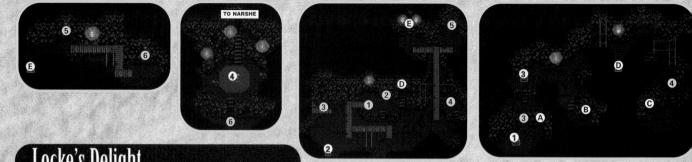

Locke's Delight

The town of Narshe is locked up tight, and hardly anyone is around. Locke is the only one in your party with the ability to unlock all of the locked doors. There's an empty house behind most of them, but the Weapon Shop is a bit different.

Speak with the Weapon Shop owner in his bedroom. He'll offer to either give you the **Ragnarok Esper** or transform the Esper into a powerful sword. The choice is yours, but remember that there are plenty of powerful weapons available and only one Ragnarok Esper!

Also, there's a house on the north side of town where you'll find a man in his bed. Speak with him and he'll give you the **Cursed Shield**. When it's worn, this shield casts several negative effects on its wearer and offers no additional defense. However, if one of your characters wears it in 250 battles, the curse will be broken and the Cursed Shield will become the **Paladin Shield**. You can counter most of the Cursed Shield's negative effects by equipping the character with a **Ribbon**.

Missing Mog

Remember where the Moogle's lair is? Head into the Narshe mines to find Mog in the Moogle's Lair. To have him join your party, simply talk to him. With Mog in your party, search where he was standing to find a rare relic, the **Moogle Charm**. This relic enables you to wander areas without randomly encountering monsters.

Mog will also mention that there's a Yeti in Narshe who would be a great asset to your party. Return to the airship and place Mog in your party. Then head for the area where you last saw the Tritoch Esper, the same area where Terra freaked out.

Ice Dragon

On the way to the Tritoch Esper, you'll find a dragon roaming the area where you earlier faced Kefka's army. This is yet another of the fabled dragons.

Equip your party with items like the **Ice Shield**, which protects against Ice magic, and you'll be nearly invulnerable. **Fire** weapons also work well. It also helps if Terra is in your party, and she knows the Phoenix's **Fire 3** spell.

Attack the Ice Dragon with constant Fire magic or weapons. If Terra morphs into her Esper and uses Fire 3, she can nearly wipe out the Ice Dragon in a single turn. Otherwise, just chip away at the dragon's health with Fire magic and it will fall in no time.

Tritoch

At the cliff, the Tritoch Esper will attack the party. This battle is similar to the one with the Ice Dragon. Just pummel the Esper with **Fire** magic, and the fight will quickly end. When the battle is won, the **Tritoch Esper** will join you and a new passage will be opened.

Umaro's Cave

After defeating the Tritoch Esper, a hole will open in the cliff, providing access to Umaro's cave. The cave is fairly small, and not too difficult to navigate. Just watch for the random holes in the floor. You must fall through some of the holes, but you must dodge others.

At the back of the cave, there's a patch of hay and a bone statue. Inspect the bone statue, and you'll discover the **Terrato Esper**. Upon taking the Esper, Umaro will appear and attack the party.

You will also encounter Pugs in this area. If they are too difficult to defeat, try the "Vanish/X-Zone" trick. This will make fighting them really easy.

Umaro

This fight is dependent upon **Fire** magic. Just immediately hit this Boss with Fire magic (especially **Fire 3**) and Umaro will soon give up. When this Boss eats a Green Cherry, it boosts Umaro's abilities to insane proportions.

TRIANGLE ISLAND

Enemies

Zone Eater
Harpy
Gloom Shell
Prussian
Tap Dancer
Covert
Wart Puck
Ogor
Karkass
Woolly

Items

1 Ether
2 Red Jacket
3 Magical Brush
4 Genji Armor
5 Fake Mustache
6 Zephyr Cape
7 Hero Ring
8 Tack Star
9 Thunder Shield

Checklist

- [ ] **Go to Triangle Island and find a Zone Eater**
- [ ] **Get eaten by the Zone Eater**
- [ ] **Cross the bridges while dodging the people on them**
- [ ] **Time your way past the smashing rock ceiling**
- [ ] **Bounce across the chests to the door on the other side**
- [ ] **Talk to Gogo**
- [ ] **Return to the entrance and step into the light to exit**

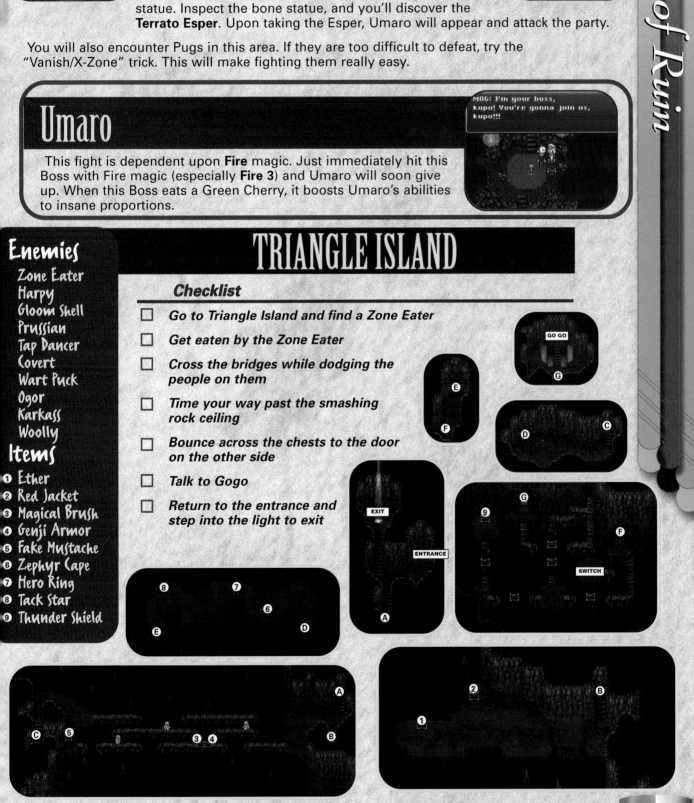

Supper for a Zone Eater

This may sound crazy, but your goal here is get everyone eaten. Zone Eaters will eat your party one by one. If you destroy the Zone Eater, the eaten party members are safely returned. However, if you allow a Zone Eater to munch on your entire party, they'll end up in the Zone Eater's belly. As nasty as that might sound, these creature's eat a lot and there's plenty to do in one's belly.

Crossing the Bridge

Some invincible people guard the bridge through Zone Eater's belly. If they touch your party, they'll knock them down to the room below. You'll want to do this once to get the items in the room below, but only once. Time your way across the bridge, and jump between the paths to avoid getting touched. Make sure you run or sprint.

Collapsing Ceiling

The room with the collapsing ceiling is very dangerous, so make sure you save before you enter. The ceiling constantly moves up and down, crushing anything that gets in its way. You must run across and make sure you stand in the few safe spots that exist. Take a peek at an area before you charge ahead to have better luck.

To get the final chest, you must pass it by and then wait until the ceiling goes up again to rush in, grab the treasure, and get out.

Chest Hopping

This puzzle is much easier than it looks. You can hop onto the open chests, causing them to launch you to the next platform. To get the treasure, you must flip the floor switch. After jumping onto the floor switch's island from the top, getting around should be a breeze.

Get Gogo

At the end of the area, you'll find Gogo. It has the ability to mimic the attacks of other characters during battle. When you select the Mimic ability in battle, Gogo will perform the same action as the last person who attacked. For example, if Sabin uses his Fire Dance Blitz just before Gogo uses the Mimic skill, Gogo will also use the Fire Dance Blitz. This is great because miming an action doesn't cost Gogo MP, and Gogo doesn't have to charge SwordTechs.

Gogo has a hidden ability to equip any type of battle commands. Go into Gogo's status screen, and select a blank space in its battle command list. A menu will appear with every command that you currently have available. You can then customize Gogo's commands however you wish. So basically Gogo can have Sabin's Blitz skill, Cyan's SwordTech skill, and Gau's Rage skill at the same time, or any other combination you see fit.

THE OPERA HOUSE

Enemies
Dirt Dragon (Boss)

Checklist

- ☐ *Speak with the Impresario in the balcony*
- ☐ *Go to the right side of the balcony and into the switch room*
- ☐ *Use the second switch from the right to reach the stage*
- ☐ *Battle the Dirt Dragon*

Getting On Stage

Talk to the Impresario in the balcony, and you'll learn that you must get to the stage. Now head for the switch room you used on your previous visit. However, instead of throwing the switch on the far right, throw the second one from the right. This drops you onto the stage. You can also throw the remaining two switches, which do funny things.

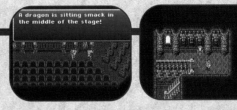

Dirt Dragon

You've located yet another of the legendary dragons, and this one is tough. Begin the battle by casting **Float** on your entire party. This will protect them from the various types of earth magic that the dragon uses. This doesn't make the battle easy, but it does make it manageable.

Keep everyone's HP up, because the Dirt Dragon can usually KO a character with a single hit of its powerful claws. You may want to cast **Haste** on your party to keep things moving. This dragon is extremely fast and may be too quick without the Haste effect.

SOLITARY ISLAND

Enemies
Peepers
Black Dragon
Earth Guard

Items
None

Checklist

- ☐ *Return to Cid's hut on Solitary Island*
- ☐ *Go to the beach and get the Palidor Esper*

Checking in on Cid

Whether or not you saved Cid's life, it's time to return and check on the island. When you get to the house, head for the beach. Along the water's edge, you'll discover the **Palidor Esper**.

DUNCAN'S HOUSE

Enemies

Geckorex
Spek Tor
Mantodea
Tyrannosaur
Bracheosaur
Tumble Weed
Reach Frog
Hoover
Cactrot
Crawler
Sprinter

Items

None

Checklist

- [ ] *Put Sabin in your party*
- [ ] *Locate Duncan's hideaway*
- [ ] *Talk to Duncan*

Duncan's Wife

Remember talking to Duncan's Wife back in South Figaro? She mentioned that Duncan was alive and well, training in a secret location north of Narshe. Well, she was almost right. The location is actually more to the northeast. Look for a cross that's made of five trees below a mountain range. When you see it, you'll know you're in the right spot.

Sabin's Training

Duncan is ready to complete Sabin's training. Just for bringing Sabin here, you'll learn Sabin's ultimate Blitz technique, the **Bum Rush**.

DUNCAN: SABIN!!
It is now time to complete
your training. Use these new
skills to smash Kefka!

TOWER OF FANATICS

Enemies

L.10 Magic
L.20 Magic
⬜ Magic
L.40 Magic
L.50 Magic
L.60 Magic
L.70 Magic
L.80 Magic
L.90 Magic
Magic Urn
White Dragon (Boss)
Mage Master (Boss)

Items

1. Safety Bit
2. Air Anchor
3. Genji Shield
4. Stunner
5. ⬜ Armor
6. Gem Box

Checklist

- [ ] *Climb the tower*
- [ ] *Get the Gem Box Relic from the top floor*
- [ ] *Exit the top room and confront Kefka's followers*
- [ ] *Battle the Mage Master*
  (Optional)
- [ ] *Fight the White Dragon*

Magic Mayhem

For whatever reason, anyone inside the Tower of Fanatics is restricted to using magic. That means no physical attacks, no special skills, and no items.

It helps to equip characters with Relics like the **Gold Hairpin** or **Economizer** because they reduce the cost of casting spells. **Wall Rings** also work well, because they reflect most of the magic used by the enemies in the tower. The down side is that you'll have trouble healing your characters. If nothing else, make sure each character can use the **Osmose** ability to draw MP from enemies.

Secret Room

There's a hidden switch on the wall to the right of the treasure chest in the first treasure room. Go back outside and you'll find a new door on the floor below. Inside you'll find an **Air Anchor**, which is a new tool for Edgar.

Fighting L.20 Magic and L.90 Magic

These two enemies are protected by Reflect magic. To attack them, you can cast **Reflect** on your own party and bounce spells off your characters, or you can use magic like **Ultima**, which can't be reflected.

White Dragon

On the third floor, you'll encounter another one of the eight legendary dragons. You can easily win this fight by casting **Reflect** on your party. You can then pound the White Dragon into submission with the spells of your choice. Just avoid using **Pearl**, because it heals the White Dragon.

Mage Master

As you attempt to leave the top floor of the tower after getting the Gem Box Relic, the Mage Master will attack. Each time you hit the Mage Master with a spell, it changes its magical strengths and weaknesses. This makes it very difficult to cause damage to the Boss.

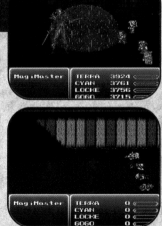

You can counter this by using spells like **Ultima** and **Meteor**, which can't be blocked by Mage Master's magical defenses. Or, you can cast **Berserk** on the Boss so that it can't change its defenses or use magic. Just make absolutely sure you cast Berserk immediately, or the Mage Master may change its defense in a way that leaves your characters powerless. If this occurs, you can always cast **Dispel** on the Boss to remove the Berserk effect. When the Mage Master changes defenses again, hit it with Berserk again. You can use **Scan** to check what the Mage Master's weakness is at any time.

You MUST first cast a **Life 3** spell on at least one of your party members (contained in the Phoenix Esper). If you don't have **Life 3**, you can't defeat the Mage Master. After weakening the Mage Master enough, he'll cast one final spell: Ultima. The Ultima spell will destroy not only the Mage Master, but your entire party as well. However, if you cast Life 3 on one or more party members, they will come back to life after the battle, enabling the player to win this battle.

Enemies
Enuo
Goblin
Figaliz
Master Pug
Boxed Set
Lethal Weapon
Katana Soul
Blue Dragon (Boss)

Items
① Ether
② Wing Edge
③ Monster-in-a-Box
④ Trump
⑤ Magicite
⑥ X-Potion
⑦ Offering
⑧ Punisher
⑨ Gold Hairpin
⑩ Blizzard Orb
⑪ X-Ether

Magicite
⑫ Odin
⑬ Raiden

Checklist

☐ Have Figaro Castle move underground

☐ When the castle stops, tell the engineer to remain stopped

☐ Go to the prison and exit through the hole in the wall

☐ Find your way through the cave to the Ancient Castle

☐ Enter the castle's main gate and find Odin

☐ Inspect Odin to get the Odin Esper

☐ Search the stairs in front of the thrones to find a hidden switch

☐ Go to the library east of the throne room

☐ Inspect the shining object in the bookcase

☐ Go into the hidden basement

☐ Battle the Blue Dragon

☐ Inspect the Queen's statue to transform Odin

☐ Return to the castle's engine room and have the castle continue its journey

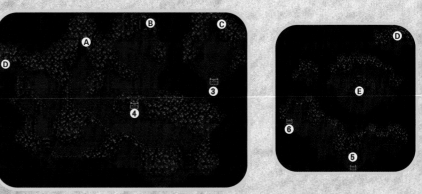

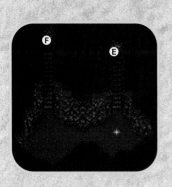

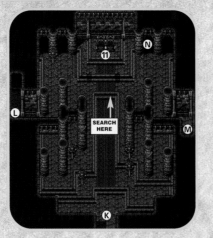

Magic Mayhem

For whatever reason, anyone inside the Tower of Fanatics is restricted to using magic. That means no physical attacks, no special skills, and no items.

It helps to equip characters with Relics like the **Gold Hairpin** or **Economizer** because they reduce the cost of casting spells. **Wall Rings** also work well, because they reflect most of the magic used by the enemies in the tower. The down side is that you'll have trouble healing your characters. If nothing else, make sure each character can use the **Osmose** ability to draw MP from enemies.

Secret Room

There's a hidden switch on the wall to the right of the treasure chest in the first treasure room. Go back outside and you'll find a new door on the floor below. Inside you'll find an **Air Anchor**, which is a new tool for Edgar.

Fighting L.20 Magic and L.90 Magic

These two enemies are protected by Reflect magic. To attack them, you can cast **Reflect** on your own party and bounce spells off your characters, or you can use magic like **Ultima**, which can't be reflected.

White Dragon

On the third floor, you'll encounter another one of the eight legendary dragons. You can easily win this fight by casting **Reflect** on your party. You can then pound the White Dragon into submission with the spells of your choice. Just avoid using **Pearl**, because it heals the White Dragon.

Mage Master

As you attempt to leave the top floor of the tower after getting the Gem Box Relic, the Mage Master will attack. Each time you hit the Mage Master with a spell, it changes its magical strengths and weaknesses. This makes it very difficult to cause damage to the Boss.

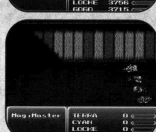

You can counter this by using spells like **Ultima** and **Meteor**, which can't be blocked by Mage Master's magical defenses. Or, you can cast **Berserk** on the Boss so that it can't change its defenses or use magic. Just make absolutely sure you cast Berserk immediately, or the Mage Master may change its defense in a way that leaves your characters powerless. If this occurs, you can always cast **Dispel** on the Boss to remove the Berserk effect. When the Mage Master changes defenses again, hit it with Berserk again. You can use **Scan** to check what the Mage Master's weakness is at any time.

You MUST first cast a **Life 3** spell on at least one of your party members (contained in the Phoenix Esper). If you don't have **Life 3**, you can't defeat the Mage Master. After weakening the Mage Master enough, he'll cast one final spell: Ultima. The Ultima spell will destroy not only the Mage Master, but your entire party as well. However, if you cast Life 3 on one or more party members, they will come back to life after the battle, enabling the player to win this battle.

Enemies
Enuo
Goblin
Figaliz
Master Pug
Boxed Set
Lethal Weapon
Katana Soul
Blue Dragon (Boss)

Items
① Ether
② Wing Edge
③ Monster-in-a-Box
④ Trump
⑤ Magicite
⑥ X-Potion
⑦ Offering
⑧ Punisher
⑨ Gold Hairpin
⑩ Blizzard Orb
⑪ X-Ether

Magicite
⑫ Odin
⑬ Raiden

Checklist

- [ ] Have Figaro Castle move underground
- [ ] When the castle stops, tell the engineer to remain stopped
- [ ] Go to the prison and exit through the hole in the wall
- [ ] Find your way through the cave to the Ancient Castle
- [ ] Enter the castle's main gate and find Odin
- [ ] Inspect Odin to get the Odin Esper
- [ ] Search the stairs in front of the thrones to find a hidden switch
- [ ] Go to the library east of the throne room
- [ ] Inspect the shining object in the bookcase
- [ ] Go into the hidden basement
- [ ] Battle the Blue Dragon
- [ ] Inspect the Queen's statue to transform Odin
- [ ] Return to the castle's engine room and have the castle continue its journey

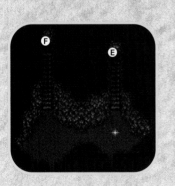

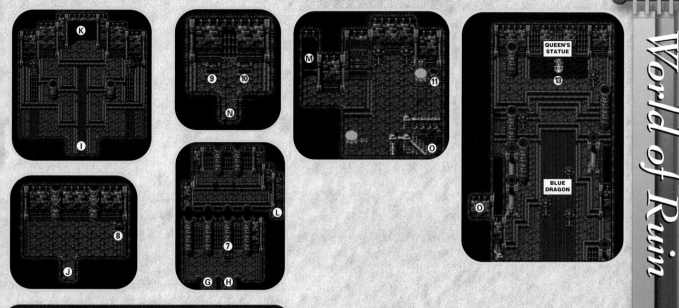

Finding a Lost Castle

The Ancient Castle is buried deep under the ocean. The only thing that can reach it is Figaro Castle, so go there and have the engineer move the castle. About half way to its destination, the castle will stop. You will then have the option to continue or check out the area. Have the castle stay put and go to the prison. You can use the entrance you used to save Figaro Castle earlier to exit into a cave that leads to the Ancient Castle.

Reflections

Most of the enemies in this area are protected by Reflect. Therefore, don't use spells that can be reflected against them unless you bounce them off of one of your own party members protected by Reflect.

Getting Odin

The Odin Esper is easy to acquire. Simply go into the Ancient Castle's main entrance, and head straight to the throne room. Inspect the petrified Odin to receive the **Odin Esper**.

Transforming Odin

The Queen of the castle can transform Odin into a more powerful Esper. Search 5 paces in front of the right-hand throne to find and trigger a hidden switch. Throwing the switch causes a hidden staircase to appear in the room to the east of the throne room. Climb down the new staircase to find a hidden room containing both the Blue Dragon and the petrified Queen.

You may have to battle the Blue Dragon before you can reach the Queen. The hall is narrow and the Blue Dragon's flight path is erratic, but you can avoid the battle if you don't feel you're ready for it.

When you have Odin, inspect the Queen's Statue once and her tears will transform Odin into **Raiden**. Raiden is a more powerful Esper than Odin. Just keep in mind that you may want to take the time to teach a character the **Meteor** spell that Odin has now, because Raiden has a different spell to teach. After trading the Odin Esper for the Raiden Esper, the Odin Esper is gone for good.

Blue Dragon

There's another legendary dragon in the hidden basement. The Blue Dragon is weak to Lightning, so have your party use **Bolt 3** against the beast. If Terra is in your party, give the **Gem Box** and **Economizer Relics** to her if you have them. Then have her Morph and cast two Bolt 3 spells each turn. The rest of the party can then focus on healing. Fighting in this fashion will make this a quick battle.

CleanSweep

Blue Drgn	TERRA	4054
	CYAN	4022
	LOCKE	3925
	GOGO	3715

Mimic	TERRA	3844
Magic	CYAN	2591
Tools	LOCKE	3362
Blitz	GOGO	2737

EBOT'S ROCK CAVE

Checklist

☐ *Place Relm and Strago in your party and return to Thamasa*

☐ *Speak with Gungho about Ebot's Rock and Hidon*

☐ *Head to Ebot's Rock north of Thamasa*

☐ *Feed Coral to the Hungry Chest*

☐ *Confront Hidon*

☐ *Return to Thamasa*

Enemies

Warlock
Cluck
Eland
Opinicus
Hipocamp
Displayer
Slatter
Hidon and Hidonites
(Bosses)

Items

None

HIDON

WARP POINT

HUNGRY CHEST

ENTRANCE

WARP POINT

Return to Thamasa

GUNGHO: It was...Hidon, the beast you and I used to hunt. I almost had it...

To start this quest, revisit Thamasa with Strago and Relm in your party. They discover that Strago's friend and rival Gungho has been injured by Hidon, a creature that Strago has been chasing his entire life. Once Strago sets out to defeat Hidon, fly to the island north of Thamasa to find Hidon's lair.

TREASURE: I'm hungry!

Received a piece of "Coral."

The Hungry Chest

There's a chest blocking your way to Hidon, and it's hungry for Coral. Fortunately, there's lots of Coral in this cave, but getting it won't be easy.

To find Coral, step on the teleporter to get thrown into a random area. Any chests you find will contain Coral of different amounts. After collecting about 50 pieces, take them to the Hungry Chest and feed them to it. This will satisfy the chest, causing it to move.

Hidon & the Hidonites

Begin the battle by casting **Float** on your entire party. This will put them out of harm's reach from your follow-up spell. Cast **Quake** as often as possible against Hidon and its Hidonites. This spell will eliminate all of the Hidonites, and should cause a lot of damage to Hidon.

However, don't destroy Hidon too quickly. It can teach Strago the **Grand Train Lore**, so give it a chance to use the spell. If you don't have the Quake spell, **Fire** and **Pearl** magic also work well.

Enemies
Doom Gaze

Magicite
Bahamut

DOOM GAZE

Finding Doom Gaze

Doom Gaze is a demon that will sometimes attack the Airship as you travel from point to point. Its appearances aren't very common, so you may have to fly for several minutes before running into it.

Doom Gaze

At the start of every battle, Doom Gaze will use the Level 5 Doom spell. Therefore, it's important that not all of your characters are at a level divisible of five. If they are, they're dead. You'll need at least one survivor to revive anyone who may have succumbed to the spell.

After Doom Gaze's opening attack, have one or two characters attack Doom Gaze with **Fire 3** and **Pearl** magic. The others should focus on healing. Again, it's good to have Terra in your party for these battles, because she can cause double damage with Fire 3 and Pearl while in Esper form.

After causing enough damage, Doom Gaze will escape from battle. You will have to find and fight Doom Gaze several times before you can finally defeat it. You may remember that someone once told the party that Doom Gaze can't heal itself between battles, so any damage you did in this battle will carry over to the next one.

When you finally defeat Doom Gaze, you receive a powerful Esper, **Bahamut**. That should make all of the extra flying time well worth the trouble.

KEFKA'S TOWER

Checklist

- ☐ Split the party into three groups
- ☐ Take control of the second group
- ☐ Battle Atma
- ☐ Have the second group find a switch to assist the first group
- ☐ Fight the Gold Dragon
- ☐ Continue to the room with three switches and change to the third party
- ☐ Challenge Inferno
- ☐ Inspect the glowing chest to open a path for the first party
- ☐ Defeat the Skull Dragon
- ☐ Continue to the room with the three switches and change to the first party
- ☐ Fight your way to the room where the other two groups are waiting
- ☐ Have the first party push the weights down off the ledges above the second and third parties
- ☐ Continue on with each group and defeat Guardian, Poltergeist, Goddess, and Doom
- ☐ Put all three parties on a switch
- ☐ Challenge Kefka

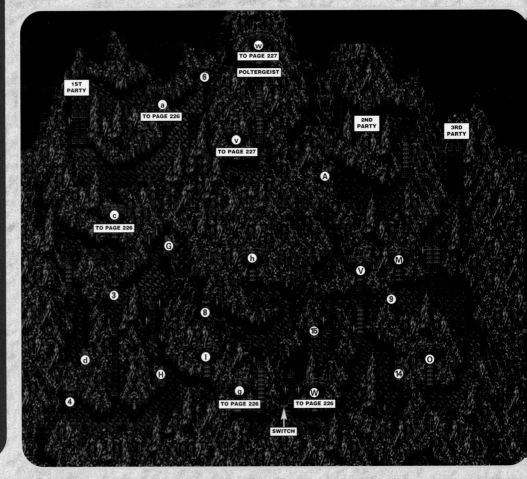

Exploring Kefka's Tower

At the start, you'll split into three groups. It's important that you have a fair balance between all three. Don't put your best warriors into one group, or you'll have a tough time getting past some of the Bosses in this area.

Also, you should remove Espers from inactive groups so that the active group can have the freedom to learn whatever spells they need. Make sure you move them around every time you switch unless you're only switching for a minor adjustment.

Start with either the second or third group. Both of these groups must find switches that open up the path for the first group. These two groups also have the dubious honor of fighting two Bosses each, so they'll need a bit more strength at first than the first group.

The path through this area isn't nearly as complex as it looks. There are a few loops, but it's fairly straightforward. Use the maps to help guide you through.

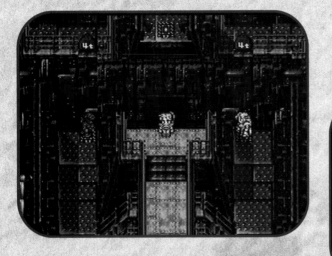

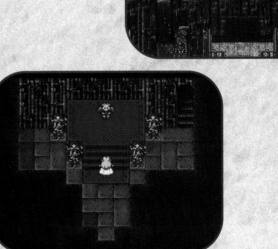

Atma

The second party will fight Atma, who's held up in Kefka's old cell. Because Atma doesn't have any weaknesses, you must rely on strong attacks and support magic. It helps to cast **Haste 2** and **Life 3** on your party. Use everyone's strongest skills, like Sabin's **Bum Rush** Blitz, and keep everyone healthy.

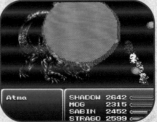

Gold Dragon

If you've followed along since the beginning of the guide, this should be the seventh of the legendary dragons. Prepare your second party for the battle by equipping anything that protects against Lightning Magic. This should help neutralize the Gold Dragon's attacks.

Attack the Gold Dragon with **Water** magic if you have any (like Strago's **Aqua Rake** Lore spell). If not, just use strong physical attacks or spells like **Ultima** and **Meteor**.

Inferno (Striker & Rough)

This creature attacks the third party as they walk through Kefka's Tower. Inferno has three body parts. You can destroy its arms, but they regenerate after a few turns. However, if you have powerful magic like **Ultima** or **Meteor**, you can attack all three parts simultaneously. Otherwise, ignore the arms and attack the torso.

Inferno's body is weak against Lightning magic, so **Bolt** spells are very effective. The other body parts are weak to other types of magic, so there's no need to spread out the Bolt spells. Just focus on the torso, and the arms will get destroyed along with it.

Skull Dragon

This is the last of the eight legendary dragons, and your third party gets the honor of finishing this quest. The Skull Dragon uses a lot of negative status effects, so **Ribbons** are a must. If not on every character, then at least on two of them. The Skull Dragon also likes to cast Doom on your party, so use **Life 2** for quick recovery.

Start the battle by casting **Haste 2** on the entire party. Then bombard the Skull Dragon with **Fire** and **Pearl** magic, because it is weak against both. If multiple characters have **Fire 3** spells, you can end this battle quickly. Make sure you keep everyone's HP high, because you may get hit with an abnormal status effect.

Guardian

Apparently the Guardian is no longer invincible, which is good news. Use lots of **Lighting** and **Water** magic. **Aqua Rake** and **Bolt 3** work wonders. Even some physical attacks, like Sabin's **Bum Rush** or **X-Fight**, work really well. If you can, summon **Ramuh** to unleash some extra damage.

Poltergeist

Poltergeist is only weak to Poison magic, so **Poison** and **Bio** work best. This won't poison the Boss, however, it will cause a lot of damage. This Boss packs quite a punch, so keep everyone's HP high. Also, make sure you use support magic like **Haste 2**, **Safe**, and **Shell**. They'll help a lot if your weaker characters are in this party.

Goddess

The Goddess doesn't have a weakness. She is protected from Lightning magic, but other strong spells like **Ultima** and **Meteor** work well. In fact, you can usually defeat her with just a few casts of the Ultima spell.

Use support magic again to make up for any weaknesses in your party. If you lack strong magic, physical attacks will work as well, but the battle will last longer. The Goddess has a tendency to confuse party members into doing her bidding. You'll want to quickly attack anyone under her control to snap him/her back to reality.

Doom

Doom is very fast and powerful. Start the battle by setting up a good defense with **Safe** and **Shell**. You may also want to summon **Golem** for added protection. Then use **Haste 2** to increase your party's speed.

Doom's only weakness is **Pearl** magic. Unfortunately, you may not have this, because it isn't easy to learn. If you don't have it, use whatever powerful magic and attacks you have at your disposal. You may want to cast **Life 3** on your weaker party members early in the fight, because a single attack can often eliminate them.

On to Kefka

Move all three parties onto the switches ahead, and then save your game. You'll soon battle Kefka, who's a lot tougher than you may remember.

In preparation, equip your four best characters with any items that block magic and your best relics. You'll want everyone to know **Cure 3**, **Life 2**, **Life 3**, **Haste 2**, and **Ultima** or **Meteor**. Also, make sure everyone is rested and you save your game.

Climbing the Tower

As the battle begins, you're asked to place your characters in the order in which you want them to fight. What you're doing is planning your battle strategy. The tower you're about to face is comprised of three powerful Bosses. At the first Boss, you're first four characters from your list will enter the battle. After destroying the first Boss, you'll progress up the tower to the second Boss and any character(s) that is knocked out during the first Boss fight will be replaced with the next character(s) from your list in the order that you selected them.

So when setting the list, place your four best characters at the top. Then continue to fill the list going in order from your strongest to your weakest characters.

Fighting the Bosses

Although each of the Bosses on the tower are very different, you'll want to use one simple strategy over and over. Begin each battle by casting **Haste 2** and **Life 3** on everyone in your party. Haste 2 will enable your characters to attack quickly, while Life 3 will automatically revive them if they're K.O.ed at any point in the battle. This will also keep them from being replaced in the next battle if they're taken down by a Boss' final attack. You will have to recast Life 3 several times if your character gets repeatedly knocked out.

Attack the Bosses by using either **Ultima** or **Meteor** spells. It helps a great deal to have your most powerful spellcaster (usually Terra) equipped with the **Gem Box Relic**, so he/she can use the X-Magic ability that enables the character to cast two spells each turn. Also, you may want to equip a strong fighter like Cyan or Sabin with a **Genji Glove** and the **Offering Relics**, so you'll have someone who can attack eight times each turn. Sabin's **Bum Rush Blitz** skill also works extremely well.

Make sure you have a character who always serves as a healer. That person should cast **Cure 3** each turn and be prepared to use **Life 2** if the situation arises. You'll also want to have another character ready to help out with healing if a particular spell lowers everyone's HP. If any of your spell casters starts to run low on MP, make sure you take a turn to draw MP from a Boss using the **Osmose** spell. This way, there's never a need to use Ether during these battles.

Kefka: The Final Boss

After facing the statues, you will then face the final Boss, Kefka. You can use similar strategies for defeating Kefka as you did for the statues.

BESTIARY

Bestiary Legend

The following is a list of enemies for FINAL FANTASY VI. Study the legend to learn how to interpret the statistics shown with each enemy.

Name	Enemy's name
Name	Enemy's name
LV.	Enemy's level of experience. The higher the level, the stronger the monster.
HP	Enemy's Hit Points or health. You must cause at least this much damage to the enemy to defeat it.
MP	Enemy's Magic Points. The enemy has this much MP available for magic attacks.
Exp.	Amount of Experience Points earned for defeating the enemy. Exp. is divided evenly among party members.
GP	Gold Pieces received for defeating the enemy.
Sp.	Enemy's Speed rating. Faster enemies attack more often.
Atk.	Enemy's physical attack power.
Def.	Enemy's defensive powers against physical attacks.
Eva.	Enemy's ability to dodge/block physical attacks.
Mag. Atk.	Enemy's magic attack power.
Mag. Def.	Enemy's defensive powers against magical attacks.
Mag. Eva.	Enemy's ability to dodge/block magical attacks.
Element	The enemy is immune or protected from these elements.
Weaknesses	The enemy is vulnerable to these elements.
Steal	Items that Locke can steal from the enemy using the Steal or Capture commands.
Drop	Items the enemy may drop after being defeated.

Name	Lv.	HP	MP	Exp.	GP	Sp.	Atk.	Def.	Eva.	Mag. Atk.	Mag. Def.	Mag. Eva.	Element	Weaknesses	Steal	Drop
1st Class	11	180	25	117	112	30	13	55	0	10	135	0	None	Poison	Tonic	None
Abolisher	24	860	82	485	525	35	16	125	0	10	150	0	None	None	Antidote	Phoenix Down
Actaneon	12	230	98	57	125	35	13	100	0	10	150	0	Water	Fire, Lightning	Potion	None
Adamanchyt	24	1305	50	1450	189	40	22	225	0	10	45	0	None	None	Gold Shield	None
Air Force	25	8000	750	0	0	35	10	150	0	12	120	0	None	Water, Lightning	Elixir	Czarina Ring
Allosaurus	38	3000	300	953	731	15	10	105	0	3	0	50	None	Holy, Fire	None	None
Allo Ver	19	8000	8000	0	0	55	13	140	0	55	160	0	Poison	Holy, Fire	Tonic, Potion	Tiger Fang
Anemone	33	2000	100	1000	550	33	10	115	0	10	145	0	Lightning, Water	Fire	None	Green Cherry
Anguiform	13	315	150	96	358	25	14	80	0	6	150	0	Water	Lightning	Potion	Phoenix Down
Apokryphos	26	1900	195	1200	525	37	18	80	0	10	150	0	None	Water, Holy, Lightning	Cure Ring	None
Apparite	20	781	60	415	300	35	17	110	0	10	150	0	Fire, Poison	Holy, Ice	Potion, Revivify	Revivify
Aquila	49	6013	820	2781	906	40	13	120	30	10	145	0	Fire	Ice	Economizer, Phoenix Down	Phoenix Down
Areneid	6	87	15	37	94	30	20	80	0	10	0	135	None	Water, Ice	Tonic	Tonic
Aspik	12	220	330	48	115	40	2	100	0	2	150	0	Water	Fire	Tonic	X-Potion
Atma	67	55,000	19,000	0	0	63	20	75	0	10	70	0	Poison, Water, Earth, Wind, Holy	None	Drainer, Crystal Orb	None
Atma Weapon	37	24,000	5000	0	0	67	45	142	20	5	97	10	None	None	Elixir, Ribbon	Elixir
Balloon	22	555	80	369	300	25	11	20	0	10	130	0	Fire	Ice, Water	Phoenix Down	None
Barb-e	39	3062	198	1410	631	30	13	100	0	10	160	0	None	Poison	None	None
Baskervor	22	750	100	465	458	35	17	110	0	10	120	0	None	None	Gaia Gear	Potion
Beakor	11	290	30	108	135	30	12	80	0	10	150	0	None	Fire	Eyedrop, Potion	Potion
Behemoth	28	5800	180	2055	0	50	25	100	0	7	135	0	None	Ice	Running Shoes	X-Potion
Black Dragon	26	4000	600	780	502	30	14	102	0	10	20	0	Poison	Holy, Fire	Revivify	Tent
Bleary	7	119	10	53	80	30	13	100	0	10	155	0	None	Fire	Tonic	Tonic
Bloompyre	26	12	400	510	896	35	13	254	0	10	254	0	Water	Fire	Echo Screen	Smoke Bomb
Blue Dragon	65	26,900	3800	0	0	75	13	110	0	10	150	0	Water	Lightning	None	Scimitar
Bogy	29	1318	100	532	1200	30	15	102	0	10	153	0	None	None	Potion	None
Bomb	8	160	50	35	80	30	10	90	0	1	150	0	Fire	Water, Ice	Tonic, Potion, Muscle Belt,	Potion
Borras	35	4771	590	2953	2500	43	23	150	105	10	145	10	None	Poison	Potion	None

Name	Lv.	HP	MP	Exp.	GP	Sp.	Atk.	Def.	Eva.	Mag. Atk.	Mag. Def.	Mag. Eva.	Element	Weaknesses	Steal	Drop
Bounty Man	13	285	50	115	55	32	16	75	0	10	140	0	None	Fire	Potion	None
Boxed Set	45	4020	105	1504	465	30	13	90	0	7	250	0	None	Holy	Antidote	None
Brachosaur	77	46,050	51,420	14,396	0	95	55	190	70	25	145	50	None	Ice	Ribbon	Economizer
Brainpan	25	1300	1000	550	600	35	24	120	0	10	110	0	Poison	Holy, Fire, Lightning	Earrings	None
Brawler	9	137	100	79	84	35	14	100	0	10	70	0	Poison	Ice	Bandana	Tonic
Brontaur	50	10,050	12,850	3000	1200	35	15	130	0	12	110	0	None	Ice	Dried Meat	None
Buffalax	26	2252	218	562	458	30	15	100	0	10	150	0	None	Water, Fire	Diamond Vest, Tincture	None
Bug	16	310	20	165	210	35	13	120	0	10	150	0	None	Ice, Water	Potion, Soft	None
Cactrot	27	3	60,000	0	10,000	39	1	255	250	50	255	250	None	Water, Ice	Soft	Soft
Cadet	13	380	48	0	144	30	13	80	0	10	140	0	None	Poison	Tonic	Tonic
Cephaler	21	420	100	214	280	30	10	100	0	10	140	0	None	Lightning	Potion, Remedy	None
Ceritops	33	2000	100	1000	850	34	10	130	0	10	150	0	Lightning	Fire	None	White Cape, Green Cherry
Chadarnook	41	30,000	7600	0	0	61	18	135	0	10	130	0	Lightning	Fire, Holy	None	None
Chaos Dragon	44	9013	1300	4881	1000	30	13	5	0	10	85	0	Fire	Ice	Phoenix Down	Phoenix Down
Chaser	19	1202	140	691	380	40	13	200	0	8	150	0	None	Water,	Bio Blaster, Lightning	None
Chickenlip	18	545	155	190	279	30	11	150	0	3	150	0	None	Ice	Sleeping Bag, Tonic	None
Chimera	22	2237	100	1144	760	45	25	100	0	10	110	0	None	None	Hyper Wrist	Gold Armor
Chitonid	26	1111	60	321	356	25	13	140	0	10	80	0	None	Lightning	Potion	Remedy
Chupon	26	10,000	40,000	0	0	10	13	100	0	10	55	0	Fire	Water, Ice	Dirk	None
Cipius	10	134	100	82	102	30	13	80	0	10	110	0	None	None	Tonic, Antidote	None
Cluck	38	2366	185	770	422	33	13	105	0	10	155	0	Poison	Ice	Warp Stone	Warp Stone
Coelecite	20	480	15	290	270	35	20	120	0	10	130	0	Fire	Ice	Potion, Antidote	Antidote
Commander	10	102	50	85	153	30	13	100	0	10	150	0	None	Poison	Tonic	None
Commando	18	580	35	252	273	30	13	210	0	10	145	0	None	Lightning, Water	Mythril Vest, Tent	Tent
Covert	44	4530	240	1757	1768	35	25	100	50	11	150	0	Poison	Holy	Tack Star, Shuriken	None
Crane (Left)	23	1800	447	0	0	35	14	145	0	4	120	0	Lightning	Water	Noise Blaster	None
Crane (Right)	24	2300	447	0	0	30	14	125	0	4	120	0	Fire	Water, Lightning	Debilitator, Potion	None
Crass Hopper	11	243	80	89	145	30	10	50	0	10	155	0	None	Wind, Fire	Antidote	Potion

Name	Lv.	HP	MP	Exp.	GP	Sp.	Atk.	Def.	Eva.	Mag. Atk.	Mag. Def.	Mag. Eva.	Element	Weaknesses	Steal	Drop
Crawler	51	3200	620	1456	1224	40	13	115	0	8	150	0	None	Ice	Remedy	None
Crawly	7	122	0	71	120	30	13	45	0	10	155	0	None	Fire	Remedy, Tonic	None
Critic	40	1200	330	1323	531	30	13	125	0	10	150	0	None	None	None	None
Cruller	28	1334	100	419	797	30	11	110	100	4	70	0	Poison	Holy, Fire	Tonic	None
Crusher	36	2095	340	788	577	30	13	145	0	5	85	0	None	Fire	Super Ball	Super Ball
Curley	47	15,000	2000	0	0	35	1	100	0	4	110	0	Fire	Water, Ice	None	Super Ball
Dadaluma	22	3270	1005	0	1210	30	12	85	0	3	143	10	Lightning	Water	Sneak Ring, Jewel Ring	Thief's Knife, Headband
Dahling	37	3580	500	1151	1260	35	1	110	20	8	145	0	None	Poison	Moogle Suit	None
Dante	28	1945	200	1150	712	40	17	105	0	10	150	0	None	Poison	Diamond Helm	Gold Shield
Dark Force	55	8940	700	2950	600	35	12	105	0	7	155	0	None	Holy	Crystal	None
Dark Side	13	255	85	165	138	30	10	100	0	8	150	0	Poison	Holy, Fire	Tonic	Potion
Dark Wind	5	34	0	28	41	30	13	55	0	10	140	0	None	Fire	Tonic	Tonic
Deep Eye	28	1334	100	385	485	30	14	100	0	10	150	0	None	Fire	Eyedrop	None
Delta Bug	26	612	80	288	211	30	11	220	0	10	5	0	None	Fire	Tonic	Sleeping Bag
Didalos	59	12,280	100	3500	0	37	13	105	0	12	150	0	Poison	Holy, Fire	None	None
Dirt Dragon	53	28,500	16,500	0	0	55	23	110	0	12	150	0	None	Water, Wind	X-Potion	Magus Rod
Displayer	38	3826	1327	1510	393	44	13	150	30	10	135	0	Poison	Holy, Fire	Warp Stone	Warp Stone
Doberman	12	465	10	0	83	35	10	100	0	10	150	0	None	Fire	Potion, Tonic	Potion
Doom	73	63,000	4800	0	0	61	60	110	0	9	160	0	Ice, Poison	Holy	Safety Bit	Sky Render
Doom Dragon	54	18,008	10,000	8500	2700	48	13	110	0	13	90	0	None	None	Pod Bracelet	None
Doom Gaze	68	55,555	38,000	0	0	95	35	150	30	8	170	0	Ice, Poison	Fire, Holy	None	None
Dragon	29	7000	850	2931	0	55	45	130	40	10	110	30	None	Lightning	Genji Glove, Potion	None
Drop	27	1000	80	398	427	30	6	100	0	10	150	0	None	Water, Lightning	Tincture	Tincture
Dueller	53	7200	1600	2500	800	35	13	185	0	10	145	0	None	Water, Lightning	Chain Saw	None
Dullahan	37	23,450	1721	0	0	55	55	130	10	7	160	0	Ice	Fire	Genji Glove, X-Potion	None
Earth Guard	23	1	18	1	0	45	6	5	0	10	5	0	None	Water	Megalixir	None
Eland	37	2470	145	775	550	32	13	110	10	10	155	0	None	Lightning	Warp Stone	Warp Stone
Enuo	46	4635	280	1429	968	30	13	50	0	10	250	0	None	Holly	X-Potion	None
Evil Oscar	56	7000	500	2800	1320	30	13	115	0	6	105	0	Ice, Lightning, Poison, Water, Earth, Wind, Holy	Fire	Warp Stone	None

Name	Lv.	HP	MP	Exp.	GP	Sp.	Atk.	Def.	Eva.	Mag. Atk.	Mag. Def.	Mag. Eva.	Element	Weaknesses	Steal	Drop
Exocite	11	196	100	162	153	30	19	100	0	10	150	0	Water	Lightning, Fire	Mythril Claw, Tonic	Tonic
Exoray	29	1200	112	449	370	33	13	105	0	10	105	0	Poison	Holy, Fire	None	Revivify
F.Boss 1 (Face)	74	30,000	10,000	0	0	44	63	140	10	12	140	0	None	Fire	Elixir	None
F.Boss 1 (Long Arm)	73	30,000	10,000	0	0	39	35	110	5	30	150	0	None	None	Elixir	None
F.Boss 1 (Short Arm)	73	33,000	10,000	0	0	37	50	115	10	10	155	0	None	Water	Elixir	None
F.Boss 2 (Hit)	73	27,000	10,000	0	0	33	6	115	0	9	153	0	None	Poison	Elixir	None
F.Boss 2 (Magic)	72	28,000	10,000	0	0	35	1	145	0	8	125	0	None	Earth	Elixir	None
F.Boss 2 (Tiger)	70	30,000	10,000	0	0	21	13	120	0	7	153	0	Earth	Ice	Elixir	None
F.Boss 2 (Tools)	73	30,000	10,000	0	0	29	13	105	0	10	153	0	None	Lightning	Elixir	None
F.Boss 3 (Girl)	58	9999	10,000	0	0	41	73	150	0	9	155	0	Fire, Ice, Earth, Lightning, Poison, Water, Wind, Holy	None	Ragnarok	None
F.Boss 3 (Sleep)	71	40,000	10,000	0	0	46	63	140	0	6	120	0	None	None	Atma Weapon	None
Fidor	13	355	80	160	180	35	25	55	0	10	170	0	None	Fire	Potion, Phoenix Down	None
Figaliz	45	4220	140	1219	554	30	29	90	0	10	250	0	None	Ice	Potion	None
Flame Eater	26	8400	480	0	0	34	13	105	20	7	150	0	Fire	Ice	Flame Sabre	None
Flan	19	255	110	160	120	30	13	13	0	10	100	0	None	Fire	Magicite, Tonic	None
Fortis	54	9800	700	3500	250	35	5	160	0	10	150	0	None	Water, Lightning	Drill	None
Fossil Fang	20	1399	219	380	1870	35	25	100	0	3	165	0	Poison	Water, Holy, Ice, Fire	Remedy, Revivify	None
Gabbldegak	15	350	20	104	126	30	13	85	0	10	155	0	None	Poison	Eyedrop, Phoenix Down	None
Garm	19	615	45	228	343	30	13	220	0	10	140	0	None	Water, Lightning	Phoenix Down, Tonic	None
Geckorex	54	5000	1020	2400	1120	35	13	135	10	10	155	10	None	Ice	Tortoise Shield	Tortoise Shield
General	19	650	30	232	308	30	13	155	0	10	105	0	None	Poison	Mythril Shield, Tonic	Green Cherry
Ghost	10	226	70	48	75	30	1	105	0	1	150	0	Poison	Holy, Fire	Tonic	Tonic
Ghost Train	14	1900	350	0	0	30	10	30	0	5	210	0	Wind	Holy, Fire, Lightning	None	Tent
Giga Toad	26	458	20	235	340	30	11	100	0	10	130	0	None	Ice	None	Sleeping Bag
Gigantos	25	6000	1120	7550	0	50	20	1	0	10	1	0	None	Poison	X-Potion	Hardened
Gilomantis	26	1412	110	559	756	35	16	115	0	10	140	0	None	Fire	Poison Claw	None
Gloom Shell	41	2905	175	1096	421	35	13	115	0	10	150	0	None	Ice	Potion	None
Gobbler	19	470	63	438	250	30	13	170	0	8	120	0	None	None	Potion, Green Cherry	None

Name	Lv.	HP	MP	Exp.	GP	Sp.	Atk.	Def.	Eva.	Mag. Atk.	Mag. Def.	Mag. Eva.	Element	Weaknesses	Steal	Drop
Goblin	46	5555	1150	2189	960	30	18	70	0	7	250	0	None	Holy	Mythril Glove	None
Goddess	68	44,000	19,000	0	0	50	13	65	0	14	150	0	Lightning, Holy	None	Minerva	Excaliber
Gold Bear	13	275	0	160	185	25	13	40	0	10	140	0	None	None	Potion, Tonic	Potion
Gold Dragon	62	32,400	4000	0	0	75	13	110	0	10	150	0	Lightning	Water	None	Crystal Orb
Grease Monk	8	132	100	53	256	35	15	100	0	10	150	0	None	Poison	Buckler, Tonic	None
Grenade	17	3000	500	190	500	30	13	0	0	10	150	0	Fire	Water, Ice	Fire Skean	None
Grunt	12	100	10	0	48	35	11	50	0	10	150	0	None	None	Tonic	Tonic
Gt. Behemoth	58	11,000	700	4100	2900	35	7	90	0	10	105	0	None	None	Tiger Fangs	None
Guard	5	40	15	48	48	30	16	100	0	6	140	0	None	Poison	Tonic, Potion	Tonic
Guardian	67	60,000	5200	0	0	80	13	150	0	25	150	0	None	Water, Lightning	Force Armor, Ribbon	None
Hades Gigas	16	1200	60	550	600	40	18	125	0	5	115	0	Earth	Poison	Atlas Armlet	None
Harpiai	29	1418	100	449	909	30	19	102	0	10	153	0	None	Wind	Phoenix Down	None
Harpy	42	3615	233	1994	1221	35	13	115	0	10	145	0	None	None	Phoenix Down	None
Harvester	16	428	85	291	314	50	13	105	0	10	150	0	None	Poison	Dragoon Boots, Goggles	Barrier Ring
Hazer	12	120	100	35	101	25	5	110	0	7	150	0	None	Holy	Potion	Tonic
Heavy Armor	13	495	150	80	195	40	53	150	0	11	110	0	None	Water, Lightning	Iron Helmet, Tonic	None
Hemophyte	56	6800	1600	3090	200	40	12	110	0	14	145	0	None	None	Tack Star	None
Hermit Crab	26	305	35	267	400	10	5	150	0	5	80	0	None	Water	Potion	Warp Stone
Hidon	43	25,000	12,500	0	0	55	13	110	0	10	160	0	Poison	Earth, Holy, Fire	Thornlet, Warp Stone	Warp Stone
Hidonite	43	3500	1000	0	0	30	13	115	0	10	120	0	Fire, Ice, Lightning, Poison, Water, Earth, Holy	None	None	None
Hidonite	43	3500	1000	0	0	30	13	85	0	10	150	0	Poison	Wind	None	None
Hidonite	43	3500	1000	0	0	30	13	95	0	10	140	0	None	Fire, Ice, Holy, ightning, Wind, Poison, Earth, Water	None	None
Hidonite	43	3500	1000	0	0	30	13	105	0	10	130	0	Poison	Fire, Holy	None	None
Hipocampus	37	2444	82	981	669	37	15	115	0	10	160	0	Poison	Holy, Fire	Warp Stone	Warp Stone
Hoover	49	12,018	10,500	7524	10,000	54	54	130	30	22	60	0	None	Water, Ice	Remedy	None
Hornet	6	92	0	48	64	30	16	100	0	10	150	0	None	Fire	Tonic	Tonic

Name	Lv.	HP	MP	Exp.	GP	Sp.	Atk.	Def.	Eva.	Mag. Atk.	Mag. Def.	Mag. Eva.	Element	Weaknesses	Steal	Drop
Humpty	27	800	100	421	326	30	8	145	0	10	135	0	Poison	Holy, Fire	Green Cherry	None
Ice Dragon	74	24,400	9000	0	0	60	13	110	0	10	150	0	Ice	Fire	None	Force Shield
Ifrit	21	3300	600	0	0	35	25	215	20	7	115	0	Fire	Ice	None	None
Inferno	67	30,800	9700	0	0	45	13	130	0	10	145	0	Fire	Ice	Ice Shield	None
Ing	21	1100	50	740	442	35	18	110	0	12	150	0	Fire, Poison	Water, Holy	Amulet	Revivify
Innoc	52	6600	390	2400	1950	33	13	155	0	12	155	0	None	Water, Lightning	Bio Blaster	None
Insecare	23	977	80	292	410	35	15	115	0	10	155	0	None	Wind, Fire	Echo Screen	Smoke Bomb
Intangir	26	32,000	16,000	0	0	50	25	150	50	10	150	0	Fire, Ice, Lightning, Poison, Water, Earth, Wind, Holy	None	Magicite	Antidote
Io	39	7862	1550	3253	1995	60	13	110	0	10	150	0	None	Water, Holy, Lightning	None	None
Ipooh	11	360	60	0	0	35	18	105	0	10	150	0	None	Fire	Potion	None
Iron Fist	15	333	65	144	249	35	13	75	0	10	145	0	Poison	None	Headband, Tonic	Mythril Knife
Iron Hitman	52	2000	800	2000	700	31	13	20	0	25	165	0	Lightning, Water	None	Auto Crossbow	None
Joker	17	467	90	194	320	35	13	125	0	10	150	0	None	Poison, Lightning	Green Beret, Tonic	Mythril Rod
Junk	53	2000	200	2200	1100	35	2	190	0	10	170	0	None	Water, Lightning	Noise Blaster	None
Karkass	43	3850	185	1399	826	33	13	105	0	10	155	0	Poison	Holy, Fire	Soul Sabre, Mythril Blade	None
Katana Soul	61	37,620	7400	0	30,000	75	25	115	20	11	175	0	None	Poison	Murasame, Strato	Offering
Kefka (Narshe)	18	3000	3000	0	0	45	25	55	0	9	160	30	None	None	Elixir, Tincture	Peace Ring
Kefka (Final)	71	62,000	38,000	0	0	72	80	117	45	8	135	0	None	None	Megalixir	None
Kiwok	33	2000	100	1000	750	33	10	105	0	10	145	0	None	Ice	None	White Cape, Green Cherry
L.10 Magic	48	1000	300	0	0	33	10	200	100	22	150	0	Poison	Holy, Fire	Tincture	Tincture
L.20 Magic	51	2000	500	0	0	35	10	200	100	21	145	0	Poison	None	Tincture	Tincture
L.30 Magic	54	3000	700	0	0	36	10	200	100	20	140	0	Holy	Poison	Tincture	Tincture
L.40 Magic	55	4000	1000	0	0	38	10	200	100	19	135	0	Poison	Lightning	Tincture	Tincture
L.50 Magic	57	5000	2000	0	0	45	10	200	100	18	130	0	Poison	Fire, Holy	Ether	Tincture

Name	Lv.	HP	MP	Exp.	GP	Sp.	Atk.	Def.	Eva.	Mag. Atk.	Mag. Def.	Mag. Eva.	Element	Weaknesses	Steal	Drop
L.60 Magic	58	6000	5000	0	0	35	10	200	100	17	125	0	Ice	Fire	Ether	Tincture
L.70 Magic	56	7000	3000	0	0	40	10	200	100	16	120	0	Fire	Water, Ice	Ether	Tincture
L.80 Magic	53	8000	2800	0	0	37	10	200	100	15	115	0	None	Poison	Ether	Tincture
L.90 Magic	55	9000	9000	0	0	38	10	200	100	14	110	0	Wind	None	Ether	Tincture
Land Worm	59	12,000	1300	4600	0	30	13	80	0	8	120	0	Earth	Ice	X-Potion	None
Larry	47	10,000	2000	0	0	30	2	90	0	5	120	0	Ice, Wind	Fire	None	None
Laser Gun	24	3300	335	0	0	30	12	130	0	9	140	0	None	Water, Lightning	X-Ether	None
Latimeria	27	1700	100	612	971	35	15	125	0	9	140	0	None	Lightning	Gaia Gear	Antidote
Leader	12	456	20	0	50	35	18	5	0	10	110	0	None	None	None	Phoenix Down, Black Belt
Leafer	5	33	0	24	45	30	13	60	0	10	140	0	Ice	Water, Fire	Tonic	Tonic
Left Blade	21	400	150			30	20	120	0	5	150	0	Ice	None	Tincture	Phoenix Down
Lethal Weapon	47	9200	1956	5848	1189	55	18	190	10	15	125	10	None	Water, Lightning	Debilitator	None
Lich	20	590	90	374	350	35	1	50	0	10	190	0	Fire, Poison	Holy	Poison Rod, Green Cherry	Green Cherry
Lizard	26	1280	70	297	356	30	14	102	0	10	153	0	Poison	Ice	Drainer	Soft
Lobo	5	27	5	37	30	35	20	80	0	3	120	0	None	Fire	Tonic	Tonic
Lunaris	26	582	25	308	247	25	13	155	0	10	145	0	None	None	Potion	None
Luridan	34	2079	122	707	1000	33	12	210	25	10	125	0	None	Wind, Fire	Potion	None
Mad Oscar	30	2900	980	780	2292	30	20	95	0	10	145	0	None	None	X-Potion	Remedy, Revivify
Madam	53	8150	900	2200	700	35	8	100	0	12	155	0	None	Poison	Goggles	None
Mag Roader 4	32	1380	70	647	284	33	14	105	0	10	150	0	None	None	Shuriken, Blot Edge	Fire Skean
Mag Roader 3	32	1777	100	621	352	33	13	115	0	10	145	0	None	None	Shuriken, Bolt Edge	Water Edge
Mag Roader 2	18	250	100	198	300	25	10	20	0	1	140	0	None	Ice	Shuriken, Bolt Edge	Fire Skean
Mag Roader 1	19	420	100	232	277	30	12	25	0	1	140	0	Ice	Fire	Shuriken, Bolt Edge	Water Edge
Mage Master	68	50,000	50,000	0	0	90	1	250	100	25	100	100	None	None	Elixir, Crystal Orb	Megalixir

Name	Lv.	HP	MP	Exp.	GP	Sp.	Atk.	Def.	Eva.	Mag. Atk.	Mag. Def.	Mag. Eva.	Element	Weaknesses	Steal	Drop
Magic Urn	31	100	10,000	0	0	40	5	220	100	35	190	0	Fire, Ice, Holy, Lightning, Poison, Earth, Water, Wind	None	Elixir, Tonic	None
Maliga	26	952	100	360	576	30	15	110	0	10	145	0	None	Water, Lightning, Ice	Tonic	None
Mandrake	23	1150	104	378	450	30	16	115	0	10	125	0	Water	Fire	Potion	Remedy
Mantodea	54	4500	420	4612	501	45	180	145	0	10	100	0	None	Fire	Imp Halberd	None
Marshal	8	420	150	0	350	40	13	110	0	9	140	0	None	Poison	Mythril Knife	Potion
Master Pug	73	22,000	1200	0	0	45	13	100	0	9	165	0	Water	None	Megalixir, Elixir	Graedus
Mega Armor	21	1000	50	350	0	45	19	120	0	10	100	0	None	Water, Lightning	Potion	None
Merchant	5	119	20	26	60	30	10	50	0	10	150	0	None	None	Plumed Hat, Guardian	None
Mesosaur	26	1112	130	459	456	30	13	110	0	10	150	0	None	Ice	Antidote	None
Mind Candy	15	290	100	128	168	30	14	105	0	10	165	0	None	Wind, Fire	Tonic, Soft	Soft
Misfit	26	1750	140	750	786	35	26	105	0	10	155	0	Poison	Holy, Fire	Back Guard	None
Missile Bay	25	3000	7000	0	0	20	12	135	0	8	150	0	None	Ice, Lightning	Debilitator	None
Moe	47	12,500	2000	0	0	25	4	80	0	6	130	0	Lightning	None	None	None
Mover	51	120	10,500	1500	0	85	20	115	225	10	254	0	Poison	None	Super Ball	Magicite
M-Tek Armor	8	210	250	0	0	25	18	30	0	3	130	0	None	Lightning	Potion, Tonic	Potion
Muus	28	900	100	189	287	30	11	110	0	10	105	0	None	None	Magicite	None
Nastidon	32	1877	100	697	298	35	13	145	0	10	105	0	None	Fire	Potion, Tonic	Potion
Naughty	24	3000	195	0	0	48	11	115	0	10	145	0	Ice	Holy, Lightning, Fire	None	None
Nautloid	11	236	100	216	173	35	18	100	0	10	150	0	Water	Fire, Lightning	Potion, Tonic	Eyedrop
Neck Hunter	28	1334	150	558	1330	30	5	102	0	10	153	0	None	Poison	Dark Hood	Peace Ring
Necromancer	48	3525	900	1510	791	25	13	100	0	7	150	0	Poison	Holy, Fire	Phoenix Down	Revivify
Nerapa	26	2800	280	0	0	48	11	105	0	10	150	0	Fire	Holy, Lightning, Ice	None	None
Nightshade	37	2200	305	872	767	35	13	110	0	9	140	0	Water	Fire	Nutkin Suit	None
Ninja	27	1650	130	694	520	37	22	135	50	5	140	0	Poison	Holy, Lightning	Cherub Down	Ninja Star
Nohrabbit	26	75	200	0	0	30	7	100	0	30	100	0	None	Water	Remedy	Potion
Number 024	24	4777	777	0	0	40	20	170	0	3	100	0	None	None	Drainer, Rune Edge	Flame Sabre, Blizzard

Name	Lv.	HP	MP	Exp.	GP	Sp.	Atk.	Def.	Eva.	Mag. Atk.	Mag. Def.	Mag. Eva.	Element	Weaknesses	Steal	Drop
Number 128	23	3276	810	0	0	30	13	120	0	3	125	0	Ice	None	Tempest	Tent
Officer	7	102	25	33	66	30	13	100	0	10	150	0	None	Poison	Potion, Tonic	None
Ogor	44	4211	219	1583	869	32	19	100	30	11	150	30	None	Poison, Lightning	Murasame, Ashura	Revivify
Opinicus	38	3210	514	1270	519	38	22	135	0	10	150	0	Poison	Holy, Fire	Warp Stone	Warp Stone
Orog	30	1584	250	510	716	35	45	105	0	10	140	0	Poison	Holy, Fire	Amulet	Amulet, Revivify
Osprey	26	850	100	249	596	25	12	105	0	10	120	0	None	Ice	None	Echo Screen
Osteosaur	30	1584	143	770	542	33	45	115	0	10	155	0	Poison	Holy, Fire	Remedy	Revivify
Outsider	18	8050	400	2600	2800	40	15	105	0	4	155	0	Poison	Holy	Break Blade	None
Over Gunk	15	492	100	219	365	30	13	125	0	10	125	0	None	Fire	Remedy, Potion	None
Over-Mind	13	390	190	65	228	30	12	55	0	7	150	0	Poison	Holy, Fire	Potion	Revivify, Green Cherry
Pan Dora	39	1522	350	622	461	25	13	140	0	10	80	0	Poison	Holy, Fire	None	None
Parasite	39	1000	230	455	461	20	1	140	0	1	5	0	None	Fire	None	None
Parasoul	47	2077	500	1620	674	30	13	80	0	10	150	0	Fire	Ice	Phoenix Down	Phoenix Down
Peepers	23	1	19	2	0	35	7	5	0	10	5	0	None	Water, Ice	Elixir	None
Phase	47	4550	1700	2600	890	30	11	105	0	10	150	0	Fire	Ice	Phoenix Down	Phoenix Down
Phunbaba (1st)	31	28,000	10,000	0	0	30	15	105	0	6	150	0	Lightning	Poison	None	None
Phunbaba (2nd)	31	26,000	10,000	0	0	35	15	100	0	6	130	0	Lightning	Poison	None	None
Pipsqueak	18	250	50	115	100	25	13	200	0	10	150	0	None	Water, Lightning	Tonic	None
Piranha	9	10	60	0	0	30	13	100	0	10	150	0	None	Lightning	None	Tonic
Pluto Armor	39	2850	220	853	629	35	13	105	0	9	150	0	None	Water, Lightning	None	None
Pm Stalker	26	265	190	258	491	20	9	140	0	6	115	0	Poison	Holy, Fire	X-Potion	None
Poltergeist	67	58,000	18,900	0	0	53	15	180	0	13	145	0	Fire, Wind	Poison	Red Jacket	Air Lancet
Poplium	11	145	25	55	55	25	13	55	0	10	150	0	Poison	Holy, Fire	Potion	Tonic
Poppers	33	1000	100	800	350	34	5	120	0	10	140	0	None	Fire	Green Cherry	Green Cherry
Power Demon	29	2058	360	485	385	40	13	145	0	10	140	0	Poison	Holy, Fire	Diamond Vest, Potion	Amulet, Revivify
Presenter	31	9845	1600	0	1000	35	75	80	0	7	150	0	Ice, Water,	Fire, Lightning	None	Dragon Claw
Primordite	11	145	10	90	115	30	13	50	0	10	150	0	None	Lightning	Tonic, Eyedrop	None
Prometheus	56	14,500	2050	5200	1300	47	13	170	0	10	150	0	None	Water, Lightning	Debilitator	None

Name	Lv.	HP	MP	Exp.	GP	Sp.	Atk.	Def.	Eva.	Mag. Atk.	Mag. Def.	Mag. Eva.	Element	Weaknesses	Steal	Drop
Proto Armor	19	670	125	499	296	30	12	230	0	7	110	0	None	Lightning	Mythril Mail, Potion	Bio Blaster
Prussian	41	3300	188	1396	773	35	13	115	0	10	155	0	None	None	Full Moon	None
Psychot	32	900	55	347	275	33	14	165	0	10	125	0	Fire	Ice	Tonic	Tonic
Pterodon	12	380	70	464	325	45	25	65	0	10	180	0	None	Fire	Guardian, Mythril Knife	Potion
Pug	27	8000	15,500	1200	3333	35	13	150	50	10	180	50	Water	Lightning, Fire	None	Tintinabar
Pugs	99	14,001	11,000	0	0	70	5	100	150	1	150	0	Water	Fire	Minerva	Minerva
Punisher	35	2191	136	1242	3000	35	28	100	115	10	155	0	None	Poison	Bone Club, Rising Sun	None
Rain Man	39	2722	180	890	485	34	13	110	0	10	145	30	None	Water, Ice, Holy	None	None
Ralph	17	620	10	255	345	35	14	135	0	10	145	0	None	None	Tiger Mask, Tonic	Potion
Reach Frog	52	3511	220	1550	2600	35	13	130	0	7	145	0	None	Ice	Tack Star, Potion	None
Red Dragon	67	30,000	1780	0	0	75	13	110	0	10	150	0	Fire	Water, Ice	None	Strato
Red Fang	14	325	20	135	185	30	13	95	0	10	150	0	None	None	Tonic	Dried Meat
Red Wolf	32	1510	110	687	412	25	10	155	0	10	140	0	None	None	Tonic	Tonic
Repo Man	5	35	0	25	25	35	19	90	0	10	120	0	None	Poison	Tonic	Tonic
Retainer	59	7050	2600	2300	2000	35	13	100	40	5	180	0	None	Poison	Aura	None
Rhinotaur	8	232	100	246	186	35	25	100	0	10	155	0	Lightning	None	Mythril Claw, Tonic	Potion
Rhinox	19	800	35	592	400	30	13	200	0	10	100	0	Lightning	None	Flash	None
Rhobite	10	135	40	53	110	30	9	70	0	10	140	0	None	Water	Potion	Tonic
Rhodox	7	119	100	59	80	30	11	100	0	10	155	0	None	None	Tonic, Antidote	None
Rider	14	1300	170	400	1290	45	48	120	0	10	150	0	None	Poison, Fire	Elixir, Mythril Vest	Remedy
Right Blade	22	700	470	0	0	30	13	120	0	5	150	0	Ice	None	Tincture	Phoenix Down
Rinn	11	110	35	95	100	25	10	55	0	10	125	0	Poison	Holy, Fire	Tonic	None
Rizopas	13	775	39	0	0	40	14	110	0	3	175	0	Water	None	None	Remedy
Rough	69	8000	770	0	0	30	13	80	0	10	190	0	Lightning	Ice	Flame Shield	None
Ryhos	36	7191	354	4928	1889	60	40	150	0	15	160	0	None	None	Gold Lance	None
Samurai	40	3000	500	1545	791	20	13	10	0	10	20	0	None	Poison	None	None
Sand Horse	27	1025	100	475	726	30	15	135	0	9	155	0	None	Water, Ice	Potion	None
Sand Ray	6	67	10	41	54	30	20	110	0	10	145	0	None	Water, Ice	Antidote	Antidote

Name	Lv.	HP	MP	Exp.	GP	Sp.	Atk.	Def.	Eva.	Mag. Atk.	Mag. Def.	Mag. Eva.	Element	Weaknesses	Steal	Drop
Scorpion	26	290	19	199	336	20	10	5	0	9	215	0	None	None	Tonic	Tonic
Scrapper	34	1759	68	797	2000	37	10	125	120	10	145	0	Poison	None	Thief's Glove	Air Lancet
Scullion	57	27,000	9000	9000	0	40	13	175	0	15	145	0	None	Water, Lightning	Air Anchor	None
Sea Flower	47	4200	200	1315	670	30	13	135	0	10	100	0	Fire, Water	Lightning, Ice	Phoenix Down	Phoenix Down
Sewer Rat	16	299	20	108	156	30	13	110	0	10	160	0	Poison	Fire	Potion	None
Shiva	21	3000	500	0	0	35	15	200	20	7	110	0	Ice	Fire	None	None
Skull Dragon	62	32,800	1999	0	400	57	15	140	0	10	120	0	Poison	Fire, Holy	None	Muscle Belt
Sky Armor	24	900	170	350	400	30	16	150	0	7	120	0	None	Wind, Lightning	Tincture	None
Sky Base	52	6000	550	2300	670	35	10	140	0	5	140	0	None	Water, Lightning	Flash	None
Sky Cap	40	3262	200	1253	441	35	13	105	0	8	150	0	None	Water, Wind, Lightning	None	None
Slam Dancer	15	392	120	224	296	35	13	115	0	10	145	0	None	Poison	Thief's Knife, Potion	None
Slatter	37	2600	97	830	415	35	13	125	20	10	145	10	None	Holy	Warp Stone	Warp Stone
Slurm	23	505	20	232	270	30	12	50	0	10	50	0	None	Fire	Potion	None
Soldier	11	100	15	0	48	30	12	80	0	10	150	0	None	Poison	Tonic, Potion	Tonic
Soul Dancer	22	2539	100	1531	769	30	1	60	0	30	170	0	None	Poison	Moogle Suit	None
Soul Saver	41	3066	566	0	0	15	50	150	0	3	175	0	Fire, Holy	Ice	None	None
Sp. Force	21	700	20	200	0	40	13	100	0	10	140	0	None	Poison	Tonic	Magicite
Speck	25	420	285	0	0	15	12	230	0	10	160	0	None	Water, Lightning	Amulet	None
Specter	19	1500	10,000	0	0	40	15	120	0	8	180	0	Poison	Holy, Fire	None	Hyper Wrist
Spectre	13	235	120	220	138	35	1	0	0	8	160	0	Poison	Fire, Holy	Ice Rod, Tonic	Tonic
Spek Tor	50	250	20	1356	1524	70	30	100	50	10	200	0	None	Water	X-Potion	None
Spit Fire	25	1400	180	550	300	35	17	155	0	4	130	0	None	Wind, Lightning	Elixir, Tincture	Tincture
Sprinter	53	4500	350	2293	1420	55	13	100	0	10	150	0	None	Lightning	None	Imp's Armor
Sr. Behemoth	43	19,000	1600	0	0	60	11	120	0	9	130	0	Ice	Poison, Fire	Murasame	Valiant Knife, Oath Veil
Sr. Behemoth	49	19,000	9999	0	0	39	27	105	0	10	150	0	Poison	Fire, Holy	None	Behemoth Suit

Name	Lv.	HP	MP	Exp.	GP	Sp.	Atk.	Def.	Eva.	Mag. Atk.	Mag. Def.	Mag. Eva.	Element	Weaknesses	Steal	Drop
Steroidite	54	25,000	350	4200	100	45	13	5	0	15	70	0	None	Holy	Thunder Shield	None
Still Going	12	200	84	54	135	30	10	100	0	10	150	0	Poison	Holy, Fire	None	Potion
Still Life	37	4889	390	2331	1574	45	13	150	0	10	150	0	None	Fire	Fake Mustache	None
Storm Dragon	74	42,000	1250	0	0	65	13	110	0	9	150	0	Wind	Lightning	None	Force Armor
Stray Cat	10	156	30	42	90	30	9	10	0	10	135	0	None	None	Potion	Tonic
Striker	67	11,000	2600	0	0	26	13	75	0	7	185	0	Ice	Fire	Flame Shield	None
Suriander	40	2912	228	1150	435	30	13	105	0	10	155	0	None	Holy	None	None
Tap Dancer	43	4452	270	1727	526	39	13	105	0	11	150	0	None	Poison	Sword Breaker, Dirk	None
Telstar	14	1800	250	0	0	35	20	120	0	13	150	0	None	Lightning, Water	X-Potion	Green Beret
Templar	11	205	50	0	96	30	16	50	0	10	150	0	None	Poison	Tonic	Potion
Tentacle	33	5000	600	0	0	35	13	102	0	8	153	0	Lightning, Water	None	None	None
Tentacle	31	7000	800	0	0	25	13	102	0	8	153	0	Fire	Ice, Water	None	None
Tentacle	34	4000	500	0	0	40	13	102	0	8	153	0	Water, Earth	None	None	None
Tentacle	32	6000	700	0	0	30	13	102	0	8	153	0	Ice, Water	Fire	None	None
Test Rider	32	3100	220	1947	520	40	27	135	0	10	155	0	None	Poison	Partisan	Spear
Toe Cutter	36	2500	187	1753	726	40	21	125	20	12	140	0	Ice	Wind, Fire	Poison Rod	Poison Rod
Tomb Thumb	33	2000	100	500	150	32	10	150	0	10	120	0	None	Water, Lightning	None	Green Cherry
Trapper	19	555	80	235	200	35	13	180	0	10	135	0	None	Water, Lightning	Auto Crossbow	None
Trilium	9	147	100	97	134	30	13	102	0	10	170	0	Water	Fire	Remedy, Tonic	None
Trilobiter	12	150	20	105	135	30	11	90	0	10	150	0	None	None	Tonic, Antidote	None
Tritoch	62	30,000	50,000	0	0	40	19	254	0	4	70	0	Ice	Fire	None	None
Trixter	49	3815	9900	1698	826	30	13	120	0	7	165	0	None	Holy	Phoenix Down	Phoenix Down
Trooper	13	255	60	90	96	25	15	100	0	10	125	0	None	Poison	Tonic, Mythril Blade	None
Tumble Weed	55	6200	600	2554	1333	30	10	120	0	10	90	0	Water	Fire	Titanium	None
Tunnel Armor	16	1300	900	0	250	40	10	29	100	15	145	0	None	Lightning	Bio Blaster, Air Lancet	Elixir
Tusker	10	270	100	163	102	30	28	100	0	10	135	0	None	Fire	Potion, Tonic	Soft
Tyranosaur	57	12,770	420	8800	0	55	33	125	0	16	160	0	None	Ice	Imp's Armor	Imp Halberd
Ultros (Airship)	26	17,000	8000	0	0	30	10	20	0	3	10	0	Water	Fire, Poison	Dried Meat	None
Ultros (Esper)	25	22,000	750	0	3	35	22	95	0	7	155	0	Water	Fire, Lightning	White Cape	None

Name	Lv.	HP	MP	Exp.	GP	Sp.	Atk.	Def.	Eva.	Mag. Atk.	Mag. Def.	Mag. Eva.	Element	Weaknesses	Steal	Drop
Ultros (River)	19	3000	640	0	0	35	13	40	0	3	140	0	None	Lightning, Fire	None	Dried Meat
Ultros (Opera)	19	2550	500	0	2	40	13	105	0	4	150	0	Water	Lightning, Fire	None	None
Uroburos	48	50	760	1780	390	40	13	252	0	10	252	0	Fire	Ice	Phoenix Down	Phoenix Down
Ursus	34	2409	74	882	2000	34	15	165	110	10	140	0	None	Fire	Sneak Ring	None
Vaporite	5	15	0	23	29	30	13	95	0	10	150	0	Lightning	Holy, Fire	Tonic	Tonic
Vargas	12	11,600	220	0	0	30	13	85	0	10	150	0	None	Wind	Mythril Claw, Tonic	None
Vectagoyle	57	7500	880	2900	900	37	22	110	30	9	150	30	None	None	Sword Breaker	None
Vectaur	59	2800	180	1400	350	30	12	110	0	7	150	0	None	Water, Ice	Ninja Star	None
Vector Pup	11	166	10	128	83	25	14	80	0	10	150	0	None	Fire	Tonic	None
Vermin	16	499	40	145	235	35	20	120	0	10	190	0	Poison	Ice	Antidote, Potion	Potion
Veteran	51	10,000	300	2820	0	30	11	110	0	17	145	0	None	None	Earrings	None
Vindr	36	885	87	653	497	30	14	100	90	10	150	0	None	Fire	Chocobo Suit	None
Vommamoth	1	115	30	50	90	25	110	75	0	0	160	0	None	Fire	Potion, Tonic	Potion
Vulture	15	412	60	160	485	30	13	100	0	10	155	0	None	Wind	Phoenix Down, Potion	Phoenix Down, Potion
Warlock	38	1300	1250	970	333	39	10	180	0	10	225	0	None	Poison,	Warp Stone, Lightning	Warp Stone
Wart Puck	44	3559	330	1595	1169	35	15	120	0	11	160	0	None	Fire	Dried Meat, Flail	None
Weed Feeder	17	480	20	278	234	30	13	115	0	10	150	0	None	Wind, Fire	Antidote	Echo Screen
Were-Rat	4	24	0	21	22	30	13	100	0	10	150	0	Poison	Fire	Tonic	Tonic
Whelk	6	1600	1000	0	0	45	22	100	0	10	155	0	None	None	None	Tincture, Potion
Whisper	12	230	90	42	125	30	12	95	0	10	150	0	Poison	Holy, Fire	Potion	Soft
White Dragon	71	18,500	12,000	0	0	55	13	110	0	9	150	0	Holy	None	X-Potion	Pearl Lance
Wild Cat	36	1115	78	701	416	30	17	100	10	10	140	0	None	Water, Fire	Tabby Suit	None
Wild Rat	12	160	10	135	135	30	10	85	0	10	100	0	Poison	Fire	Tonic	None
Wirey Dragon	26	2802	200	895	1300	31	35	150	0	10	115	0	None	None	Dragoon Boots	None
Wizard	32	1677	200	587	388	33	13	50	0	10	160	0	None	Poison, Lightning	Ice Rod, Thunder Rod	Fire Rod

Name	Lv.	HP	MP	Exp.	GP	Sp.	Atk.	Def.	Eva.	Mag. Atk.	Mag. Def.	Mag. Eva.	Element	Weaknesses	Steal	Drop
Woolly	43	3609	300	1385	826	32	17	105	20	11	150	0	Ice, Lightning, Poison, Water, Earth, Wind	Fire	Imperial	None
Wrexsoul	53	23,066	5066	0	0	40	27	70	0	5	220	0	Fire, Holy	Ice	Safe Ring	Pod Bracelet
Wyvern	18	892	95	484	434	30	15	140	0	10	155	0	None	Ice	Dragoon Boots, Tonic	None
Yeti	33	17,200	6900	0	10	45	25	100	0	11	150	0	Ice	Fire	None	None
Ziegfried	7	100	5	0	1	30	1	50	0	10	150	0	None	None	None	Green Cherry
Zombone	21	1991	160	1072	309	40	29	150	0	10	100	0	Poison	Holy, Fire	Potion, Phoenix Down	Phoenix Down
Zone Eater	61	7700	57,000	2000	2000	60	23	120	0	10	150	0	Ice	Holy	Warp Stone	None

Weapons, Armor, Relics, & Items

The following pages contain lists of Weapons, Armor, Relics, and Items found in FINAL FANTASY VI.

Legend

Healing Items	These items can be used to restore HP, MP, or to cure abnormal status ailments.
Misc. Items	These rare items have unusual uses.
Tools	Only Edgar can use these items with his "Tool" command.
Throwing Weapons	Only Shadow can use these items with his "Throw" command.
Relics	Every character can equip two of these at a time. They give special bonuses that can drastically alter a character's performance.
Weapons	Nearly every character can use weapons. They strengthen a character's attack and often have special properties that can be advantageous if used properly.
Armor	Most characters can also equip armor to increase their defense against both physical and magical attacks.
Price	The cost of such an item if it can be purchased from a shop.
Effect	If an item has a special property, you'll find it noted here.
Users	A list of all characters that can make use of a piece of armor or a weapon. Not all items have such restrictions.

Healing Items

Item	Price	Effect
Antidote	50	Cures "Poison" status
Dried Meat	150	Restores 150 HP
Echo Screen	120	Cures "Mute" status
Elixir	N/A	Completely restores HP and MP
Ether	N/A	Restores 150 MP
Eyedrop	50	Cures "Dark" status
Phoenix Down	500	Revives a K.O.ed ally/Destroys undead enemies
Green Cherry	150	Cures "Imp" status
Megalixir	N/A	Completely restores party's HP and MP
Potion	300	Restores 250 HP
Remedy	1000	Cures abnormal statuses except "Zombie" and "Imp"
Revivify	300	Cures "Zombie" status/Damages undead enemies
Sleeping Bag	500	Completely restores one character's HP and MP. Can use at Save Points and Outdoors only
Soft	200	Cures "Petrify" status
Tent	1200	Completely restores party's HP and MP. Can use at Save Points and Outdoors only
Tincture	1500	Restores 50 MP
Tonic	50	Restores 50 MP
X-Ether	N/A	Completely restores MP
X-Potion	N/A	Completely restores HP

MISC. ITEMS

Item	Price	Effect
Magicite	N/A	Randomly summons an Esper to aid your party in battle
Rename Card	N/A	Allows you to change a character's name
Smoke Bomb	300	Allows party to escape from battle
Super Ball	10,000	Causes damage by bouncing off enemies
Warp Stone	700	Allows party to escape from battles and dungeons

TOOLS

Item	Price	Effect
Air Anchor	N/A	Causes enemies to self-destruct
Auto Crossbow	250	Attacks all enemies
Bio Blaster	750	Poisons enemies
Chain Saw	2000	Randomly dispatches an enemy
Debilitator	5000	Creates an elemental weak point in an enemy
Drill	3000	Drills through enemy defenses
Flash	1000	Blinds enemies
Noise Blaster	500	Confuses enemies

THROWING WEAPONS

Item	Price	Effect
Bolt Edge	500	Thunder-elemental attack against multiple enemies
Fire Skean	500	Fire-elemental attack against multiple enemies
Inviz Edge	200	Makes thrower invisible
Shadow Edge	400	Creates an illusion of the thrower
Water Edge	500	Water-elemental attack against multiple enemies

RELICS

Item	Price	Effect
Amulet	5000	Protects against "Poison", "Dark", and "Zombie"
Atlas Armlet	5000	Increases attack power
Back Guard	7000	Protects against "Back Attacks" and "Pincer Attacks"
Barrier Ring	500	Casts "Shell" on a character when his/her HP runs low
Beads	4000	Increases wearers "Evade" rate
Black Belt	5000	Allows character to counterattack enemies
Blizzard Orb	N/A	Allows Umaro to cast Blizzard spells
Charm Bangle	N/A	Lowers random encounter rate

Item	Price	Effect
Cherub Down	6300	Causes character to float during battle
Coin Toss	N/A	Changes Setzer's "Slot" command to "GP Rain"
Crystal Orb	N/A	Increases wearer's MP by 50%
Cure Ring	8000	Character slowly regains HP during battle (like Regen)
Cursed Ring	N/A	Bares a terrible curse, but increases defenses
Czarina Ring	3000	Casts "Safe" and "Shell" on a character when his/her HP is low
Dragon Horn	N/A	Makes character "Jump" every turn
Dragoon Boots	9000	Changes a character's "Fight" command to "Jump"
Earrings	5000	Increases wearer's magic power. Effect can be doubled by equipping a pair
Economizer	N/A	Cuts spell casting cost down to one Magic Point
Exp.Egg	N/A	Doubles the amount of Exp earned after battles
Fairy Ring	1500	Protects wearer from "Poison" and "Dark" spells
Fake Mustache	N/A	Changes Relm's "Sketch" command into "Control"
Gale Hairpin	8000	Increases party's chances for a "Preemptive Attack"
Gauntlet	N/A	Allows wearer to hold a weapon with both hands increasing attack power
Gem Box	N/A	Changes wearers "Magic" command to "X-Magic" allowing wearer to cast two spells each turn
Genji Glove	N/A	Allows wearer to equip and attack with two weapons
Goggles	500	Protects against "Dark"
Gold Hairpin	N/A	Cuts spell casting cost in half
Guard Ring	5000	Casts "Safe"
Hero Ring	N/A	Increases character's physical and magical attacking power
Hyper Wrist	8000	Increases a character's "Vigor"
Jewel Ring	1000	Protects against "Petrify"
Marvel Shoes	N/A	Causes a variety of positive status effects when a character wears them

(RELICS Cont.)

Item	Price	Effect
Memento Ring	N/A	Protects the wearer from mortal attacks
Merit Award	N/A	Allows wearer to equip heavy armor
Mythril Glove	700	Casts "Safe" on a character when his/her HP is low
Moogle Charm	N/A	No random enemy encounters
Muscle Belt	N/A	Increases a character's max HP by 50%
Offering	N/A	Changes wearers "Fight" command into "X-Fight" allowing him/her to attack four times each turn
Peace Ring	3000	Protects wearer from "Berserk" and "Muddle" spells
Pod Bracelet	N/A	Allows a character to cast Safe and Shell spells
Rage Ring	N/A	Strengthens Umaro's Rage attack/Umaro Only
Relic Ring	N/A	Makes wearers body cold
Ribbon	N/A	Protects wearer from all abnormal status ailments
Running Shoes	7000	Casts "Haste" in battle
Safety Bit	N/A	Protects wearer from mortal magic attacks
Safety Ring	N/A	Protects wearer from mortal magic attacks
Sneak Ring	3000	Increases Locke's chances of stealing items during battle
Sniper Sight	3000	Increases wearer's hit ratio to 100%
Sprint Shoes	1500	Walk faster in towns and dungeons when holding the "Circle" button
Star Pendant	500	Protects wearer from "Poison" spells
Thief Glove	N/A	Changes Locke's "Steal" command to the "Capture" command
Tintinabar	N/A	Wearer slowly recovers HP while walking
True Knight	1000	Allows character to protect other characters who are low on HP during battles
Wall Ring	600	Casts "Reflect" on wearer
White Cape	5000	Protects wearer from "Imp" and "Mute" spells
Zephyr Cape	7000	Increases wearer's "Evade" rate

WEAPONS

Weapons	Price	Effects	Users
Air Lancet	950	Wind-elemental	Locke, Strago, Gogo, Relm
Ashura	N/A		Cyan
Assassin	N/A	Randomly dispatches an enemy	Shadow, Locke
Atma Weapon	N/A	Transforms at Level Up, Grows stronger as HP increases	Celes, Edgar, Locke, Terra
Aura	N/A		Cyan
Aura Lance	N/A		Mog, Edgar
Blizzard	7000	Randomly casts "Ice"	Celes, Edgar, Locke, Terra
Blossom	3200		Shadow
Bone Club	N/A	Intricately carved	Locke
Boomerang	4500	Same damage from back row	Locke
Break Blade	12,000	Randomly casts "Break"	Celes, Edgar, Terra
Cards	N/A		Setzer
Chocobo Brush	N/A		Relm
Crystal	15,000		Celes, Edgar, Terra
Darts	10,000		Setzer
DaVinci Brush	7000		Relm
Dice	5000		Setzer
Dirk	150		Terra, Locke, Edgar, Celes, Setzer, Mog, Strago, Shadow, Relm, Gogo
Doom Darts	N/A	Randomly dispatches an enemy	Setzer
Dragon Claw	N/A	Holy-elemental	Sabin
Drainer	N/A	Absorbs damage as HP	Celes, Edgar, Terra, Locke
Enhancer	10,000	Magic power up	Terra, Celes, Edgar
Epee	3000		Celes, Edgar, Terra
Excalibur	N/A	Holy-elemental	Celes, Edgar, Locke, Terra
Falchion	17,000		Celes, Edgar, Locke, Terra
Fire Knuckle	10,000	Randomly casts "Fire"	Sabin

Weapons	Price	Effects	Users
Fire Rod	3000	Casts "Fire 2" when used as an item, and then breaks	Gogo, Relm, Strago
Fixed Dice	N/A		Setzer
Flail	2000	Same damage from back row	Gogo, Relm, Strago, Celes, Terra
Flame Sabre	7000	Randomly casts "Fire"	Celes, Edgar, Locke, Terra
Forged	1200		Cyan
Full Moon	2500	Same damage from back row	Locke
Gold Lance	12,000		Mog, Edgar
Graedus	N/A	Holy-elemental	Terra, Locke, Edgar, Celes, Setzer, Mog, Strago, Shadow, Relm, Gogo
Gravity Rod	1300	Casts "Quarter" when used as an item, and then breaks	Gogo, Relm, Strago
Guardian	N/A	Randomly evades an enemy's attack	Locke
Hardened	N/A		Shadow
Hawk Eye	6000	Same damage from back row	Locke
Heal Rod Strago	N/A	Recovers target's HP	Gogo, Relm,
Ice Rod	3000	Casts "Ice 2" when used as an item, and then breaks	Gogo, Relm, Strago
Illumina	N/A	Same damage from back row	Celes, Edgar, Locke, Terra
Imp Halberd	N/A	??? if equipped while an Imp	Terra, Locke, Edgar, Sabin, Cyan, Gau, Celes, Setzer, Mog, Strago, Shadow, Relm, Gogo
Imperial	N/A		Shadow
Kaiser	1000		Sabin
Kodachi	1200		Shadow
Kotetsu	800		Cyan
Magical Brush	10,000		Relm
Magus Rod	N/A	Magic power up	Gogo, Relm, Strago
Man Eater	11,000	Doubles damage to a human target	Terra, Locke, Edgar, Celes, Setzer, Strago, Shadow, Relm, Gogo

(WEAPONS Cont.)

Weapons	Price	Effects	Users
Metal Knuckle	N/A		Sabin
Morning Star	5000	Same damage from back row	Gogo, Relm, Strago, Celes, Terra
Murasame	N/A		Cyan
Mythril Blade	450		Celes, Edgar, Locke, Terra
Mythril Claw	800		Sabin
Mythril Knife	300		Terra, Locke, Edgar, Celes, Setzer, Mog, Strago, Shadow, Relm, Gogo
Mythril Pike	800		Mog, Edgar
Mythril Rod	500		Gogo, Relm, Strago
Ninja Star	500	Used with "Throw" command	Shadow
Ogre Nix	N/A	Consumes MP to inflict mortal blow	Celes, Edgar, Terra
Partisan	13,000		Mog, Edgar
Pearl Lance	N/A	Randomly casts "Pearl"	Mog, Edgar
Pearl Rod	12,000	Casts "Pearl" when used as an item, and then breaks	Gogo, Relm, Strago
Poison Claw	2500	Randomly poisons an enemy	Sabin
Poison Rod	1500	Casts "Poison" when used as an item, and then breaks	Gogo, Relm, Strago
Punisher	N/A	Uses MP to inflict mortal blow	Gogo, Relm, Strago
Ragnarok	N/A		Celes, Edgar, Locke, Terra
Rainbow Brush	N/A		Relm
Regal Cutlass	950		Celes, Edgar, Terra
Rising Sun	N/A	Same damage from back row	Locke
Rune Edge	7500	Consumes MP to inflict mortal blow	Celes, Edgar, Terra
Scimitar	N/A	Randomly dices up an enemy	Celes, Edgar, Cyan, Terra
Shuriken	30	Used with "Throw" command	Shadow

Weapons	Price	Effects	Users
Sky Render	N/A		Cyan
Sniper	15,000	Same damage from back row	Locke
Soul Sabre	N/A	Absorbs damage as MP, randomly casts "Doom"	Celes, Edgar, Locke, Terra
Stout Spear	10,000		Mog, Edgar
Strato	N/A		Cyan
Striker	N/A	Randomly dispatches an enemy	Shadow
Stunner	N/A	Randomly casts "Stop"	Shadow
Sword Breaker	16,000	Randomly evades an enemy's attack	Gogo, Relm, Strago, Shadow, Locke
Tack Star	N/A	Used with "Throw" command	Shadow
Tempest	N/A	Randomly casts "Wind Slash"	Cyan
Thief's Knife	N/A	Randomly steals an enemy's item	Shadow, Locke
Thunder Blade	7000	Randomly casts "Bolt"	Celes, Edgar, Locke, Terra
Thunder Rod	3000	Casts "Bolt 2" when used as an item, and breaks	Gogo, Relm, Strago
Tiger Fangs	N/A		Sabin
Trident	1700		Mog, Edgar
Trump	13,000	Randomly casts "Doom"	Setzer
Valiant Knife	N/A	Gains power as HP decreases	Locke
Wing Edge	N/A	Same damage from back row	Locke

ARMOR

Armor	Price	Effects	Users
Aegis Shield	N/A	Randomly evades magic attack	Terra, Locke, Edgar, Sabin, Cyan, Gau, Celes, Setzer, Mog, Strago, Shadow, Relm, Gogo
Bandana	800		Terra, Locke, Edgar, Sabin, Cyan, Gau, Celes, Setzer, Mog, Strago, Shadow, Relm, Gogo

(ARMOR Cont.)

Armor	Price	Effects	Users
Bard's Hat	3000	Raises MP a little	Terra, Locke, Edgar, Sabin, Cyan, Gau, Celes, Setzer, Mog, Strago, Shadow, Relm, Gogo
Behemoth Suit	N/A	Made of Behemoth hide	Relm, Strago
Beret	3500	Raises success rate of "Sketch"	Relm
Buckler	200		Terra, Locke, Edgar, Sabin, Cyan, Gau, Celes, Setzer, Mog, Strago, Shadow, Relm, Gogo
Cat Hood	N/A	Doubles GP earned in battle	Relm
Chocobo Suit	N/A	Feel like a Chocobo!	Relm, Strago
Circlet	7000		Terra, Locke, Edgar, Sabin, Cyan, Gau, Celes, Setzer, Mog, Strago, Shadow, Relm, Gogo
Coronet	N/A	Raises success rate of "Control"	Relm
Cotton Robe	200		Gogo, Relm, Strago, Terra
Crystal Helm	10,000		Setzer, Celes, Edgar, Terra
Crystal Mail	17,000		Setzer, Celes, Edgar, Cyan, Locke, Terra
Crystal Shield	7000		Setzer, Celes, Edgar, Cyan, Terra
Cursed Shield	N/A	Causes several abnormal status ailments	Terra, Locke, Edgar, Sabin, Cyan, Gau, Celes, Setzer, Mog, Strago, Shadow, Relm, Gogo
Czarina Gown	N/A		Relm
Dark Gear	13,000		Gogo, Gau, Setzer, Sabin, Shadow, Locke
Dark Hood	7500		Gogo, Gau, Mog, Sabin, Shadow, Locke
Diamond Armor	15,000		Setzer, Celes, Edgar, Cyan, Terra

Armor	Price	Effects	Users
Diamond Helm	8000		Setzer, Celes, Edgar, Cyan, Terra
Diamond Shield	3500		Setzer, Celes, Edgar, Cyan, Terra
Diamond Vest	12,000		Terra, Locke, Edgar, Sabin, Cyan, Gau, Celes, Setzer, Mog, Shadow, Gogo
Flame Shield	N/A	Absorbs Fire-elemental attacks	Terra, Locke, Edgar, Sabin, Cyan, Gau, Celes, Setzer, Mog, Strago, Shadow, Relm, Gogo
Force Armor	N/A	Magic Defense up	Setzer, Celes, Edgar, Cyan, Locke, Terra
Force Shield	N/A	Protects against magic attacks	Terra, Locke, Edgar, Sabin, Cyan, Gau, Celes, Setzer, Mog, Strago, Shadow, Relm, Gogo
Gaia Gear Sabin,	6000	Absorbs Earth-elemental attack	Terra, Locke, Gau, Celes, Setzer, Mog, Strago, Shadow, Relm, Gogo
Genji Armor	N/A		Setzer, Celes, Edgar, Cyan, Locke, Terra, Shadow
Genji Helmet	N/A		Terra, Locke, Edgar, Sabin, Cyan, Gau, Celes, Setzer, Mog, Strago, Shadow, Relm, Gogo
Genji Shield	N/A		Terra, Locke, Edgar, Sabin, Cyan, Gau, Celes, Setzer, Mog, Strago, Shadow, Relm, Gogo
Gold Armor	10,000		Mog, Setzer, Celes, Edgar, Cyan, Terra
Gold Helmet	4000		Mog, Celes, Egar, Cyan, Terra
Gold Shield	2500		Mog, Setzer, Celes, Edgar, Cyan, Terra
Green Beret	3000	Raises HP a little	Terra, Locke, Edgar, Sabin, Cyan, Gau, Celes, Setzer, Mog, Strago, Shadow, Relm, Gogo

(ARMOR Cont.)

Armor	Price	Effects	Users
Hair Band	150		Relm, Celes, Terra
Head Band	16,000		Gau, Mog, Sabin, Shadow, Cyan, Locke
Heavy Shield	400		Setzer, Celes, Edgar, Cyan, Locke, Terra
Ice Shield	N/A	Absorbs Ice-elemental attacks	Terra, Locke, Edgar, Sabin, Cyan, Gau, Celes, Setzer, Mog, Strago, Shadow, Relm, Gogo
Imp's Armor	N/A	??? if equipped while an Imp	Terra, Locke, Edgar, Sabin, Cyan, Gau, Celes, Setzer, Mog, Strago, Shadow, Relm, Gogo
Iron Armor	700		Setzer, Celes, Edgar, Cyan, Locke, Terra
Iron Helmet	1000		Gau, Setzer, Celes, Edgar, Cyan, Locke, Terra
Kung Fu Suit	250		Gau, Sabin, Shadow, Locke
Leather Armor	N/A		Terra, Locke, Edgar, Sabin, Cyan, Gau, Celes, Setzer, Mog, Strago, Shadow, Relm, Gogo
Leather Hat	N/A		Terra, Locke, Edgar, Sabin, Cyan, Gau, Celes, Setzer, Mog, Strago, Shadow, Relm, Gogo
Light Robe	11000		Gogo, Relm, Strago
Magus Hat	600		Gogo, Mog, Relm, Strago, Setzer, Terra
Minerva	N/A	Raises MP by 1/4	Celes, Terra
Mirage Vest	N/A	Creates an illusion	Terra, Locke, Edgar, Sabin, Cyan, Gau, Celes, Setzer, Mog, Strago, Shadow, Relm, Gogo

Armor	Price	Effects	Users
Moogle Suit	N/A	Be a moogle! Kupo!!	Relm, Strago
Mystery Veil	5500		Relm, Celes, Terra
Mythril Helm	2000		Gogo, Gau, Setzer, Celes, Edgar, Shadow, Cyan, Locke, Terra
Mythril Mail	3500		Setzer, Celes, Edgar, Cyan, Locke, Terra
Mythril Shield	1200		Terra, Locke, Edgar, Sabin, Cyan, Gau, Celes, Setzer, Mog, Strago, Shadow, Relm, Gogo
Mythril Vest	1200		Terra, Locke, Edgar, Sabin, Cyan, Gau, Celes, Setzer, Mog, Strago, Shadow, Relm, Gogo
Ninja Gear	1100		Gogo, Gau, Setzer, Sabin, Shadow, Locke
Nutkin Suit	N/A	A squirrel costume	Relm, Strago
Oath Veil	9000		Relm, Celes, Terra
Paladin Shield	N/A	Cursed Shield after "curse" is broken	Terra, Locke, Edgar, Sabin, Cyan, Gau, Celes, Setzer, Mog, Strago, Shadow, Relm, Gogo
Plumed Hat	250		Terra, Locke, Edgar, Sabin, Cyan, Gau, Celes, Setzer, Mog, Strago, Shadow, Relm, Gogo
Power Sash	5000		Gau, Sabin, Shadow, Cyan, Locke
Red Cap	N/A	Raises HP by 1/4	Terra, Locke, Edgar, Sabin, Cyan, Gau, Celes, Setzer, Mog, Strago, Shadow, Relm, Gogo
Red Jacket	N/A	Houses legendary grappler's spirit	Sabin, Edgar
Regal Crown	N/A		Sabin, Edgar
Silk Robe	600		Gogo, Mog, Relm, Strago, Celes, Terra
Snow Muffler	N/A		Gau, Mog
Tabby Suit	N/A	Resembles a tabby cat	Relm, Strago

(ARMOR Cont.)

Armor	Price	Effects	Users
Tao Robe	13000		Gogo, Relm, Strago
Thornlet	N/A	Slowly drains HP from wearer	Terra, Locke, Edgar, Sabin, Cyan, Gau, Celes, Setzer, Mog, Strago, Shadow, Relm, Gogo
Thunder Armor	N/A	Randomly casts Bolt 2, casts Bolt 3 when used as an item, and then breaks	Terra, Locke, Edgar, Sabin, Cyan, Gau, Celes, Setzer, Mog, Strago, Shadow, Relm, Gogo
Thunder Shield	N/A	Absorbs Thunder-elemental attacks	Terra, Locke, Edgar, Sabin, Cyan, Gau, Celes, Setzer, Mog, Strago, Shadow, Relm, Gogo
Tiara	3000		Relm, Celes, Terra
Tiger Mask	2500		Gau, Sabin, Shadow, Locke
Titanium	N/A	Cures "Imp" status	Terra, Locke, Edgar, Sabin, Cyan, Gau, Celes, Setzer, Mog, Strago, Shadow, Relm, Gogo
Tortoise Shield	N/A	??? if equipped while an Imp	Terra, Locke, Edgar, Sabin, Cyan, Gau, Celes, Setzer, Mog, Strago, Shadow, Relm, Gogo
White Dress	2200		Relm, Celes, Terra

ESPERS

In the early stages of the game only two of your characters, Terra and Celes, can use magic. It isn't until later in the game, when you begin to collect **Magicite crystals**, that the other characters will be able to cast spells.

Magicite is what remains of an Esper when its life has ended. You can equip these crystals one at a time on a character. When equipped, the character will slowly learn spells that the Esper was once able to cast. The character can also summon the Magicite's Esper once during a battle.

There are many different Espers to collect. You'll find a complete list of these Espers and their powers on the following pages.

Equipping an Esper

After collecting an Esper, you can equip it on a character. To do so, go to the Main Menu and select the Skills option. Select the character you want to equip, and then choose the Esper option. You'll then see a complete list of all of the Espers you've collected up to that point.

Espers in white are unequipped, while Espers in gray are currently equipped on a character. You can see which character has a particular Esper equipped by selecting it.

You can only equip one Esper on a character at a time. After the character has learned all it can from the Esper, you can then remove the equipped Esper and select another.

Learning from Espers

When you equip an Esper, you'll see a complete list of the spells the Esper can teach a character, the Learning Rate for each spell, and a percentage that indicates how far (or close) your character is to learning a particular spell.

After most battles, your characters will earn Magic Points if a character is currently learning a spell from an Esper. The amount earned varies from one to 10 Magic Points. These points are given to all of your active characters and applied toward every spell the characters are currently learning.

The Learning Rate next to a spell acts as a multiplier. The amount of Magic Points earned is multiplied by the Learning Rate and added to the percentage learned. For example, say your character is learning Cure 3 and the Learning Rate is x2. After a battle, the character earns five Magic Points. Those five points are multiplied by two, so the character's percentage learned is 10 percent. (5 Magic Points x 2 = 10%)

You can learn many spells from several different Espers. The Learning Rate will be different with each Esper, so you should always look for the quickest way to learn the spell. So, if you're trying to teach a character Cure, it's better to have Starlet, which has a x25 Learning Rate for Cure than Shiva, whose learning rate is only x3 for Cure. Always keep this in mind so that you avoid wasting valuable Magic Points.

Summoning an Esper

Each character can summon the Esper they have equipped once during a battle. To do so, select the Magic command and go to the top of the screen and press up. Select the Espers' attack, and it will perform the attack the next time the character acts. Esper attacks consume a lot of MP, so be careful when using them.

Level Bonuses

Most Espers have a Level Bonus, which is given to a character if it is equipped with the Esper when the character goes up a level. For example, let's say Locke has a Stamina of 30 and he's equipped with Golem when he goes up a level. Because Golem has a Level Bonus of Stamina +2, Locke's Stamina would increase to 32.

You can maximize the benefits of such Level Bonuses by paying close attention to your character's experience points. Just before your character goes up a level, equip an Esper with the Level Bonus you desire. Then, once the character goes up a level, go back to the Esper that the character was learning from. This takes a lot of work on your part, but it can be well worth the effort.

ALEXANDER

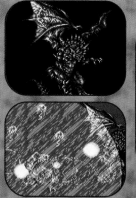

You can find Alexander on the throne in Doma Castle after you've defeated Wrexsoul in the World of Ruin. Alexander uses Justice, a ray of holy light, to attack a group of enemies. The Justice attack is a Holy attack and works best against undead creatures.

Level Bonus: None

Attack	MP Used
Justice	90 MP

Spells	Learn. Rate
Pearl	x2
Shell	x10
Safe	x10
Dispel	x10
Remedy	x15

BAHAMUT

You receive Bahamut after your party defeats the terror of the skies, Doom Gaze, in the World of Ruin. Bahamut attacks enemies with the Sun Flare attack, which causes massive damage to the entire group.

Level Bonus: HP +50%

Attack	MP Used
Sun Flare	80 MP

Spells	Learn. Rate
Flare	x2

BISMARK

You can find Bismark in the MagiTek Research Facility located in the town of Vector. Its Sea Song attack engulfs enemies in a blast of bubbling water. Sea Song is a Water elemental attack.

Level Bonus: Vigor +2

Attack	MP Used
Sea Song	50 MP

Spells	Learn. Rate
Fire	x20
Ice	x20
Bolt	x20
Life	x2

CARBUNKL

You can find Carbunkl in the MagiTek Research Facility located in the town of Vector. This Esper uses its Ruby Power to cast Reflect on your entire party.

Level Bonus: None

Attack	MP Used
Ruby Power	36 MP

Spells	Learn. Rate
Reflect	x5
Haste	x3
Shell	x2
Safe	x2
Warp	x2

CRUSADER

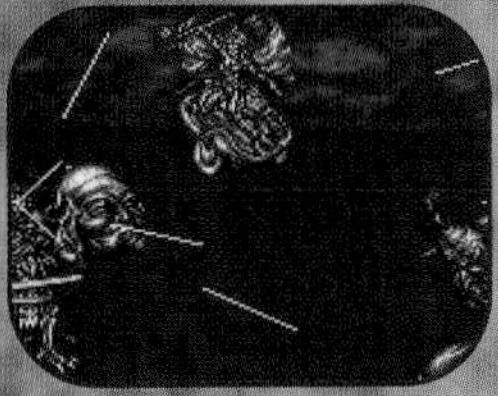

You receive Crusader after defeating all eight of the legendary Dragons. Its Purifier attack damages everyone on the screen—even your party. Be VERY careful when using this Esper.

Level Bonus: MP +50%

Attack	MP Used
Purifier	96 MP

Spells	Learn. Rate
Merton	x1
Meteor	x10

FENRIR

You receive Fenrir after defeating Phunbaba in Mobliz. Its Moon Song spell makes the party much harder to hit than normal.

Level Bonus: MP +30%

Attack	MP Used
Moon Song	70 MP

Spells	Learn. Rate
Warp	x10
X-Zone	x5
Stop	x3

GOLEM

You can purchase Golem for 20,000 GP in the Jidoor Auction House any time after the party escapes Vector. Its Earth Wall spell helps protect the party from physical attacks.

Level Bonus: Stamina +2

Attack	MP Used
Earth Wall	33 MP

Spells	Learn. Rate
Safe	x5
Stop	x5
Cure 2	x5

IFRIT

You can find Ifrit in the MagiTek Factory located in the town of Vector. Its Inferno attack blasts enemies with a huge firestorm. The Inferno spell is a Fire elemental attack.

Level Bonus: Vigor +1

Attack	MP Used
Inferno	26 MP

Spells	Learn. Rate
Fire	x10
Fire 2	x5
Drain	x1

KIRIN

You can find Kirin at the top of the tower in Zozo after the battle with Dadaluma. Kirin casts a regeneration spell on your entire party that causes them to slowly regain lost HP.

Level Bonus: None

Attack	MP Used
Life Guard	18 MP

Spells	Learn. Rate
Cure	x5
Cure 2	x1
Regen	x3
Antidote	x4
Scan	x5

MADUIN

You can find Maduin in the MagiTek Research Facility located in the town of Vector. Its Chaos Wing attacks enemies with powerful bolts of energy.

Level Bonus: Magic Power +1

Attack	MP Used
Chaos Wing	44 MP

Spells	Learn. Rate
Fire 2	x3
Ice 2	x3
Bolt	x3

ODIN

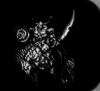

You can find Odin in the Ancient Castle, which can only be found in the World of Ruin. Odin charges through a group of enemies with its Atom Edge attack, which slices them in two.

Level Bonus: Speed +1

Attack	MP Used
Atom Edge	70 MP

Spells	Learn. Rate
Meteor	x1

PALIDOR

You can find Palidor on the beach on the Solitary Island where Celes begins in the World of Ruin. This Esper won't appear until you've received the second Airship. Palidor's Sonic Dive attack picks up the entire party and drops them onto any enemies below.

Level Bonus: None

Attack	MP Used
Sonic Dive	61 MP

Spells	Learn. Rate
Haste	x20
Slow	x20
Haste 2	x2
Slow 2	x2
Float	x5

PHANTOM

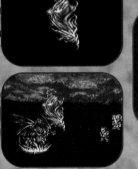

You can find Phantom in the MagiTek Research Facility located in the town of Vector. It casts Fader on your party, which makes the entire party invisible to the enemy.

Level Bonus: MP +10%

Attack	MP Used
Fader	38 MP

Spells	Learn. Rate
Berserk	x3
Vanish	x3
Demi	x5

PHOENIX

You receive Phoenix after locating Locke in the Phoenix Cave in the World of Ruin. When summoned, it uses Rebirth to bring any K.O.ed party members back to life.

Level Bonus: None

Attack	MP Used
Rebirth	110 MP

Spells	Learn. Rate
Life	x10
Life 2	x2
Life 3	x1
Cure 3	x2
Fire 3	x3

RAGNAROK

You can find Ragnarok inside the Weapon Shop at Narshe in the World of Ruin. The player must choose to keep the Ragnarok as a stone rather than turning it into a sword.

When used in battle, the Ragnarok attempts to turn an enemy into an item using its Metamorph attack. You can increase the odds of this working by lowering the opponent's HP and casting Vanish on the enemy.

Level Bonus: None

Attack	MP Used
Metamorph	6 MP

Spells	Learn. Rate
Ultima	x1

RAIDEN

Raiden is a transformed version of Odin. To get the transformation to take place, you must get the Odin Esper from the Ancient Castle and then find the Queen's statue. The statue will transform Odin into Raiden. When summoned, Raiden charges into battle and uses the True Edge to cut enemies in two.

Level Bonus: Vigor +2

Attack	MP Used
True Edge	80 MP

Spells	Learn. Rate
Quick	x1

RAMUH

You can find Ramuh at the top of the tower in Zozo after the fight with Dadaluma. He attacks with the powerful Bolt Fist, a lighting elemental attack that strikes all enemies.

Level Bonus: Stamina +1

Attack	MP Used
Bolt Fist	25 MP

Spells	Learn. Rate
Bolt	x10
Bolt 2	x2
Poison	x5

SHIVA

You can find Shiva in the MagiTek Factory located in the town of Vector. Using the Gem Dust attack, Shiva blasts all enemies with shards of ice. Gem Dust is an Ice elemental attack.

Level Bonus: None

Attack	MP Used
Gem Dust	27 MP

Spells	Learn. Rate
Ice	x10
Ice 2	x5
Rasp	x4
Osmose	x4
Cure	x3

SHOAT

You can find Shoat in the MagiTech Research Facility located in the town of Vector. Shoat uses the Demon Eye attack to petrify your enemies.

Level Bonus: HP +10%

Attack	MP Used
Demon Eye	45 MP

Spells	Learn. Rate
Bio	x8
Break	x5
Doom	x2

SIREN

You can find Siren at the top of the tower in Zozo after the battle with Dadaluma. Siren's Hope Song casts Silence on all enemies when she's summoned into battle.

Level Bonus: HP +10%

Attack	MP Used
Hope Song	16 MP

Spells	Learn. Rate
Sleep	x10
Mute	x8
Slow	x7
Fire	x6

SRAPHIM

You can find Sraphim any time after the party's assault on Vector. You must pay a thief 3000 or 30 GP for the Esper in the town of Tzen, depending on whether you purchase it during the World of Balance or the World of Ruin. When summoned, Sraphim's Reviver spell heals the party's wounds.

Level Bonus: None

Attack	MP Used
Reviver	40 MP

Spells	Learn. Rate
Life	x5
Cure 2	x8
Cure	x20
Regen	x10
Remedy	x4

267

STARLET

You can find Starlet in Owzer's bookcase after defeating Chadarnook in Owzer's house in the World of Ruin. Starlet's Group Hug heals your party and awakens any sleeping characters.

Level Bonus: Stamina +2

Attack	MP Used
Group Hug	74 MP

Spells	Learn. Rate
Cure	x25
Cure 2	x16
Cure 3	x1
Regen	x20
Remedy	x20

STRAY

You can find Stray at the top of the tower in Zozo after the battle with Dadaluma. Stray confuses the party's enemies with its Cat Rain.

Level Bonus: Magic Power +1

Attack	MP Used
Cat Rain	28 MP

Spells	Learn. Rate
Muddle	x7
Imp	x5
Float	x2

TERRATO

You can find Terrato in the bone statue inside Umaro's cave located above Narshe during the World of Ruin. Terrato's Earth Aura attack causes a huge shockwave that damages all enemies.

Level Bonus: HP +30%

Attack	MP Used
Earth Aura	40 MP

Spells	Learn. Rate
Quake	x3
Quarter	x1
White Wind	x1

TRITOCH

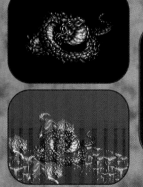

You can find Tritoch on a cliff above Narshe during the World of Ruin. You must defeat the Tritoch Esper before it will join you. Its Tri-Dazer attack combines Fire, Ice, and Thunder magic into powerful elemental bolts of energy.

Level Bonus: Magic Power +2

Attack	MP Used
Tri-Dazer	68 MP

Spells	Learn. Rate
Fire 3	x1
Ice 3	x1
Bolt 3	x1

UNICORN

You can find Unicorn inside the MagiTek Research Facility located in the town of Vector. Its Heal Horn removes some abnormal status effects for your entire party.

Level Bonus: None

Attack	MP Used
Heal Horn	30 MP

Spells	Learn. Rate
Cure 2	x4
Remedy	x3
Dispell	x2
Safe	x1
Shell	x1

ZONESEEK

You can purchase ZoneSeek for 10,000 GP at the auction in Jidoor any time after the party escapes from Vector. ZoneSeek's Wall spell creates a barrier that protects your entire party from magic attacks.

Level Bonus: Magic Power +2

Attack	MP Used
Wall	30 MP

Spells	Learn. Rate
Rasp	x20
Osmose	x15
Shell	x5

Magic
Magic Spells

As the game progresses, your characters will begin to learn the art of casting spells. On the following pages, you'll find a complete listing of those spells and information about each one. Keep this section handy to help you determine which Espers to equip and what spells to learn first.

Legend

(1) Spell Name

(2) Spell description/effect

(3) Magic Point consumption for a single use

(4) The number of allies/enemies the spell can target with each use

(5) The Espers from which your characters can learn the spell

(6) The rate at which the spell is learned from each Esper

(1) → Cure

(2) → *Restores a small amount of HP.*

(3) → MP Used — 5

(4) → Range — Single/All

(5) → Esper

Esper	**(6)** → Learn. Rate
Starlet	x25
Sraphim	x20
Kirin	x5
Shiva	x3

Recovery Magic

Cure

Restores a small amount of HP.

MP Used	5
Range	Single/All

Esper	Learn. Rate
Starlet	x25
Sraphim	x20
Kirin	x5
Shiva	x3

Cure 2

Restores three times as much HP as Cure.

MP Used	25
Range	Single/All

Esper	Learn. Rate
Starlet	x16
Sraphim	x8
Golem	x5
Unicorn	x4
Kirin	x1

Cure 3

Restores seven times as much HP as Cure.

MP Used	40
Range	Single/All

Esper	Learn. Rate
Phoenix	x2
Starlet	x1

Antidote

Cures a character of the Poison status.

MP Used	3
Range	Single

Esper	Learn. Rate
Kirin	x4

Life

Revives wounded allies and destroys undead enemies.

MP Used	30
Range	Single

Esper	Learn. Rate
Phoenix	x10
Sraphim	x5
Bismark	x2

Life 2

Revives wounded allies and completely restores their HP.

MP Used	60
Range	Single

Esper	Learn. Rate
Phoenix	x2

Life 3

Similar to Life, but this spell is cast on a fighter before he/she is knocked out during battle. If the character is critically wounded later in the battle, he/she is automatically revived.

MP Used	50
Range	Single

Esper	Learn. Rate
Phoenix	x1

Remedy

Cures all abnormal status effects except Zombie and Imp.

MP Used	15
Range	Single

Esper	Learn. Rate
Starlet	x20
Alexander	x15
Sraphim	x4
Unicorn	x3

Regen

Slowly restores a character's HP over time.

MP Used	10
Range	Single

Esper	Learn. Rate
Starlet	x20
Sraphim	x10
Kirin	x3

Offensive Magic

Fire

This small blast of heat causes a limited amount of damage to opponents.

MP Used:	4
Element:	Fire
Range:	Single/All

Esper	Learn. Rate
Bismark	x20
Ifrit	x10
Siren	x6

Fire 2

A larger blast of heat that causes three times as much damage as the Fire spell.

MP Used:	20
Element:	Fire
Range:	Single/All

Esper	Learn. Rate
Ifrit	x5
Maduin	x3

Fire 3

Bombs the enemy with an explosive blast that causes six times the damage of Fire.

MP Used:	51
Element:	Fire
Range:	Single/All

Esper	Learn. Rate
Phoenix	x3
Tritoch	x1

Bolt

Strikes an enemy with a lightning bolt.

MP Used:	6
Element:	Lightning
Range:	Single/All

Esper	Learn. Rate
Bismark	x20
Ramuh	x10

Bolt 2

Enemies are shocked with a larger lightning bolt that causes three times as much damage as Bolt.

MP Used:	22
Element:	Lightning
Range:	Single/All

Esper	Learn. Rate
Maduin	x3
Ramuh	x2

Bolt 3

Blasts the enemy with a huge lightning bolt that causes six times as much damage as Bolt.

MP Used:	53
Element:	Lighting
Range:	Single/All

Esper	Learn. Rate
Tritoch	x1

Ice

Freezes enemies with a blast of cold air.

MP Used:	5
Element:	Ice
Range:	Single/All

Esper	**Learn. Rate**
Bismark	x20
Shiva	x10

Ice 2

Ice shards engulf the enemy, causing three times as much damage as Ice.

MP Used:	21
Element:	Ice
Range:	Single/All

Esper	**Learn. Rate**
Shiva	x5
Maduin	x3

Ice 3

Huge ice boulders crash down on the enemy, causing six times as much damage as Ice.

MP Used:	52
Element:	Ice
Range:	Single/All

Esper	**Learn. Rate**
Tritoch	x1

Bio

A more powerful version of the Poison spell that can target multiple enemies.

MP Used:	26
Element:	Poison
Range:	Single/All

Esper	**Learn. Rate**
Shoat	x8

Poison

Engulfs an enemy in poisonous gas that causes damage and the Poison status effect.

MP Used:	3
Element:	Poison
Range:	Single

Esper	**Learn. Rate**
Ramuh	x5

Drain

Sucks HP from an enemy and transfers it to the spell caster.

MP Used:	15
Element:	None
Range:	Single

Esper	**Learn. Rate**
Ifrit	x1

Break

This spell attempts to petrify enemies.

MP Used:	25
Element:	None
Range:	Single

Esper	**Learn. Rate**
Shoat	x5

Pearl

Showers an enemy with holy light.

MP Used:	40
Element:	Holy
Range:	Single

Esper	**Learn. Rate**
Alexander	x2

Demi

This magic attack cuts an enemy's HP in half.

MP Used: 33
Element: None
Range: Single

Esper	Learn. Rate
Phantom	x5

X-Zone

Sends enemies to a different dimension from which they can never return.

MP Used: 53
Element: None
Range: All

Esper	Learn. Rate
Fenrir	x5

Doom

Summons the Grim Reaper whose touch brings instant death.

MP Used: 35
Element: None
Range: Single

Esper	Learn. Rate
Shoat	x2

Flare

A powerful explosive blast focused on a single enemy.

MP Used: 45
Element: None
Range: Single

Esper	Learn. Rate
Bahamut	x2

Quarter

This is stronger version of the Demi spell that cuts an enemy's HP down to one quarter.

MP Used: 48
Element: None
Range: All

Esper	Learn. Rate
Terrato	x1

Meteor

A meteor shower rains down from above.

MP Used: 62
Element: None
Range: All

Esper	Learn. Rate
Crusader	x10
Odin	x1

Ultima

This is the ultimate attack spell, which causes massive damage to entire groups of enemies.

MP Used: 80
Element: None
Range: All

Esper	Learn. Rate
Ragnarok	x1

W.Wind

Creates a powerful tornado that saps 90% of everyone's HP.

MP Used: 75
Element: None
Range: All (Enemies & Allies)

Esper	Learn. Rate
Terrato	x1

Quake

Causes a massive earthquake that damages anyone with their feet on the ground.

MP Used:	50
Element:	Earth
Range:	All (Enemies & Allies)

Esper	Learn. Rate
Terrato	x3

Merton

This powerful magical attack effects everyone within its path.

MP Used:	85
Element:	Fire
Range:	All (Enemies & Allies)

Esper	Learn. Rate
Crusader	x1

Effect Magic

Scan

Displays an enemy's Level, HP, MP and elemental weaknesses.

MP Used:	3
Range:	Single

Esper	Learn. Rate
Kirin	x5

Slow

Reduces an enemy's speed so that it takes longer between attacks.

MP Used:	5
Range:	Single

Esper	Learn. Rate
Palidor	x20
Siren	x7

Rasp

Reduces an enemy's total MP.

MP Used:	12
Range:	Single

Esper	Learn. Rate
Zone Seek	x20
Shiva	x4

Slow 2

Slows an entire group of enemies, so they all take longer between actions.

MP Used:	26
Range:	All

Esper	Learn. Rate
Palidor	x2

Safe

Increases the target defenses against physical attacks.

MP Used:	12
Range:	Single

Esper	Learn. Rate
Alexander	x10
Golem	x5
Carbunkl	x2
Unicorn	x1

Sleep

Temporarily puts an enemy to sleep so that it cannot perform any actions. If the target is struck by a physical attack, it will awaken.

MP Used:	5
Range:	Single

Esper	Learn. Rate
Siren	x10

Muddle

Confuses the target, making use of random commands against random targets.

MP Used:	8
Range:	Single
Esper	**Learn. Rate**
Stray	x7

Haste

Raises target's speed so that it takes less time between actions in battle.

MP Used:	10
Range:	Single
Esper	**Learn. Rate**
Palidor	x20
Carbunkl	x3

Haste 2

Speeds up the entire party, so everyone takes less time between actions.

MP Used:	38
Range:	All
Esper	**Learn. Rate**
Palidor	x2

Shell

Increases the target's defenses against magic attacks.

MP Used:	15
Range:	Single
Esper	**Learn. Rate**
Alexander	x10
ZoneSeek	x5
Carbunkl	x2
Unicorn	x1

Reflect

Creates a magical barrier that blocks most magic attacks. Reflected spells are bounced back at the caster's party. Reflect cannot block a spell that has already been reflected off of another character.

MP Used:	22
Range:	Single
Esper	**Learn. Rate**
Carbunkl	x5

Float

Causes the target to float in the air. Earth magic does not affect floating characters.

MP Used:	17
Range:	Single/All
Esper	**Learn. Rate**
Palidor	x5
Stray	x2

Imp

Turns the target into an Imp, limiting it's battle options. Can also be used to cure the Imp status effect.

MP Used:	10
Range:	Single
Esper	**Learn. Rate**
Stray	x5

Berserk

The target loses control of its actions and can only use physical attacks against random targets.

MP Used:	16
Range:	Single
Esper	**Learn. Rate**
Phantom	x3

Vanish

Makes the target temporarily invisible, which makes it immune to physical attacks. Character reappears when taking some actions or when magic is used against it.

MP Used: 18
Range: Single

Esper	Learn. Rate
Phantom	x3

Mute

Silences the target, making it impossible for the enemy to use magic.

MP Used: 8
Range: Single

Esper	Learn. Rate
Siren	x8

Quick

Makes the target super fast, allowing it to immediately take two additional turns.

MP Used: 99
Range: Caster

Esper	Learn. Rate
Raiden	x1

Stop

Stops the target temporarily so that it cannot perform actions during battle.

MP Used: 10
Range: Single

Esper	Learn. Rate
Golem	x5
Fenrir	x3

Osmose

Absorbs MP from and enemy and transfers it to the spell caster.

MP Used: 1
Range: Single

Esper	Learn. Rate
ZoneSeek	x15
Shiva	x4

Warp

Allows the party to escape from battles or dungeons instantly.

MP Used: 20
Range: All

Esper	Learn. Rate
Fenrir	x10
Carbunkl	x2

Dispel

Removes some abnormal status spells from characters.

MP Used: 25
Range: Single

Esper	Learn. Rate
Alexander	x10
Unicorn	x2

Colosseum

The following is a list to assist you with your betting in the Colosseum. With each item, you'll find the name of the monster you'll be fighting when the item is bet and what you stand to win if your fighter is victorious. Take special care when betting rare items. There's never such a thing as a sure win.

ARMS

Bet	Challenger	Prize
Blizzard	Scullion	Ogre Nix
Assassin	Test Rider	Sword Breaker
Strato	Aquila	Pearl Lance
Atma Weapon	Gt. Behemoth	Graedus
Fixed Dice	Trixter	Fire Knuckle
Trump	Allosaur	Trump
Striker	Chupon	Striker
Magus Rod	Allosaur	Strato
Wing Edge	Rhyos	Sniper
Ogre Nix	Sr. Behemoth	Soul Sabre
Stunner	Test Rider	Strato
Graedus	Karkass	Dirk
Crystal	Borras	Enhancer
Aura Lance	Land Worm	Sky Render
Imp Halberd	Allosaur	Cat Hood
Hardened	Phase	Murasame
Thunder Blade	Steroidite	Ogre Nix
Scimitar	Covert	Ogre Nix
Doom Dart	Opinicus	Bone Club
Sniper	Borras	Bone Club
Soul Sabre	Opinicus	Falchion
Tiger Fang	Mantodea	Fire Knuckle
Thief	Wart Puck	Thief Glove
Dragon Claw	Test Rider	Sniper
Fire Knuckle	Tumble Weed	Fire Knuckle
Punisher	Opinicus	Gravity Rod

ARMS (continued)

Bet	Challenger	Prize
Valiant Knife	Woolly	Assassin
Heal Rod	Pug	Magus Rod
Falchion	Outsider	Flame Shield
Drainer	Enuo	Drainer
Break Blade	Lethal Weapon	Break Blade
Flame Sabre	Evil Oscar	Ogre Nix
Pearl Lance	Sky Base	Strato
Bone Club	Test Rider	R. Jacket
Aura	Rhyos	Strato
Sky Render	Scullion	A. Lance
Murasame	Borras	Aura
Rising Sun	Allosaur	Bone Club
Illumina	Scullion	Scimitar
Ragnarok	Didalos	Illumina
Rainbow Brush	Test Rider	Gravity Rod

Items

Bet	Challenger	Prize
Air Anchor	Bronotaur	Zephyr Cape
Elixir	Cactrot	Rename Card
Tack Star	Opinicus	Rising Sun
Ninja Star	Chaos Dragon	Tack Star
Phoenix Down	Cactrot	Magicite
Megalixir	Ziegfried	Tintinabar
Rename Card	Doom Dragon	Marvel Shoes

Armor

Bet	Challenger	Prize
Imp's Armor	Rhyos	Tortoise Shield
Ice Shield	Innoc	Flame Shield
Aegis Shield	Borras	Tortoise Shield
Thornlet	Opinicus	Mirage Vest
Paladin Shield	Hemophyte	Force Shield
Crystal Helmet	Dueller	Diamond Helmet
Crystal Mail	Covert	Ice Shield
Genji Helmet	Fortis	Crystal Helmet
Genji Shield	Retainer	Thunder Shield
Genji Armor	Borras	Air Anchor
Tort Shield	Sterdite	Titanium
Tabby Suit	Vectaur	Chocobo Suit
Titanium	Brachosaur	Cat Hood
Snow Muffler	Retainer	Charm Bangle
Chocobo Suit	Veteran	Moogle Suit
Tao Robe	Test Rider	Tao Robe
Nutkin Suit	Opinicus	Genji Armor
Cat Hood	Hoover	Merit Award
Coronet	Evil Oscar	Regal Crown
Force Armor	Sr. Behemoth	Force Armor
Force Shield	Dark Force	Thornlet
Czarina Gown	Sky Base	Minerva
Flame Shield	Iron Hitman	Ice Shield
Behemoth Suit	Outsider	Snow Muffler
Minerva	Pug	Czar Gown
Mirage Vest	Vectagoyle	Red Jacket
Moogle Suit	Madam	Nutkin Suit
Thunder Shield	Outsider	Genji Shield
Red Cap	Rhyos	Coronet
Red Jacket	Vectagoyle	Red Jacket
Regal Crown	Opinicus	Genji Helmet

Relics

Bet	Challenger	Prize
Rage Ring	Allosaur	Blizzard Orb
Safe Ring	Chupon	Safe Ring
Gauntlet	Vectagoyle	Thunder Shield
Gale Hairpin	Evil Oscar	Dragon Horn
Crystal Orb	Borras	Gale Hairpin
Exp. Egg	Steroidite	Tintinabar
Merit Award	Covert	Rename Card
Genji Glove	Hemophyte	Thunder Shield
Relic Ring	Sky Base	Charm Bangle
Economizer	Vectagoyle	Dragon Horn
Safe Bit	Pug	Dragon Horn
Gem Box	Sr. Behemoth	Economizer
Charm Bangle	Retainer	Dragon Horn
Tintinabar	Dark Force	Exp. Egg
Sneak Ring	Tap Dancer	Thief Glove
Thief Glove	Harpy	Dirk
Cursed Ring	Steroidite	Air Anchor
Dragon Horn	Rhyos	Gale Hairpin
Blizzard Orb	Allosaur	Rage Ring
Hero Ring	Rhyos	Pod Brace
Muscle Belt	Allosaur	Crystal Orb
Pod Brace	Hemophyte	Hero Ring
Marvel Shoes	Tyranasaur	Tintinabar
Moogle Charm	Outsider	Charm Bangle
Ribbon	Dark Force	Gale Hairpin

FINAL FANTASY® VI Secrets

Secrets

The following pages contain many secrets from FINAL FANTASY VI. Many can be considered **spoilers**, so you shouldn't dive into this section right away. This is best viewed once you've already played through the game. Those of you who can't wait will have to pay the price of knowing a bit more than you probably should.

Bonus Menus

Anytime you complete FINAL FANTASY VI, be sure to wait through the credits and you'll get a special surprise. The game will create a "System File" on your memory card that will allow you to see all of the features in the Bonus Menu. You can then access the Bonus Menu when you first load the game. The new menus allow you to watch the game's cinemas, peek at the bestiary, look at production art, and much more. You'll need one empty block on your Memory Card for the System File.

The Legendary Vanish/X-Zone Trick

Spells like Doom and X-Zone don't seem to be very valuable since they usually fail to do what they're supposed to do. If you combine these spells with the Vanish spell, however, they almost always work. In battle, cast Vanish on your enemy. This makes the enemy invisible and protects it from physical attacks but makes it vulnerable to nearly any type of magic. Follow up with either Doom or X-Zone, and you're almost guaranteed they'll work. This trick works on just about every enemy, including Bosses! You can also use the Vanish trick to make it easier to transform enemies into items when using the Ragnarok Esper in battle.

Curing the Cursed Shield

In Narshe, during the World of Ruin, you'll find a man hiding in his house who'll give your party a Cursed Shield. You must have Locke in your party in order to unlock the door to his house. Anyone who wears the shield will suffer from several abnormal statuses in battle, and the shield fails to provide any additional protection. Why would anyone equip such a thing?

If you're willing to equip the Cursed Shield for 255 battles, the curse will be broken. Once the curse is gone, the Cursed Shield becomes the Paladin Shield, which is arguably the best shield in the game.

Should you choose to take on this challenge, be sure to equip the character that'll be using the shield with a Ribbon, which will counter most of the abnormal status effects. Then you'll want to go some-where like Solitary Island and fight a bunch of easy battles to help you quickly reach the necessary 255.

281

FINAL FANTASY VI Limit Breaks?

Believe it or not, even FINAL FANTASY VI has Limit Breaks. When a character's HP is extremely low, there's a chance that a character can perform an unusually powerful attack in place of its normal fight command. Such occurences are rare, but you should see it happen at least once during your adventure.

Time Extension

Sometimes, in battle, an enemy will curse your characters. Should this happen, a timer will appear over the cursed character's head. If it reaches zero, the character is petrified. Should time be running short on a character's life, you can always give it a small boost.

Quickly select each of your characters' attacks, but have the last character open the Magic menu and wait. As long as the menu is open, the timer won't move. But your characters that have already selected an attack will still be able to act. This may not be useful all of the time, but it can help if you've almost got the battle won.

Relic Ring

This is an item that may seem a bit useless to you. If a character has this item equipped, you can actually use a Doom spell as a healing spell. Cast Doom on the character with the Relic Ring, and suddenly you'll understand just what a great thing the Relic Ring can be.

Powerful Relic Combinations

Try these Relic combinations. Equipping the Genji Glove and the Offering on a character allows the character to attack a total of eight times each turn. The Offering also works well with Locke's Thief Glove, allowing him to attack and steal four times.

Give a powerful spell caster like Terra the Gem Box Relic and an Economizer Relic. Now the equipped character can cast two spells each turn for one MP each. If your character has learned the Quick spell, it can cast Ultima and then Quick to get two more turns immediately. So, you can cast Ultima four more times for only six MP.

Counter Cold

There are many enemies in the game that use a freezing attack to paralyze your characters. As long as one character isn't frozen, you can counter this by casting a weak fire spell on the party. You can also counter other abnormal statuses by attacking your own characters. Hitting a sleeping character with a physical attack wakes them. Doing the same with a confused character snaps them out of the daze. Casting Imp on a character that's been turned into an Imp changes the character back to normal.

Life is Death

Undead creatures can be killed instantly by using certain healing magic and items. Magic with this effect includes Life and Life 2. Items include Phoenix Down, Revivify, and X-Potions. Keep in mind that things that normally cause death will heal the undead.

Dinosaur Forest

In the World of Ruin, there's a forest north of the Veldt that looks like a dinosaur head. In the forest, you'll encounter tough enemies like the Tyranosaurs and the Brachosaur. Tyranosaurs are hard to beat, but the Brachosaur is the worst. Use the Vanish/X-Zone trick to quickly win these battles. Not only do you get ten Magic Points, but you can also randomly find an Economizer. These rare Relics cut casting costs down to one Magic Point for any spell. You can also steal extra Ribbons from them if you're brave enough to try. Always be sure to save before wandering into the dinosaur forest.

Super Save Points

In any area where you must split your characters into two or more groups, you can perform a useful trick with Save Points. Having a party use a Tent on a Save Point heals that party but not others. If you switch to the other groups, however, they can also use a Tent as long as one of the parties is still standing on a Save Point.

Early Level-Up Trick

In the World of Balance, you can give your characters an early advantage by spending some time on the Lete River. Hop onto the raft outside the Returner's Hideout. At the first Save Point, go into the sub-menu. Go to "Cmd. Set", select "short" and press the ⊗ button. You can now place Banon's Health spell in place of the Fight command. This means that he will cast his health spell every turn.

Back on the river, go up the river at the first intersection and then tape down the ⊗ button and tape the D-pad in the up position. The raft will then circle the area, and your characters will fight and heal automatically. Leave the game running in this fashion overnight. The next day, you'll find that your character's level has increased significantly.

Hunting for Cactrots

If you really want to gain a lot of Magic Points and GP quickly, you'll want to seek out the elusive Cactrot. It can be found in a desert southwest of Maranda in the World of Ruin. Defeating the Cactrot isn't easy. Its evading skill is unmatched, and most magic isn't effective against it. You can whittle away at its HP by using a character's special skill. Edgar's Drill, Sabin's Pummel Blitz, and Cyan's Dispatch SwordTech all work well. You can also equip a character with the Sniper Sight Relic, which ensures you'll hit the spiny, little beast. For defeating a Cactrot, you're given 10 Magic Points and 10,000 GP.

Shadow's Past

If you want to learn more about the mysterious ninja, Shadow, you must have him in your party when you stay at Inns. Each time you do, there's a fair chance you'll see one of several flashbacks into Shadow's past.

AMANO'S
HERO

A LEGEND OF THE FUTURE

WORLD
PREMIERE
EXHIBITION

OCTOBER 6 THRU
OCTOBER 31, 1999

ANGEL ORENSANZ FOUNDATION
172 NORFOLK STREET, NEW YORK CITY

212-625-3367

www.amanosworld.com

SANDMAN

Featuring artwork from *THE SANDMAN: The Dream Hunters*, the New SANDMAN Graphic Novel by Neil Gaiman and Yoshitaka Amano coming in October from Vertigo/DC Comics

FINAL FANTASY

Concept Illustrator for the FINAL FANTASY® series Featuring FINAL FANTASY Anthology by SquareSoft.

Square Electronic Arts Game Tips

Be sure to check out Square's hit game!

Got the game? Get the book!
Official Final Fantasy® VIII Strategy Guide

from

///IIBradyGAMES
STRATEGY GUIDES

Lv 10 HP 92/92

21F Lv 19 HP 190/110 37%

January, 2000

February, 2000

SQUARESOFT®
www.squaresoft.com
Published by Square Electronic Arts L.L.C.